THE
Baseball ◇24 Research
JOURNAL

Another View of Dick Allen	Craig R. Wright	2
The Oriole—Verse	Jonathan Boyd	15
If Not Larson, Who?	Charles Blahous	17
The Parker Brothers and Other Cincinnati Oddities	Joseph Cardello	21
The Matty–Alex Tie	Joseph M. Wayman	25
Triple Milestone Hitters	Bill Gilbert	27
The Pumpkin and Cabbage Tournament of 1866	Tony Kissel	30
The SABeRhagen Syndrome	Michael McBride	34
Dominant Starting Pitchers	Tony Blengino	39
Dominant Pitchers of the 20th Century	Alan S. Kaufman and James C. Kaufman	47
Minor League Big Guns	Ernest J. Green	53
Bobby Brown: Hitting Hard to All Fields	Talmage Boston	58
Which Yankee Teams Were Best?	Russell O. Wright	62
1969: Carew Steals Home	Ron Marshall	66
Pinch-Hitting Pitchers	Gene Noll	69
Czech Baseball	Ted Kapnick	73
The 1910 White Sox	Ted Farmer	76
Streaks: Statistics vs. Serendipity	Neal Moran	79
The D-Score: Managers and Close Games	Bob Boynton	81
Tommy McCarthy: Maybe Not So Heavenly	Eddie Gold	88
Jimmie Reese	James D. Smith III	89
Rube Parnham	Mike Ross	92
Batting Champs in the World Series	Stan Grosshandler	94
The Six Greatest Throwing Outfielders in History	Cappy Gagnon	96
Ted Williams, Premier Batting Coach	Jerry Hannan	101
The Mysterious Case of Rodney Pedraza	Jim Storer	103
The California Winter League of 1921	R. Scott Mackey	106
The Walk-A-Game Club	Lary Bump	108
Rookie Umps	Ted Di Tullio	111
Standardized Range Factor	Scott McClellan and Mark Schreiber	113
Pants Rowland: The Busher from Dubuque	Joseph P. Murphy, Jr.	117
RBI Average	Daniel Lee Swetman	123
Total Production Average	Eugene E. Heaton, Jr. and Alan W. Heaton	127
1938: England Beats the U.S.	Ian Smyth	131
Goldie Rapp's Rookie Hitting Streaks	Jamie Selko	134
No-Hitters Lost in the Ninth	Stew Thornley	137
The Thief—Verse	Harry J. Rothgerber, Jr.	141
"Mr. October"? Not!	Alan Hirsch	142
The Average Length of a World Series	Bob Brown	144
Ham Hyatt and the Development of Pinch Hitting	John T. Hannon, Jr.	146
They Didn't Know How To Quit	Henry C. Mayer	150
Competitive Imbalance	Campbell Gibson	153
How Voters Decide the Cy Young Award	Stuart Miller	157
Tim McNamara	Jim Kreuz	160
From a Researcher's Notebook	Al Kermisch	162

Editor: Mark Alvarez
Designated Readers: Dick Thompson, Bob Tiemann
Copy Editor: A.D. Suehsdorf

THE BASEBALL RESEARCH JOURNAL (ISSN 0734-6891, ISBN 0-910137-63-3), Number 24. Published by The Society for American Baseball Research, Inc. P.O. Box 93183, Cleveland, OH, 44101. Postage paid at Birmingham, AL. Copyright The Society for American Baseball Research, Inc. All rights reserved. Reproduction in whole or in part without written permission is prohibited. Printed by EBSCO Media, Birmingham, AL.

Another View of Dick Allen

The most misunderstood player of his generation

Craig R. Wright

In recent years, I have been surprised at the harsh assessments of the career of Dick Allen, from his brief bio in *Total Baseball* to Bill James' scathing comments in his otherwise excellent book on the Hall of Fame, *The Politics of Glory*. A grudging respect is given to Allen's offensive numbers, which are easily understood and irrefutable in their excellence, but in the grayer areas of player evaluation, it seems that great liberties have been taken to shed the worst possible light on his career.

For example, the assessment of Allen's defense in *Total Baseball* begins with the mocking comment, "He came to the Phillies a professed third baseman," and goes on to note that he led the league in errors a couple times and ended up being shifted to first base. The truth is that Allen never played third base in the minors, and had the unenviable task of learning the position while breaking into the majors at age 21. Allen was error prone, but it is inaccurate to suggest to future generations that he was a brutal third baseman whose poor fielding led to his move to first base.

From 1964 to 1967, Allen had more assists and started more double plays at third base than any NL third baseman except Gold Glover Ron Santo. And that was true even though a dislocated throwing shoulder kept Allen from playing third base for nearly half the 1966 season.

Chances Fielded Cleanly Per Game
1964-67 NL 3B (400 games, min.)

1.	3.40	Ron Santo
2.	**2.84**	**Dick Allen**
3.	2.81	Ken Boyer

That's two pretty good gloves to be sandwiched between, and that stat deserves to be mentioned at least as much as Allen's poor .932 fielding percentage—which, incidentally, is better than Santo's fielding percentages over his first four seasons as a professional third baseman. Allen may never have developed into a good third baseman—he never did throw as well after the injury to his shoulder—but there was no thought of moving him off third base until the 1967 hand injury that damaged the nerves in his throwing hand and made it difficult for him to grip and throw the ball accurately. *That* is why was moved to first base.

Yet this slanted assessment of Allen's fielding is nothing compared to the wild things that have been written about his influence in the clubhouse. James concluded that Dick had such a negative clubhouse presence that despite his heavy hitting he did "more to keep his teams from winning than anybody else who ever played major league baseball."

When Dick Allen was a spring training instructor with the Rangers in 1982, I got to know him a bit and

Craig R. Wright *is a consultant to several of the major league teams. He also assists STATS Incorporated as their Director of Major League Operations. As a hobby he researches and writes the radio show* A Page from Baseball's Past.

talked with him about his career. In the intervening years I have had the chance to talk with several people who were also there at various points in Allen's career. Their accounts are consistent, and it is clear there are some gross factual errors in many of these harsh written assessments of his career and the impact he had on his teams, managers, and teammates.

I interviewed Gene Mauch, Bob Skinner, Red Schoendienst, Chuck Tanner, and Danny Ozark. Except for Walter Alston, who died in 1984, that covers every big league manager who had Allen for at least half a season. While I could not interview Alston, I did discuss Dick's year in L.A. with two Dodger coaches, Caroll Beringer and Danny Ozark. I also interviewed Roland Hemond, who was the GM in Chicago during Dick's White Sox days, and I spoke with many others who had personal contact with Allen.

The most helpful in that regard was Pat Corrales, who was an early teammate of Allen's in the minors and in his first two years in Philadelphia. Gene Mauch recommended Corrales as someone from those early days who knew Dick Allen "better than anyone, perhaps better than Dick himself." I tried to contact Allen to refresh my memories of our 1982 conversations about his career. He did not respond to my messages relayed through the Phillies. That did not surprise me. This is not a project he would welcome, and my guess is that he would be happy to leave things as they are, content to be known only by those close enough to know him firsthand.

Philadelphia—Keeping in mind James' claim that Allen actually hurt his teams, I made it a point to ask each of the managers if, after their experiences with Allen, they would have traded fair market value to have Dick on their team again. Gene Mauch managed Allen longer than anyone else, and in his mind there was no question that the pluses outweighed the minuses.

> I've never been in contact with a greater talent. He was held in absolute awe by every player in the league. He had tremendous power. He had a great feel for the game, and he was one of the finest base runners—which is different from base stealing—that I ever saw. If I was managing California today and Allen was in his prime, I'd take him in a minute.

In our interview Gene downplayed any problems that he had managing Allen, with the exception of Dick's being frequently late getting to the ballpark.

> One year I fined him probably more than the minimum salary over times he got to the park late. He never missed a game—wasn't late for the game itself, but he was late getting to the park. And I fined him for that. I should say he fined himself. He knew what he was doing.

Pat Corrales also mentioned Dick's chronic tardiness early in his career.

> He got better after a while, but being on time definitely wasn't something that came naturally to [Allen]. He just wasn't careful with the clock. If I have to be someplace at three, I'm there at 2:45, if not sooner. Dick would shoot for 2:58, and if he got there at 3:15, 3:30, he didn't care."

James' basic complaint against Allen is that he was a divisive presence on his teams: "Every team that he played for degenerated into warring camps of pro-Dick Allen and anti-Dick Allen factions." I asked Mauch if that was true with any of his teams; he was emphatic in his denial, "Never. His teammates always liked him. You could go forever and not meet a more charming fellow." Later in the interview he came back to this topic to make the following point:

> ...he wasn't doing anything to hurt [his teammates] play of the game, and he didn't involve his teammates in his problems. When he was personally rebellious, he didn't try to bring other players into it.

That last part is important, as some critics have suggested that Allen was a manipulative clubhouse lawyer. Corrales did not accept that view, "No, I didn't see that. He wasn't a guy who would use people." And Mauch's famous line, "Richie Allen walks to the beat of a different drummer," also suggests individualism more than a clubhouse politician.

Allen's critics invariably mention the fight that took place in 1965 between Allen and teammate Frank Thomas. Their theme has been that this fight disrupted team harmony and kept the Phils from improving on their 1964 performance, when they won 92 games, finishing one game back. Bill James describes it this way: "In 1965, when the Phillies were trying to overcome the memory of having blown the pennant in the last few days of the 1964 season, Allen got into a fight with a teammate early in the season, forcing a trade."

An important correction to that interpretation is that the fight actually took place in the *middle* of the season, on July 3. The team was already well off its 1964 pace. The Phillies pitching wasn't nearly as good, and they had a couple of older players who had been key figures in 1964 who were on their way out in 1965. One of them was 36-year-old Frank Thomas who had lost his outfield job, and when the fight took place he was hitting .250 with 0 HR in 76 at bats. Pat Corrales remembers it this way:

> It had really started earlier on our road trip in Chicago. Thomas was your tough bully type, and he had been picking on Johnny Briggs [21-year-old black outfielder], saying 'Boy this' and 'Boy that.' Dick didn't go for that, and there were some words between them.
>
> We get back to Philly, and during early BP I'm down the line talking with Mauch, when we see this commotion down at the cage. They were just pulling them apart at this point, after Thomas swung the bat. During the fight, Thomas had hit Dick with a bat, on the shoulder.

The fight bothered Thomas so much that in the following game he hit his first homer of the year, but his career continued to slide away. He finished the year as a weak reserve with Houston and Milwaukee, hitting .187 in 91 at bats.

When Mauch told Allen that Thomas was being put on irrevocable waivers, Dick protested on Frank's behalf. Mauch ordered Allen and his teammates not to speak to the press about the fight and backed it up with a threat of stiff fines. As a result the press and the fans heard just Thomas' side, and they did not take kindly to a young black guy popping a white veteran. Mauch told me,

> They really turned on him after the Thomas fight. From there, if he did one little thing wrong, they would see it as so much worse because it was Allen. They got it in their heads that this was a bad guy, and they booed his every move.

But the view of the fans and the press was not the view in the clubhouse. Both Mauch and

Corrales saw no effect on team morale, and Corrales noted that his teammates backed Allen in this dispute. In the book *Crash*, teammate Johnny Callison said,

> Thomas rubbed a *lot* of people the wrong way. Mauch wanted him gone—and here was his excuse. …Thomas got himself fired when he swung that bat at Richie. In baseball you don't swing a bat at another player—ever.

Allen hit well in the game after the fight, going 3 for 4. At that point, he led the NL in hitting with a .341 average. But overnight, Allen's shoulder swelled to twice its normal size. Corrales remembers, "He couldn't lift that shoulder for a while, and it bothered him for some time." Dick continued to play and led the team with 161 games played, but it appears the injury affected his hitting.

Allen in 1965	BA	AB	HR	RBI	Team Record W-L	Win%
Thru July 3rd	.341	279	11	49	40-35	.526
After July 3rd	.271	340	9	36	45-41	.523

Rather than hurting team morale, it looks like Allen's teammates picked him up as they managed to play at about the same level as they did earlier when Allen was stinging the ball.

James wrote that the 1964 Phillies were a "young team…that never did come together, and were never in position to win again," and suggests that Allen's disruptive presence was responsible. But most of their young players simply weren't that good. Bobby Wine (25) couldn't hit; Tony Gonzalez (27) was an outfielder who lacked power, and John Herrnstein (26) was a weak hitting first baseman who had to be replaced by 32-year-old Dick Stuart the very next year. Johnny Callison (25) had talent, but subsequent injuries limited him to just one big year after 1964. With the exception of Allen, there was no one under 32 on that team who went

Gene Mauch

Transcendental Graphics

on to become a star.

Still, Mauch's Phillies did well with Allen until their pitching started to collapse in 1968. And if Allen was holding them back, you sure couldn't tell by the way they played the two times he was on the disabled list. In April of 1966 Allen dislocated his shoulder and the team went 11-13 without him in the starting lineup. After his 1967 season was ended by the serious hand injury the Phils went 19-21, including six 1-0 losses.

1964-67 Best Team Winning Percentages

1. .570 San Francisco
2. .553 St. Louis
3. .542 Philadelphia (Allen not disabled)
    .469 Philadelphia (Allen disabled)

But playing in Philadelphia was an increasingly hellish experience for Allen. In 1967 Allen asked the Phillies several times to trade him. He was getting threatening hate mail, and some of his friends were even urging him to hire a bodyguard. The response to his hand injury was the final straw. While he was trying to deal with an injury that doctors felt could end his career, rumors were spread that his story of the accident was a cover-up, that Allen had been knifed in a bar fight or jumped through a window after getting caught sleeping with a teammate's wife.

For the record, Allen was pushing a stalled car up his driveway when his right hand slipped and went into a headlight. Pat Corrales: "I asked his Momma about it. She was there. She wouldn't lie about it. Dick wouldn't lie about it." To this day Allen has little sensation in the two middle fingers on his throwing hand. He would have trouble with his throws—particularly in cold weather—the rest of his career. Dick told me, "Those two fingers would stay on the ball, and I would be throwing sliders."

The roughest years—In his biography *Crash*, Allen talks about how the steady abuse wore on him mentally and emotionally. "I'd been hearing I was a bum for so long that I began to think maybe that's just what I was." With free agency not yet even a gleam in Marvin Miller's eye, in the spring of 1968 he began a campaign of minor transgressions of team rules in hopes that it would cause Philadelphia to trade him.

1968 was the team's first losing season with Allen, and Mauch resigned about a third of the way into the season. By Dick's own admission he had been far more of a problem player that spring, so I was surprised when Mauch insisted in our interview that, "Allen wasn't a factor. I'd been there a long time, and...I was ready to move on."

Mauch also refused to blame Allen for the team's poor play in 1968, but he did seem to second-guess himself and ownership about whether they were being fair to Dick and the team by forcing him to stay in Philadelphia. I asked Gene if he felt Allen ever had a negative influence on the team:

> Never. Well, there are a lot of ways to look at that. His trouble with the fans might have been distracting. It was a bad situation....they booed his every move. When they gave him a tough time over his hand injury—questioning his story about how it happened—that's when Allen wanted out.

That led me to ask Gene whether he felt any of his teams might have been better off if Allen had been traded away.

> No. He was irreplaceable as a player. Maybe that last year in '68. I don't know. He wanted out, and that team wasn't going anywhere anyway. It might have been better to trade him then.

Mauch was right about the 1968 Phillies being a team going nowhere. The team had been burned by some bad deals. They were stuck with an aging Bill White on first base, who at age 34 hit .239 with little power. Worse, they had 37-year-old Larry Jackson in the rotation, whom they had acquired by trading away a young Fergie Jenkins who was now 24 years old and winning 20 games with the Cubs. Their pitching staff collapsed, going from the fourth-best ERA in 1967 to the league's third worst in 1968.

And Dick Allen? In this extreme year of the pitcher he hit 33 homers and drove in 90 runs for a team on which no one else had more than 48. Only Willie McCovey had more homers or a higher percentage of his team's RBIs.

New manager Bob Skinner, who managed the last two-thirds of the season, did not remember having any problems with Allen that year. "I don't recall any real incidents in '68, nothing that would make him stand out from most players. He wasn't late; he didn't miss any games."

Corrales made the point that Dick "was years ahead of us [players] in seeing that it was wrong for the owners to have such complete control over our careers." In the off-season, on January 1, the players' union had a historic meeting of 130 players n which they discovered the solidarity of their feelings in battling the owners for their rights. Over 20 years later, in Marvin Miller's book, *A Whole Different Ballgame*, Dick Allen's voice was the one he remembered best.

> He did not speak in the early part of the meeting but later spoke with quiet dignity in a fashion that indicated he had been listening carefully. He was eloquent and forceful, and the other players listened intently. He didn't speak as a superstar, but as a player who understood both the issues and the importance of the players moving forward as a group.

But in 1969 it was still just Allen versus the Phillies' right to retain his services for the rest of his career. Allen described 1969 to me as a year of anger and confusion. He was a figure of ambivalence; he still had the desire to play well but there was no joy to it. His heart wasn't fully in it.

In May, for the first time in his career, Allen arrived at the park after the game had started. Skinner fined him $1,000, a huge fine for that era. A month later, Allen forgot that the starting time for a doubleheader in New York had been moved up. He was on his way to the ballpark when he heard on the radio that the first game had started and that Skinner had suspended him. While acknowledging that he was wrong and had no excuse, Allen had reached a point of such misery that he could not remember the last time he had fun playing ball. He finally decided he would rather retire than continue to play in Philadelphia.

At the time Allen was hitting .318 and was on pace for his best HR year. (He had hit 19 in 62 games, which projects to 50 in a full season). A month later Allen was reinstated and came back only after ownership made him a firm promise to trade him at the end of the year.

From my interviews with his managers, it is safe to say that his extreme offenses in 1969 were something that Allen had never done before and would never do again. Mauch had trouble with Allen getting to the park on time, but he also noted that he was never late for a game and never missed a game. With the Cardinals, Red Schoendienst said, "He was always on time for me. He never gave me any trouble." Chuck Tanner and L.A. coach Caroll Beringer said pretty much the same thing. Danny Ozark was very emphatic: "He wasn't any problem for me, ever, not in L.A. or Philly. He was super. He did everything I asked him to."

But even if 1969 was a unique season in Allen's career, there is still a stubborn perception that Allen was the reason the 1969 Phillies were such a horrible team. The simple truth is that the 1969 Phillies *improved* their offense relative to the league. The problem was the continued demise of their pitching. Chris Short, their number one starter in 1968, threw only ten innings in 1969 before being shelved by back surgery. Only the two expansion teams had worse ERAs than the Phillies.

Despite a late-season slump and missing 44 games, Allen led the team in batting average, homers, and RBIs. The question is, how much should Allen's 1969 transgressions be held against him? There have been some analysts who suggest that Allen didn't help the team at all in 1969. They point to the fact that the Phillies had their longest winning streak of the year while Allen was suspended. What they don't mention about that winning streak is that nearly half the wins came against Montreal, the new expansion team that lost 110 games, and that shortly after that streak—still without Allen—they lost seven in a row. Despite playing Montreal nine times in those 31 games, they were only 13-18 during Allen's suspension. That is hardly a strong endorsement that they were a better team without him. I asked Bob Skinner if he ever felt his 1969 team was better off without Dick.

> No, I had a poor team, and he was way above everyone else. He was a good player, a damn good player. We certainly weren't a bad team because of him. I didn't appreciate some of his antics or his approach to his profession, and I told him so, but I understood some of it. I do believe that he was trying to get them to move [trade] him. He was very unhappy. He wanted out. There were people in Philadelphia treating him very badly, throwing garbage on his lawn, things like that.

I also asked Skinner my standard question about whether Allen had been a divisive presence on the team.

> I didn't see any of that in the time I had him. He obviously did some things that weren't team oriented, but his teammates did not have a sense of animosity toward him. Not that I saw. They had some understanding of what was going on.

I asked Skinner if he would have okayed a trade for Allen in 1970 if he had been managing somewhere else and could have gotten him at a reasonable price:

> At any price. Any time you have a shot at a player of that caliber, you want to take it. He was a great hitter; one of the best base runners you'd ever

want to see, and he had great instincts for the game. He had some throwing problems with the bad hand, but you could play him at first base well enough. I'd gladly have taken him.

Skinner resigned in August, after ownership gave Allen permission to skip an exhibition game with their AAA farm team. When I asked if his problems with Allen contributed to his resignation, Skinner said, "No. In my eyes, Allen was just another player. My problem was with the front office."

There is no excuse for Allen's transgressions in 1969. Regardless of how desperate or how justified Allen may have been in trying to reach his personal goal, it doesn't change the fact that those actions negatively affected the team. But historians of the game must assess the damage in a realistic manner, and must refrain from unfairly projecting that negative effect into the evaluation of the rest of his career.

Why are we more forgiving of, say, Roger Clemens in 1987 than we are of Dick Allen in 1969? In 1987, as a young player without arbitration rights, Clemens refused to accept Boston's right to renew his contract when their negotiations broke down—a right his union had agreed to in forming the same salary structure that would be so lucrative to Clemens in subsequent years. On the day the spring exhibition schedule was to begin, Clemens walked out of camp and didn't return until April 4. He was not ready to pitch when the season started. He didn't win a game until April 21, and through June he was only 6-6. He pitched very well after that, but by then his team had already fallen out of the race.

Now where is the difference between Clemens and Allen? The Red Sox were coming off a season in which they came within one strike of being World Champions. If I had been a Red Sox player, I would have been upset with Clemens taking a hike the next spring. At least Allen's personal battle was not hurting the Phillies in a year when they had a chance to win anything.

It has been suggested to me that the difference between the two is that the Red Sox players "understood" Clemens' battle, were sympathetic to his stand, and so it was less disruptive to the team. Well, Boston was disrupted enough to misplace 18 wins from their 1986 total, but never mind; if that's the difference between Clemens and Allen then there is no difference. The manager of Allen's team has told us that his teammates "did not have a sense of ani-

mosity toward him…They had some understanding of what was going on."

Both players hurt their teams by putting a personal goal ahead of the team. Both had reasons that did not alienate them from their teammates. Both helped their teams with their play. Neither deserves to have his whole career colored by that single season. It has not happened with Clemens; it should not happen with Allen.

The 1969 season ended Allen's first tour of duty with Philadelphia. Even with those two weak final seasons, it is still a far better six-year period than the Phillies had before Allen arrived, and better than the six-year period they had after he left. The difference was the big bat of Dick Allen.

	Phillies	W-L	Win%	Runs	NL Avg.	Diff.
Before Allen	1958-63	407-532	.433	3,740	4060	-320
With Allen	1964-69	485-486	.499	3,843	3811	+32
After Allen	1970-75	436-529	.452	3,708	3982	-274

Even with the Phillies trading with their back to the wall, there was a good market for Allen's services. There were a couple of minor players exchanged on both sides, but the deal that sent Allen to St. Louis boiled down to Allen for Tim McCarver, a fine catcher in his physical prime (just five months older than Allen), and Curt Flood, a Gold Glove center fielder.

There is irony in Allen being in this particular deal. Flood, who is black, did not want to go to Philadelphia, and challenged baseball's reserve clause, setting in motion the chain of events that would bring about the present system of free agent rights after six years of service. Under the modern rules of free agency, Allen would have been able to play through that last season in Philly knowing he would be a free agent at the end of the year. We can only guess at what a difference that could have made in how he is viewed today.

St. Louis—In our interview Manager Red Schoendienst remembered Dick this way:

> He did a real fine job for me. He had a great year, led our team in RBIs, and he never gave me any trouble…I planned on using him at first base, but with [Mike] Shannon's illness, I had to use him some at third base, and I played him a few games in the outfield, too. He was good about that.

When asked if Allen was a divisive presence among

his teammates, Red said,

> Absolutely not. He was great in our clubhouse. He got along with everybody. He wasn't a rah-rah guy, but he came to play. They respected him, and they liked him.

Allen played a good portion of the year with an Achilles tendon injury that was aggravated by the Cardinals' new artificial turf, and then in August he tore a hamstring while sliding into second base. Despite being limited to 122 games, Allen not only led the team in RBIs, but hit 34 homers, which is a remarkable feat in Busch Stadium.

The lineup was hampered by Mike Shannon's career-ending kidney ailment and by the presence of two young rookies who struggled to replace McCarver and Flood. (Leron Lee, Ted Simmons, and Shannon combined to hit .230 in 722 at bats.) Yet the Cardinals scored a lot more runs (+149), and Allen was the biggest reason why.

The team did slip in the standings, but this was primarily a pitching problem. After leading the league in ERA in 1969 (2.94), the staff ERA exploded to 4.06. Maybe having Joe Torre and Allen at third base for over 100 games took a toll, but lack of control was the pitchers' downfall. The staff walked 121 more batters than the year before.

Allen told me in 1982 that he had been very happy in St. Louis, that he wished he could have played the rest of his career there. He was very disappointed to be traded at the end of the year. Schoendienst recalls that the trade took place strictly for baseball reasons. "I was happy with Allen. [Julian] Javier was on his way out, and I guess the front office figured we needed a second baseman more than a first baseman."

That seems logical looking back at the situation. Javier would be 34 and was coming off a poor year with the bat. The Cardinals felt that Ted Simmons would be a star (indeed, he hit .304 playing full-time the next year), and they had three first base talents in Allen, Torre, and Joe Hague (who was only 26 and had just hit .271 and slugged .417 in 451 at bats as an outfielder-first baseman).

The Dodgers were loaded at second base, with young Ted Sizemore, veteran Jim Lefebvre, and a young Davey Lopes converting to second in the minors. Sizemore had earned the 1969 Rookie of the Year Award by hitting .271 and playing good defense and had followed that up by hitting .306. He was also only 25, over three years younger than Allen. On October 7 the Cardinals traded Allen for Sizemore.

Los Angeles—This team did not look like a contender early in the year. They had finished 14-1/2 games back the year before and almost immediately lost one of their best players. Twenty-five-year-old Billy Grabarkewitz had led the team with 17 HRs and was second in RBIs. But early in 1971 he broke his ankle and had only 71 at bats for the year.

Rookie Steve Garvey was brought in to play third base, but he hit only .227 and broke his hand. L. A. had Wes Parker on first base and had acquired Allen to play in the outfield, but with their Bermuda triangle at third, Allen ended up appearing in more games there (67) than he did in the outfield (60) or at first (28).

Despite the injuries, the team improved their record and found themselves in a fierce pennant race. In September Walter Alston was quoted as saying, "If we win this year, I'll be more proud of this team than any I've ever managed." They just missed, finishing one game behind San Francisco.

Allen was a huge part of their success, playing 155 games and hitting a strong .295. The fences were deeper in Dodger Stadium then, and Dick's 23 homers were nearly double those of anyone else on the team (Lefebvre had 12). Allen's 90 RBIs led the team by a margin of 16, and in runs scored he was only two behind Willie Davis.

Danny Ozark, the Dodgers' third base coach, remembers,

> [Allen] did a great job for us in LA. He was a great base runner, the best I ever coached. I'd take the extra base with him, and I don't think he was ever thrown out the whole year.

When I asked Ozark how Allen and Manager Walt Alston got along, he said:

> Walt was a quiet guy. He didn't talk a lot to the players. If he didn't say anything, you assumed it was all right. He never said anything bad about Allen, not that I know of.

When I read that quote to fellow coach Caroll Beringer, he laughed and said, "That's exactly how he was," and added:

> I don't remember any problems with Richie. I do remember one thing that may have hurt Allen with the Dodgers. L. A. was very big on 'image.' They cultivated that with the fans and the community. They demanded that the players make appearances—well, not de-

manded, but it was very much expected of you. I can remember being in Alston's office when Walter O'Malley called and wanted Richie to show up for some appearance. Alston told him that he would ask Richie, but he could tell him right now that he would say 'no.'

Well, Richie did say 'no.' He just didn't do those things, you know, and I remember Alston saying that would hurt Allen's chances to stay on the club. O'Malley didn't ask for a lot, but he expected to get it.

When the Dodgers traded Allen for Tommy John and a minor shortstop prospect, they replaced him with an aging Frank Robinson. Ozark suggested it may have been done because the Dodgers were committed to Wes Parker at first base and Robinson was a true outfielder, which Allen was not. Whatever the reason, the trade did not work out for the Dodgers. John had a good year (11-5, 2.89 ERA), but Frank didn't come close to filling Allen's shoes. The team scored 79 fewer runs, and even though their improved staff led the league in ERA, they won four fewer games and finished 10-1/2 games back.

Chicago - Allen failed to report for spring training and contemplated retiring rather than entering what he feared would be a situation similar to the one he'd faced during his final years in Philadelphia. He did not want to be on a weak team where the focus would be so totally on him as to whether the team was a success or a failure.

Allen told me a story that I don't believe has ever appeared in print before. He actually *was* there at the start of spring training, watching the team incognito for a couple days from beyond the center field fence. He wanted to see for himself how weak the team was. Roland Hemond remembered a rumor, "that Dick was in town watching the team." Allen was discouraged by what he saw and went home with the intention of retiring. His mother persuaded him to give it a try and to help out manager Chuck Tanner who had grown up as a neighbor of theirs.

That year Allen was a major factor in turning the sub-.500 team into a surprise contender. With Tommy John gone, the staff ERA rose 39 points relative to the league, but the difference in adding Allen to the offense was immense. His 37 HR set a franchise record, and his 113 RBIs led the league. The Sox finished second, just 5-1/2 games behind the powerhouse Oakland A's.

White Sox GM Roland Hemond:

He came in with a tremendous amount of respect from our players. And that was always there. He was a very analytical player with a great memory for past situations. A smart player, an outstanding base runner. I'll never forget him, and I'll always be grateful to him.

He gave us great years; he made it fun. He revitalized baseball in Chicago. Attendance had been down for years...Dick got them out to the ballpark again. He had a tremendous impact on our attendance.

Compared to the average attendance in the seasons before and after Dick's time with the Sox, the average yearly attendance was up over 50 percent during Allen's three years.

White Sox Manager Chuck Tanner:

He was the greatest player I ever managed, and what he did for us in Chicago was amazing. In Pittsburgh I had guys like Willie Stargell, Dave Parker, Phil Garner, Bill Madlock, but in Chicago it was Dick Allen and, what, Bill Melton? There just wasn't a lot of talent there. With Dick—well, we were able to battle the Oakland A's, one of the greatest teams ever. Without him we simply weren't a first division team.

They talk about his hitting, but I want to tell you that in nineteen years in the majors, the two best base runners I ever saw were Don Baylor and Dick Allen. They ran aggressively and never made a mistake.

Dick was the leader of our team, the captain, the manager on the field. He took care of the young kids, took them under his wing. And he played every game as if it was his last day on earth.

When I asked Roland whether the team ever divided into pro-Allen and anti-Allen groups, he said, "No, there was none of that." When I asked Tanner, he was astounded at the question. I explained why I was asking, and I read to him Bill James' criticism of Allen as a disruptive presence on a team. Tanner said, "He's full of shit, and you be sure to tell him that."

In Allen's second year with the Sox, they were one game out of first place when he broke his leg in a collision at first base. He was hitting .310 and was second in the league in HRs. He had only five at bats the rest of the year. Without Allen, the team played .430 ball and dropped to fifth place.

It was a cracked fibula, not a displaced fracture, and some critics expressed doubts about why it knocked Allen out for virtually the rest of the year. I asked Roland to respond to that.

What may have thrown people is that the doctor felt that a cast wasn't necessary, that he could simply stay off the leg while it healed. So Dick was on crutches, but then at the All-Star game, he was there in the seats with his son, and when the team was announced, he climbed over the rail—leaving his crutches behind—and walked out there to stand on the line with the other players in his civilian clothes.

[Barely a month later, Allen tried to play on the leg. On July 31 he went 3-for-4, but he had no power, and he had a notice-able limp running to first base. He had a hitless pinch-hit at bat on August 2 and never played again in 1973.]

Chuck Tanner

The leg wasn't healed. The doctor knew it, but Dick wanted to try. He was trying to help the team, but we saw he couldn't do it, and playing wasn't going to help it heal. His teammates appreciated the effort, but some people in the press may not have understood. He seemed indestructible to them.

I also asked Roland whether the leg was ready in September when the team was out of contention, and whether they had kept Allen back for any reason. Hemond said, "No, it still wasn't healed yet." Chuck Tanner backed up Hemond's memories:

He played hurt for us so many times that [the media] thought he was superman. But he wasn't; he was human. If anything, he was hurting himself trying to come back too soon.

Early retirement—In 1974 Allen was having another superb year. After the game of August 20, his average stood at .310; he had a huge lead in the HR race and was slugging roughly 100 points higher than anyone else in the league. But his shoulder had been bother-ing him, and the pain expanded into his back. He continued to play for about three weeks but hit only .214 in that period, and, more alarming, all his hits were singles. On September 13 he announced his re-tirement.

The outrageous, callous, and cynical comments about Allen's motivation are what originally spurred me to do this article. The Allen profile in *Total Base-*

ball trips over itself with a ton of inaccuracies, but none are so wild as the contention that "[Allen] miffed [Tanner by] taking the last month of the season off to go tend his prize horses." Bill James doesn't do much better in his es-say. He claims that Allen "'voluntarily retired' to force a trade." That contradicts what Allen told me in 1982, and I quizzed both Hemond and Tan-ner carefully on this point. This is Hemond's account:

He talked to us a few days be-fore he did it. September eleventh? He had a meeting with Chuck and me. He was very sincere about retir-ing. I knew he was having some physical problems, but I told him, "Oh no, Dick, you don't want to retire," but he said it was what he wanted, he wanted to hang 'em up. It was a very emotional meeting; we all had tears in our eyes.

I talked him out of retiring [officially]. I told him that if he did that and changed his mind later, he would be ineligible to play for the first forty-two days of the season. Let us put you on the restricted list, and that's what we did.

Just to be sure on this point, I asked Hemond again if Allen had ever expressed an interest in being traded when he discussed his retirement. He replied: "Abso-lutely not, there was none of that. He was very sincere about retiring."

Tanner confirmed Roland's account of the emo-tional meeting two days ahead of Allen's announcement, agreed that Dick made no mention of a desire to be traded, and confirmed that Hemond had talked Allen out of filing the official retirement papers. I asked Tanner if he knew what prompted Dick's retirement:

I really don't know for sure. I know he was hurt-ing physically. I told him not to retire, to just let me sit him down, that I'd protect him. But he said he couldn't do that. I knew he was feeling a lot of pressure. The day after [announcing his retirement], when he came in to say goodbye, he told me he felt good, that it was like a piano was lifted off his head.

In December Atlanta acquired Dick's contract on

the chance that he might come out of retirement. I asked Tanner whether he would have taken Allen back if Chicago had retained his contract:

> You better believe it. I'd have carried him on my shoulders. But we knew that would have been a tough situation, and he really needed a fresh start. I always had a place for him if it could be worked out. I tried to get him to come out of retirement in 1979 and join us in Pittsburgh. I would have loved to have him coming off the bench, and he would have been a World Champion with us.

The role of Allen's injuries in his decision to retire has been overlooked and ignored, perhaps because he never went on the disabled list. Allen generally declined to talk about injuries or to use them as an excuse. Corrales emphasized that several times to me, and gave several examples, including a case where no one knew that Allen was playing with an injury—not Corrales, not Dick's wife—and it was discovered only by accident.

In 1974 it was an apparent enough problem that Hemond knew he was in pain; Tanner knew he was hurting, and if you get out your *Baseball Guide* for that year, you can read, "Allen…endured a sore shoulder in the later stages of the season, and although he said little about it, the pain settled in his lower back." Years later, in the biography *Crash*, Allen acknowledged that injuries were a factor in his decision to follow through on his retirement, "I'd been injured six times, and each one had taken its toll. I was hurting physically and mentally."

But it was also clear that Allen did not believe his injuries were career threatening. I don't remember a single clear answer from him when I asked about his retirement in Chicago. My impression is that it was related to a fear of repeating his miseries in Philadelphia. The way he was attacked over his "slow" recovery from the broken leg was reminiscent of the response to his hand injury in Philly. He thought he would be crucified if he took Tanner's offer to sit and heal, and he was too worn down phyically, and possibly mentally, to meet the pressure put on him to perform and carry the team.

Ultimately, his vague shoulder injury appears to be more serious than anyone suspected at the time. Allen's shoulders had taken an unusual beating starting with Thomas using one of them for batting practice, then a dislocation the next year, and finally this 1974 shoulder strain. During his comeback in 1976 Allen had several bouts of shoulder trouble in-cluding another dislocation. But even without a clear medical delineation, there certainly is a statistical one.

Allen's Career	AB	BA	SLG	OBA
Through 8/20/74	5,405	.300	.556	.389
After 8/20/74	927	.245	.401	.334

And if you want to make a Hall of Fame argument for Allen, you have to use the peak value approach, focusing on his extreme excellence in those first eleven seasons. Allen is the only non-Hall of Famer on these two lists.

1964-74 Major League Leaders (4,000 PA Minimum)

	Slugging Percentage			Runs Created per Game
1.	.561	Hank Aaron	1. 8.0	Willie McCovey
2.	.554	**Dick Allen**	2. 7.8	**Dick Allen**
3.	.541	Willie Stargell	3. 7.8	Hank Aaron
4.	.541	Willie McCovey	4. 7.4	Frank Robinson
5.	.524	Frank Robinson	5. 7.2	Willie Stargell
6.	.513	Willie Mays	6. 7.2	Roberto Clemente
7.	.511	Roberto Clemente	7. 7.1	Willie Mays
8.	.510	Billy Williams	8. 7.1	Carl Yastrzemski
9.	.502	Reggie Jackson	9. 6.9	Harmon Killebrew
10.	.501	Harmon Killebrew	10. 6.9	Billy Williams

Before leaving Allen's years in Chicago, I want to add some balance to the charges that he avoided spring training and that he thought he was too good for batting practice. Like a lot of good hitters Allen felt that he did not need a long spring training period, but I know of only three times where he was late for spring training. Once was the spring after his hand injury. He had taken a lot of B.P. prior to arriving in camp, and he went to see his doctor when he feared he had overdone it and reinjured the hand. In 1972 he was late reporting while he contemplated retiring rather than joining the White Sox. He would also miss spring training in 1975 when he was on the re-stricted list and still unofficially retired. That does not justify writing something like, "[Dick] found spring training a waste of time and avoided [it] as much as possible" (excerpt from *Total Baseball*).

His detractors never mention that he reported *early* to spring training as a Dodger in 1971. And you rarely hear that when he did decide to join the White Sox in 1972 and the players' union went out on strike, Allen stayed in Florida and took part in the daily workouts and pickup games organized by the players. (He told me it was his favorite spring training.) And here is a story I never heard until Chuck

Tanner shared it with me. In 1973 Allen was coming out early to hit buckets of balls and would wear a weighted belt as he went through the drills. Tanner was concerned that he was wearing himself down rather than building himself up, and against Allen's protests, barred him from camp for a couple of days.

It is true that Tanner allowed Allen to decide whether or not he would take batting practice. This was not revolutionary. Other managers have done this with veteran hitters whom they felt were good monitors of their own swings. Throughout his career Allen swung one of the heaviest, if not *the* heaviest, bat in the majors (40 to 42 ounces). When he felt his swing was sound, he preferred to save his strength for the game. When he felt his swing needed tuning, he took batting practice. It is hard to argue with the results. In his three years under Tanner's system, he hit over .300 every year and took the only two home run crowns of his career.

Back to Philadelphia—Allen felt that his poor showing with the Phillies in 1975 was a result of his long layoff and lack of spring training. (He joined the team in mid-May and went right into the lineup). But when I went through his daily logs, that theory comes up short. He did pick up his power hitting late in the year, but from August 1 on he still hit only .246 in his final 167 at bats.

Allen did have some good streaks in 1976 where it looked like he was coming back, but he suffered disabling shoulder problems again, and when he came back from the last occurrence he was swinging very poorly. He hit just .228 in the final 241 at bats of his career.

But there is a silver lining to this precipitous decline in Allen's performance. It allows us to ask some very unsettling questions of Allen's critics. Some have suggested that everywhere Allen went his team eventually wised up and didn't want him around anymore. How, then, did he end up back in Philadelphia? He was certainly no stranger to the Phillies. The front office had shuffled a bit, but it was essentially the same people who had dealt with him in 1969. The Carpenter family still owned the team; Bill Giles had moved up from GM to executive VP; Paul Owens had gone from Farm Director to GM, and Dallas Green had gone from Assistant Farm Director to Director of Scouting. Manager Danny Ozark had been Dick Allen's coach during his year in L. A. The contingent that went to Allen's farm to talk him out of retirement was led by Richie Ashburn, who broadcast the Phillies games during Allen's whole career. (As a player, Ashburn had also been the friend and roommate of Frank Thomas.) They knew all they would ever need to know about this guy.

If Dick Allen was as bad an apple as some people have painted him, why would the Phillies go to such lengths to bring him back? And if Dick Allen was such a horrible influence that he kept his teams from winning even when he was crushing the ball—Bill James' conclusion—then how did the 1975 Phillies go from a losing record to 86-76 even though Allen had a horrible year (.233 with only 12 HR in 416 at bats)?

And if Allen was such a divisive presence that his teams split into pro- and anti-Allen camps, why would the Phillies ask him back after the worst year of his career? And if Allen kept his teams from winning, how did they improve to 101 wins in his second year, capturing their first championship in over twenty-five years?

His detractors dance around his teams' earlier second place finishes in Philadelphia, Los Angeles, and Chicago. What are we supposed to think about this second tour in Philadelphia? That if Allen had been a nicer fellow, the '76 Phillies would have broken the all-time win record?

I asked Ozark if he was consulted and had made a recommendation on Allen's acquisition:

> Sure, they asked me, and I told them I wanted him. Definitely. I admired him. He played through injuries. He never said 'I don't want to play.' When he first hurt his shoulder—it was May or June [1976]—he didn't want to go on the DL. Even when he wasn't at his best, he was helping us. He did things right, if you know what I mean. He did things you can't find in the stats. He did things as a power hitter that you'd expect a number two hitter to do. He knew the game; he was a team player.
>
> ...he did a lot of good things that nobody saw. He helped other players. He liked to help the young guys. He helped Mike Schmidt more than anyone. Mike will back that up. He got people talking in the dugout—what a pitcher was doing, base running. He made them think.

The Phillies did not re-sign Allen after the 1976 season. Bill James suggests that Allen left the Phillies under a cloud, that Allen's "group" had held a separate victory party from the rest of the team, and that Allen had threatened not to play in the playoffs unless they made a spot for one of his teammates on the postseason roster. When I asked Ozark if he would have been willing to have Allen on the team in 1977, he said, "I would have been happy to have him back. They thought we might do better with a few changes. It was just a move. He wasn't the only change we made."

The Phillies brought in lefty Richie Hebner to replace Allen at first base. This helped balance out a lineup that lacked lefty power and had only one true lefty regular, Jay Johnstone (Larry Bowa switch-hit). In 1977 Hebner hit .285 with a .484 slugging percentage, and that was an improvement over either of Allen's final years in Philly.

The Phillies also had reason to be concerned about Allen's health and his ability to swing a productive bat. The last time he dislocated his shoulder he had been out forty days, and after his return he was only 14-for-70 (.200) with two home runs, and in the playoffs he was just 2-for-9. Allen's performance in Oakland before his final retirement supports this theory. For Finley's bargain basement A's, he hit .240 with little power.

I asked Ozark about the incidents described in James' book:

> I'll tell you what happened [with that party story]. We clinched in Montreal, winning the first game of a doubleheader. I didn't play the regulars during the second game. While the game was going on, they had a little party back in the clubhouse—I think some even had a prayer meeting. It was no big deal. I knew about it. It was okay with me. It was okay with Carpenter and Owens who were at the game.
>
> As for that other stuff [threatening to sit if a teammate was left off the post-season roster], I just don't remember it. Do you know the player's name? I'm not saying it didn't happen, but people say things, and sometimes reporters make them an issue when they're not. For me—for us—it was probably just nothing.

It did happen. The player was Tony Taylor, a 40-year-old veteran who was in his final season and had played fifteen years for the Phillies. Allen, and probably many others, felt it was unjust that the Phillies, on the eve of the playoffs, would take Taylor's uniform away. Allen did threaten not to play, saying that they could take his uniform as well. By speaking up, Allen brought about a compromise that seemed fairer to everyone: Taylor would be in uniform in post season play as a coach.

This incident, which seems so important to James, is considered so insignificant by the manager of the team that he doesn't even remember it today. That's

something that James and others should stop and think about as they assess Allen's career. Do they really have an understanding of the types of personalities that a winning team cannot abide, or the types of storms and internal conflicts that a team cannot weather?

When we talk about contributions beyond a player's performance, most players are a mixture of pluses and minuses, and Dick Allen was no exception. On the negative side he is stubborn, lacks tact, and has a problem with rules and authority. In my talks with Allen, I found that he had a good mind for a lot of subjects, but he had little grasp of the hierarchy of group management, how it works and what it requires. Dick sincerely felt that everyone should be treated at a personal level under any and all circumstances. Given his unusual philosophy, at some point every manager was going to do something out of the innocent necessity of his job that would be seen as hurtful betrayal from Dick's perspective. This naturally made Dick a tougher player to manage.

The positive side—But it would be grossly unfair to stop there. Beyond the raw results of his performance, he deserves credit for being a student of the game as well as for his willingness and his ability to share his knowledge. His managers appreciated his setting an example of playing hurt and not making excuses. And he deserves to be praised for his competitiveness, courage, and confidence. (In my career, I have learned to never underestimate the value of anyone who brings those three C's to a team.)

And don't hesitate to give Allen a few points for being kind and likeable. It is amazing how far those qualities will go in healing the incidents where you say or do something that potentially could hurt the team. I'm sure his critics would be stunned to find how warmly he is remembered by those who shared a clubhouse with him. Many echo what Beringer told me, "I admired him. Not just as a ballplayer, but as a person." A number of those I interviewed told stories of Allen's generosity and kindness.

For all of his shortcomings, a lot of people who were actually there considered Allen a good teammate and a team player. In 1970 Gene Mauch surprised a lot of folks by publicly praising Allen and stunned them with the statement, "He's a good team man." And without any prompting, I note that both Tanner and Ozark specifically called Allen a "team player" in our interviews.

As I finished up my interview with Pat Corrales, I posed this question to him: "All of these managers felt that Allen's teammates liked him. You were there in those early years in Philly, and you tell me he was well-liked as a teammate. That's all I ever hear from his old teammates. My question is, why wasn't there more resentment toward his casual approach to team rules, his chronic lateness?" This was Pat's answer:

> I guess it's because we were ballplayers, and that's how we would judge him first. There's always going to be some guy who has trouble with the rules. Look, I played with and against him, and on the field he gave 110 percent. He was ready for the game and he played it to the max. It wasn't just raw talent either. He knew how to play; he had an instinct for this game. We knew that if everyone played the way he did, there wouldn't be many losses. That's what mattered to us. If he gave it to us on the field and he was late getting to the park, that wasn't such a big deal to us.

It is time to lay some of the wilder notions about Dick Allen to rest. When someone writes that Allen "never did anything to help his teams to win," you now know that's not true. You have heard from the men in the best position to judge that. They unanimously disagree with that notion, and the record supports them.

When someone says that once a team had Allen around a while it never wanted him again, you know that's not true. The Phillies took him back and won with him. And every one of these managers, even Mauch and Skinner, said they would want him again. And think about this: If Allen left Philadelphia on such bad terms, then why are they employing him today and allowing him to work with their young players in the spring?

When someone says that Allen had a divisive presence that kept his teams from winning, you now know that's not true. You

have heard it denied here by the people who would be the first to complain if it were true, and again the record supports them.

When someone writes that Allen's teams split into pro-Allen and anti-Allen factions, or that he was disliked by many of his teammates, you now know that's not true. All of these managers deny that, and most added that they saw exactly the opposite.

So why has Allen ended up being painted so harshly? In my years around the game, I have seen how easy it is for images to be built that often do not relate to reality. Consider how much easier it would be to paint a false image for a man like Allen. Writers have often referred to Allen as an "enigma," but in my interview with Gene Mauch he referred to him as an "uncomplicated man." Pat Corrales said roughly the same thing, and in the time I spent with Allen, it was easy to see what they meant. He liked to keep things as simple as possible. He was a modest, private person who disliked being the center of attention.

Dick was not interested in being known, and he was content to present a blank canvas to the media and fans and to let us paint on it what we would. For the most part, with the dips and turns in Allen's career, we took that opportunity to paint our archetype of the troublemaker, the disruptive player. I suspect that if Allen had started off with another team, in another city, or just in a later time, our attitudes toward him and our perceptions of him would be entirely different. And even then we would need now to ask if we were really seeing him or simply what we wanted to see.

By virtue of his not wanting to be known, the "uncomplicated man" remains an "enigma" for baseball fans, writers, and historians. If you think you know Dick Allen, look again.

Dick Allen

Transcendental Graphics

The Oriole

With thanks to Baltimore's own Edgar Allan Poe

Jonathan Boyd

Now upon these midnights dreary, while I ponder, weak and weary,
Puzzling out the hopes of all who yearn to hear a baseball score—
While I wonder why, I ask, "Have summer's games become a task
Begrudged, though so beloved before?" In volumes of forgotten lore
I dig—compelled to find a time when fans were asked to render more,
                                        Seasons lost like 'Ninety-four.

When I think upon this year, the hope—but no, more like the fear—
Springs up within my mind unbidden, "Will I see the game e'ermore?
Will the men who run The Show give in, and share their treasure trove?"
'Ninety-five draws near the door, ungainly son of 'Ninety-four,
"Last chance" (they moan) to heal the grievous wounds we scarcely can ignore,
                                        Wounds not they, but fandom bore.

Dollars lost or dollars won…Number crunchers rush to run
The tape they'll use to tell the tales their bosses need to grab for more.
"Don't you see our sacred interest?" All I see is old Big Business!
Once again who pays the price? The fan who roots despite the score,
The fan who gazes at the stars, who stays through nine despite the score:
                                        To us they always turn for more.

Thoughts like these, and plenty others, keep us grousing with our brothers,
Keep our minds from restful pleasures—pitching duels, a rallying score.
Worst, I say, *this* bitter fruit: the cynicism which follows suit.
Who can claim to be untouched? Who'll forget such wrongs and more?
Shall we yield and soon forget these wrongs and baseball's countless more?
                                        Quoth the Oriole, "Nevermore."

Jonathan Boyd is a PhD candidate in history at Johns Hopkins University.
Baltimore made him a baseball fan.

For yes! that splendid bird has lit upon my arm and with his wit
Pours forth a stream of sad lament for baseball's year of 'Ninety-four.
(Orange and black his feathers gleam, speaking of his favorite team
Upon their verdant playing field, the Yards in downtown Baltimore.
He loves most parks in every league, but ask him which he loves the more,
                                        And he'll tell you, "Baltimore.")

He it is who takes my hand and, lifting me above the land,
Shows me baseball all around, rich treasures from our nation's store
Lost: like Ripken's June-planned game, or Donny's chance at playoff fame.
Waiting long, too long, is Erie's Tribe, assembled by the shore;
No chance to put on war-paint now, canoes embarking from the shore?
                                        Quoth the Oriole, "Nevermore."

Smoke from Boog's sweet barbecue lofts us high in visions true:
Umps unlimber; announcers laugh; fielders stretch, endure the chore
The diamond asks to grant success in this most playful business.
Parks resound with hometown cheers, and fans there love to keep the score.
So baseball satisfies our love, so baseball fills us to the core—
                                        And rightly pray we, "Evermore!"

Now elites who run the game insist instead that here the same
Code that twists our public life turns friendly partners round to war.
Games of 'ball in my hometown are better played, though less renowned:
Friends in contest learn to lose, or sacrifice a fly to score.
Will the moguls learn the same? Will they earn our trust once more?
                                        Quoth the Oriole, "Nevermore."

Return we will, of this one thing be sure if teams come back in spring
To ply their trade and sell their wares (from caps and 'dogs to cards and more).
But much, of course, now nonetheless is spent in baseball's pettiness:
Trust exemption, union power, market share, perhaps—but *more!*
A season gone, the Series broken! To get them back may we implore?
                                        Quoth the Oriole, "Nevermore."

GAME 2 Thursday, September 29, 1955

Brooklyn   000 110 000 - 2 5 2
New York   000 400 00x - 4 8 0

BROOKLYN (0-1)

7 Gilliam	k	7	s'	463p
6 Reese	9	D	k	s
8 Snider	9	s'x	43	k
2 Campanella	5^f	w	9	6^
9 Furillo	w	7	3^	7
3 Hodges	9	7	wc	k
5 JRobinson	6^	W	9	
4 Zimmer	k	sx	kp	
1 Loes	63			
1 Bessent 4				
o Kellert 5	643p			
1 Spooner 5				
o Hoak 8	wx			
1 Labine 8				

NEW YORK (1-0)

9 Bauer	sc			
8 Cerv 3	k	43	63	
5 McDougald	kp	sx	k	k
7/8 Noren	8	36p	wx	e4x
2 Berra	p	S	s	k
3 Collins	k	W	k	8
9/7 Howard	k*	S'	53	f64
4 Martin	k	S'	k	
6 Rizzuto	sx			
o ERobinson 4	p			
6r JColeman 4	k			
1 Byrne	463p	s"	13	

* e4 on sb attempt by Berra

Pitchers: BROOKLYN, Loes L (99xx), Bessent (xx1x), Spooner (xx82), Labine (xxx4). NEW YORK, Byrne W.
Left on Base- Bkl 4, NY 5. T- 2:28. A- 64,707.
Ump-Ballanfant, Honochick, Dascoli, Summers, Flaherty, Donatelli.

If Not Larsen, Who?

Don did it, but which pitcher was most likely to do it?

Charles Blahous

Along with DiMaggio's 56-game hitting streak, which we analyzed in last year's *BRJ*, the World Series perfect game of Don Larsen seems to be one of the two baseball events most intriguing to students of probability. In defining the improbability of Larsen's perfect game, however, we have to take proper account of why it was such a remarkable achievement: it occurred *in a World Series*. So if we're going to define just how improbable it was, we want to define, not Larsen's likelihood of throwing a perfect game at any time in his career, but his likelihood of doing it in one of his few Series starts. Similarly, in identifying the best candidate to do what Larsen did, we want to identify not the pitcher most likely to throw a perfect game at any point, but the pitcher most likely to have pulled it off in the World Series.

First, a few remarks about what it means to throw a perfect game. The odds of throwing a perfect game are quite different from those of throwing a no-hitter. A pitcher's likelihood of throwing a no-hitter is defined largely by what batting average opposing players achieve against him. The main reason that Nolan Ryan is the all-time no-hit king is that he holds opposing batters to a lower batting average than any pitcher in history.

Throwing a no-hitter is like winning a card game in which the object is to draw 27 cards marked "win" before drawing one card marked "loss." Getting the batter out is a "win" for the pitcher. A hit is a "loss."

Walks, hit batsmen, errors, and the like might be thought of as cards marked "draw again." They don't get the pitcher closer to his goal, but they don't spoil the effort, either. The principle that must be understood is that no matter how many "draw again" cards you have in the deck, it's the ratio of those "win" and "loss" cards (outs and hits) that determine your likelihood of getting to 27.

With no-hitters, some complexities are introduced by the possibilities of double plays, sacrifices, sacrifice flies, and so forth. Suppose you have two pitchers who are identical in every respect except ground-ball frequency. They have an equal chance of yielding a walk — but an unequal chance of its being erased by a double play — thus the one who gets more GIDPs might have a slightly better chance of getting that extra two-out step toward his no-hitter.

A different set of considerations—Fortunately for us, perfect games don't feature this problem. The pitcher must retire every batter. It's like playing the card game and having only two kinds of cards, "win" and "loss." There are no "draw agains," and there are always exactly 27 draws whenever the game is played to a successful conclusion.

To figure a pitcher's likelihood of throwing a perfect game, therefore, we must take into account his chances of yielding a hit, of yielding a walk, of hitting a batter, and of seeing an error committed behind him. I'm sorry to say that hit batsmen is something I am going to have to leave out of these calculations. I

Charles Blahous is legislative director for U.S. Senator Alan Simpson, a lifelong Pirates fan, and an opponent of wildcard playoffs and the DH.

don't have them for every pitcher we're going to consider; I will say that I'm confident their inclusion would not appreciably alter the relative chances of our candidates to throw no-hitters, although their absolute likelihoods would, unavoidably, be altered.

The other considerations, though, clearly matter a lot. A pitcher with a low opposing batting average does not necessarily have a relatively good chance of throwing a perfect game. He must have good control, too. It is a pitcher's baserunners allowed per out that determines his chances.

Errors and evolutionary theory—One of the fascinating things found in such a study is how errors come into play. We do not have data on how many errors were committed behind each pitcher, but we do quickly find that error propensity can make a very significant difference in a pitcher's chances. I have therefore taken each pitcher's support-team error frequency, as figured by the number of balls in play turned successfully into outs by the fielders (roughly, outs minus strikeouts) compared with errors committed. Then I took each pitcher's number of outs made on balls fielded by the team behind him, and figured the number of errors the team should have committed behind him if it fielded at a level consistent with its seasonal performance. Bear in mind that you can't, and I didn't, simply assume that a pitcher's proportion of team innings will bear the same proportion of errors. You have to consider the balls in play; some pitchers have many more balls in play than others, because they strike out fewer batters.

What you find when you're done with all this is just how much the game has evolved over the years. There were some truly great pitchers in the early part of this century—Mathewson, Alexander, and Brown, to name a few—who pitched in World Series and who yielded few hits and few walks. Yet their chances of pitching a perfect game were never all that good, because they played in an era when fields were rough, gloves were small and strikeouts were rare. Most balls were put in play, and errors were frequent.

The questions—There are two questions I sought to answer. First, in which World Series were we most likely to see a perfect game pitched? How unlikely was it? Who should have thrown it? I figured this by taking a pitcher's statistical profile for a given season and taking into account also how many chances he got in the Series that year to throw one.

The other question was this: if a perfect game was going to occur some time in World Series history, who would have been most likely to throw it? The answer that comes to your mind, possibly, is the one that came to mine: Whitey Ford. Was he the pitcher with the best chance, since he started twenty-two Series games, and no one else started more than eleven? I won't give you the answer yet, because it reveals a lot about how the probabilities of perfect games work.

Figuring—The calculations work like this: Every pitcher has a certain probability of getting a batter out for each batter he faces. You take the pitcher's chance of retiring the batter, versus the batter's chance of reaching via a walk or a hit or an error. Suppose the pitcher's chance of retiring the batter is 70 percent each time. His chances of throwing a perfect game, in a given game, would be .70 to the 27th power. Then you take that probability and determine what would have been his likelihood of throwing at least one perfect Series game, given his number of Series starts.

Of course, the pitcher's hit-yield data is what he gives up against average competition. In each batter-pitcher confrontation, the probability of the outcomes is determined by the interaction between the batter's and pitcher's statistical profiles. In order to do this right, you'd have to take all the lineups that were faced by these pitchers in the Series, and figure out the probability of an out for each batter-pitcher confrontation. As I described last year in the DiMaggio article, this is not an exact calculation. But we can reliably say that each of the probabilities we'll see here is probably a bit high, because the pitchers were often facing some of the other league's best hitters. We also have to acknowledge that the quality of opposing hitting would probably not affect each pitcher equally, since they faced offenses of varying quality. In this study, though, I am determining the probabilities intrinsic in the pitcher's own statistical profile.

When?—To the first question: When were we most likely to see a perfect game in the World Series? With the above approximations, the best candidates were:

Pitcher	Year	Chance
Sandy Koufax	1965	0.2054%
Bob Gibson	1968	0.1928%
Denny McLain	1968	0.1522%
Babe Adams	1909	0.1205%
John Tudor	1985	0.1179%

You might be tempted to place an asterisk next to

Don Larson, hurling his perfect game.

the name of Babe Adams. He pitched only 130 innings that year, so you might not consider his stats truly representative. I would argue that they are. He pitched magnificently in winning three World Series games, but more importantly, there were *four times* in his career when he led the league in fewest hits plus walks per inning pitched. Although something of a phenom in 1909, clearly he had the type of statistical profile that makes him a great candidate for a perfect game. We should also perhaps put a qualifier next to the name of John Tudor, whose chances would have been adversely affected by the fact that he had to face a lineup including a DH in one of his starts in the 1985 World Series.

You have probably noticed already that the single year most likely to have produced a perfect game in the World Series was 1968. It was the Year of the Pitcher, after all, and in the Series Gibson (of the 1.12 ERA) and McLain (and his 31 wins) each had three starts.

Other good candidates include Sandy Koufax in 1963 (despite only two starts), Grover Cleveland Alexander in 1915 (probably would be among the top five with better defensive support), and Catfish Hunter in 1972 (pinpoint control and very tough to hit that year). Not every pitcher who made the top five had three starts in the Series. But Koufax, Gibson, and McLain all were the best pitchers in their leagues, while Tudor's 1985 season would have been similarly dominant in most years.

Who—What about career chances? Who had the best chance of throwing a perfect game at some time in his career? The answers:

Pitcher	Chance
Sandy Koufax	0.337%
Bob Gibson	0.254%
Whitey Ford	0.170%
Catfish Hunter	0.159%
Denny McLain	0.152%

A few questions may be coming into your mind: Why isn't Whitey Ford first? Why are the probabilities for a career not that different than the probabilities for one season? Why is Denny McLain still on the list even though he only appeared in one Series?

If you think about it for a moment, one mathematical reality lies behind all three answers.

Bear in mind how the calculation works. Suppose you have a Sandy Koufax-level pitcher. Suppose an opposing batter only has a 24 percent chance of reaching base against him—whether by hit, walk, or error. Compare this with another great pitcher—say Whitey Ford in 1958. The batter has a 28 percent chance of reaching against him. A 76 percent chance versus a 72 percent chance of retiring the batter may not seem like that big a difference—until you take it to the 27th power. Then there is practically a five times ratio between the two pitchers' chances of success.

This is a principle familiar to most of you. Consider two teams—a .550 team and a .450 team. On any given day one team's chance of winning is almost as large as the other. But when we compare their chances of putting together a 12-game winning streak, we find that one team's chance is several times that of the other, due to the exponent to which the relative probabilities are being raised.

So you see—if I have five times the chance that you do of doing something, I still have a better chance even if you get three times as many shots at it. That's what's happening between Koufax and Ford. Similarly, a pitcher's career chances of throwing a World Series perfect game are largely defined by the number

of chances he has of pitching in the Series at his peak level of performance. That's why the career figures aren't orders of magnitude different from the first ones, and why Denny McLain is on the list while several who appeared more frequently are not.

Other worthy candidates are John Tudor and Christy Mathewson. Mathewson was undone by the number of errors committed behind him, while Tudor simply didn't add enough to his chances in 1987 and 1988, because he never again approached his phenomenal level of performance of 1985.

One final note about Don Larsen. He actually was a comparatively *good* candidate to throw a no-hitter in the Series. In 1956, he was the second toughest pitcher in baseball to hit (after Herb Score), and the toughest to appear in the Series. He had two starts, and therefore two chances.

Where Larsen would have been expected to come up short was with his control. He walked a fair number of hitters. Due to this factor, his chances of throwing a perfect game in the Series that year were only 0.00781 percent. Larsen was tough to hit; he simply struggled with his accuracy. Even in the other Series game that year, when he was knocked out of the box early, he only yielded one hit. The rest of what he yielded was due to wildness.

How unlikely?—My own conclusion after all of this is that Larsen's perfect game was comparable in improbability to DiMaggio's hitting streak. At first glance it's not obvious. One involves an individual doing something he normally has 80 to 90 percent chance of doing (getting at least one hit in a game) and doing it 56 consecutive times. The other involves something one has 75 percent chance of doing (retiring the batter) and doing it 27 consecutive times.

The kicker comes in the number of opportunities each had to perform his magic. Larsen, in the 1956 Series, had two chances. DiMaggio had dozens of 56-game bunches over which a streak could be measured. DiMaggio also had a full career of opportunities. Larsen only had the years in which his team appeared in the Series.

Larsen's perfect game could have been the bigger miracle. The biggest baseball miracle of all time? A loaded question—and a worthy topic of speculation for any baseball fan.

The Parker Brothers and Other Cincinnati Oddities

One had an infinite ERA; the other pitched the century's worst game

Joseph Cardello

A small group of family and friends gathered at the funeral of an elderly man. The mourners sat patiently but in growing discomfort as those who knew the deceased took turns eulogizing him at the podium. Each speaker struggled to find something good to say about the dearly departed. Sadly, since the deceased man had been almost universally disliked, the eulogies spoke remarkably ill of the dead.

With the negative commentaries piling up, one of the departed's closest acquaintances rose from his chair to take his turn at the podium. He walked up to the lectern and faced the mourners. But before he could launch into his own diatribe, a confused member of the audience—who perhaps did not know the subject quite so well—jumped up suddenly and yelled out: "What kind of tribute is this!? Can't anybody think of anything good to say about this poor soul!?" The man at the podium paused. He frowned and stared up at the ceiling, thinking hard. After a few minutes he looked down at the audience and nodded ever so slightly. He shrugged his shoulders and said: "His brother was woise."

Much the same could be said of the Parker brothers—although it's not at all clear which one was actually worse. Each has his distinctive claim.

Take Jay Parker. He appeared as the starting pitcher for Pittsburgh on September 27, 1899. He pitched to two Chicago hitters, walked them both, and was re-moved from the game. Both runners later scored. Since the game ultimately ended in a 7-7 tie, Jay received no decision. But, since he never appeared in any other major league game, he received something else much more rare: a career earned run average of infinity.

While the description "brief" cannot fully capture the career of Jay Parker, his brother's claim to shame involved a different and much longer story.

Harley "Doc" Parker, two years his brother's senior, had already proven beyond a doubt that he did not belong in the major leagues. For three years, 1893-95-96, he'd compiled a 5-7 record as a pitcher for Chicago, giving up 170 hits in 126-1/3 innings. He certainly earned the obscurity he enjoyed. But one day in June 1901 all that changed. Doc was pitching for minor-league Louisville, just down the river from Cincinnati. He hadn't pitched in the National League for five years. Then, suddenly, he got a call to report to the Reds.

Doc Parker's trip up the Ohio River would land him a place in baseball infamy. And it was all the fault of one desperate man: Cincinnati manager, Bid McPhee.

John Alexander McPhee could trace his career in Cincinnati back to 1882, when he first appeared as the second baseman for the city's American Association club. When the team switched to the National League in 1890, McPhee went with them. He retired in 1899, after putting in 18 solid years as Cincinnati's regular second baseman—perhaps the best in baseball at that position in the 1880s and 1890s. But in all

Joseph Cardello is a statistical analyst for Beyer Associates, supplying data to The Daily Racing Form. He lives in Columbia, Maryland.

those years his team won only one pennant—in 1882, McPhee's rookie year. For the next seventeen years Cincinnati came close a few times, but usually finished harmlessly in the middle of the pack.

In 1901 Bid McPhee took over as manager of a Cincinnati team which had finished seventh the previous year with a 62-77 record. But the club started fast in 1901, holding first place for a time in April and May. On June 8 the Reds were 20-14, in second place just behind the Giants. Then they started to lose. Day by day they sank lower and lower in the standings. On June 19 they dropped their eighth in a row, losing 10-6 to Brooklyn. The next day Brooklyn hammered them again, 8-1, battering the Reds' best pitcher, Noodles Hahn. In two days the Brooklyn batters had pounded out 29 hits against the Reds' hapless pitching staff. And there had been other massacres along the way, including a 12-1 loss to St. Louis.

Bid McPhee was a quiet, sober, unemotional man, but at this point he began to show signs of panic. The early hopes of April and May had been shattered. His pitchers were getting clobbered. He searched for some help. Precisely how he came up with Doc Parker we do not know for certain. One newspaper suggested that Tom Loftus, the Chicago manager who had managed McPhee and Cincinnati in 1890-1891, recommended this "gold brick." You can just imagine McPhee asking around and getting some sort of story from Loftus about how he'd heard this guy Parker was pitching well for Louisville and maybe Bid should give him a call.

Whatever the real story, one thing is clear: the recruiting of Doc Parker betrayed a deep desperation in the Cincinnati camp, and on June 21, in Brooklyn's Washington Park, Doc Parker took the mound for the fast-fading Reds.

Doc's game started quietly enough. The tall right-hander gave up a run in the first inning when Willie Keeler doubled, stole third, and scored on an infield out. He yielded another run in the second on an error, a wild pitch, and a double. But Cincinnati actually came back and took the lead, 3-2, in the top of the third. Then came the Brooklyn half of the third, and the game took a very distressing turn. Keeler led off with a single. Jimmy Sheckard followed with another single. Tom Daly also singled. One run. After a double steal, Bill Dahlen hit a double to right, scoring two more. Duke Farrell singled, scoring Dahlen. Four runs. Brooklyn now led, 6-3. In the fourth inning they added another run.

Then came the disastrous fifth inning. Shortstop George "Maggie" Magoon contributed an error to get things started, muffing Farrell's ground ball. Farrell then stole second. Frank Gatins sacrificed him to third. Deacon McGuire then scored him with a single. Brickyard Kennedy also singled. As did Keeler. And Sheckard. Daly added some variety, reaching first on an error. Sheckard rubbed it in by stealing home. Dahlen doubled. Tom McCreery bunted safely. When Farrell finally flied to center for the second out, Jake Beckley, the Reds first baseman, had seen enough. He let out a roar, announced that there were three outs, and began to trot off the field. He later said he knew perfectly well that there were only two outs, but he felt that, "He'd been working long enough for more to be out whether such was the case or not." Instead of laughing along with Beckley, the next Brooklyn batter singled, driving in the seventh and last run of the inning. Brooklyn now led, 14-3.

After scoring only one run in the sixth on a Willie Keeler home run, Brooklyn set out to make the seventh inning as memorable as the fifth. Dahlen led off with a single. McCreery flied out, Farrell singled, and Magoon fumbled another grounder. And the bases were loaded.

Now, it's hard to know just when the idea occurred to him, but at some point in the slaughter Doc Parker improvised a unique approach to the game. He abandoned the traditional notion of trying to get the batters out himself. Instead, he decided to just toss the ball up there and let them hit it, hoping his fielders might get in the way of enough of the balls before it got dark. "The only thing that I could do," Doc remarked after the game, "was to keep the ball on the plate after I found that they were going to hit me, and perhaps you noticed what happened." Indeed. And, for a time, it just *kept* happening. McGuire walked with the bases full. Kennedy singled. But then came the first ray of hope: Doc's "batting practice" approach began to have an impact. Players started getting tired. Keeler was the first casualty. He was due up next, but refused to bat, claiming he was so tired that he couldn't take another step if his life depended on it. He was already five-for-five, and had bunted, stolen, and scored enough for one afternoon. "'Six-day walking matches aren't in it with this sort of thing,' said he, breathlessly, as he sat on the bench and tried to collect his wind." Or so the Cincinnati *Enquirer* reported, or at least imagined. (The Brooklyn *Eagle* later denied this story, claiming that their man Keeler *never* got tired.) No matter. Harry "Cozy" Dolan, batted in Keeler's place. And—what else?—he singled. Followed by a Sheckard double, a Daly single, and a total of six more runs. At the end of seven innings the score was Brooklyn 21, Cincinnati 3.

Doc's strategy really began paying dividends in the eighth. According to the Brooklyn *Eagle*, the home-town boys simply tired of the whole lopsided business and "allowed themselves to be retired without attempting to run out the hits, which were fielded slowly and painfully by the tired and weary Cincinnatis." After Brooklyn absolutely refused to score in the eighth, the Reds cooperated by going down meekly in the ninth, and the game ended, 21-3.

Metaphors of warfare and violence filled the next morning's newspapers. "FUSILLADE OF HITS SOUNDED LIKE A SHAM BATTLE," said one headline.

> "There has not been such a slaughter of the innocents in Brooklyn since the day that trolley cars were first run and knocked every other man down.
>
> "The great majority of the hits were singles, and they snapped off the bat like dynamite were behind them.
>
> "After the exhibition this afternoon a Brooklyn baseball enthusiast suggested that it would be a good thing to have Hanlon's team arrested for baseball homicide in the first degree.
>
> "Frank Bancroft looked the field over after the last of the dead and wounded had been removed, and in a reminiscent tone said: 'There is only one thing that this reminds me of. This is the first game that Rusie pitched at Cleveland way back in 1889. We had much the same kind of a time, with much the same result if my memory serves me right. At one time this afternoon I thought the field was a tannery. There seemed to be nothing but pigskin in the air so far as I could see.'"

Doc Parker took his misfortune well. "I didn't expect to get out and win hands down the first time," he said. "But to tell the truth I didn't think there was quite so much coming my way. The next time that I get into the box I hope to give a better account of myself." These postgame platitudes proved a bit optimistic. The next day McPhee sent Parker back down the Ohio. Doc never pitched again in the major leagues.

Nobody knew it at the time, of course, but Doc Parker had done something special, something memorable. He had made baseball history. He'd pitched the National League's worst twentieth-century game: 21 runs, 26 hits, 48 official at bats in only eight innings.

And all of this was indeed the fault of Bid McPhee. Why did he leave Doc in there for the entire game? Of course, it's true, as the statisticians tell us, that 87.3 percent of starting pitchers completed their games in 1901. But surely an exception could have been made in this case. Surely Doc deserved to be among the 12.7 percent who couldn't finish what they'd started. Did McPhee have something personal against Doc, other than his horrible pitching? Apparently not, because just three days later—on Monday, June 24—McPhee proved that his stoic display of tolerance and patience in Doc's case reflected no individual or personal animosity. On that Monday in Philadelphia he sat by as Reds' pitcher Bill Phillips completed the second game of a double header against the Quakers. Silver Bill made a serious run at Doc Parker's freshly minted record, but he fell just short: in 8 innings he gave up only 19 runs on 22 hits. His teammates helped out with seven errors. All this after the Reds had dropped the first game of the twin bill, 8-0.

But this was not the end of it. In fact, the sound of National League bats hammering Cincinnati pitchers did not reach its final crescendo until three months later, on September 23 and 24 against Brooklyn. In all of Brooklyn's long baseball history, the team never again had two days of hitting like these against the Reds. And, if you could go by recent form, you might actually have predicted just such a disaster for Reds' pitching. In 1901 Brooklyn led the league in hitting, thanks mostly to their abuse of Cincinnati hurlers. They had a 14-6-1 record against the Reds, outscoring them 168-96. That's 8 runs per game, compared to only 5 runs per game against the rest of the league. Still, even with all this precedent, and even after the many poundings administered to Reds' pitchers by teams *not* from Brooklyn, these two games in late September were something to behold.

Once again, only metaphors of the bloody battle-field seemed adequate to describe what had happened to Cincinnati's pitchers:

CARNAGE.
JUST PLAIN SLAUGHTER.
BROOKLYN POUNDS STIMMEL TO THE BENCH.

On September 23 Brooklyn battered the Reds, 25-6, on 26 hits—twelve of them in the fifth inning alone. The biggest difference between this slaughter and the earlier one in June was that there were two pitching victims this time: Archie Stimmel and Johnny Suthoff. Virtually everything else was the same, including this commentary by the Brooklyn *Eagle*: "In the last two innings the Champions checked themselves out of sheer exhaustion and permitted the Reds to retire them in order." The Brooklyn pitcher, Jimmy Hughes, rubbed salt in Cincinnati's wounds: "Hughes stood in the box during the last two innings and informed the batters as they came up the exact style of ball he intended to deliver." This must have been hard for McPhee to take.

McPhee replaced Stimmel after he had surrendered 11 runs on 12 hits in the fifth inning alone. That gave the Reds' pitcher a total of 18 runs allowed on 20 hits, in only five innings—putting him way ahead of Doc Parker's record pace. But McPhee brought in Suthoff to pitch the rest of the way. Brooklyn continued with him where they'd left off with Stimmel, until they tired of it all in the final two innings.

September 24 was nearly as bad, variously described as "a batting bee," "a swatting festival," and "another baptism of base hits." This time Bill Phillips took the punishment: a total of 21 hits and a 16-2 loss. The Cincinnati *Enquirer*, apparently tired of the same old martial rhetoric, strained to find some equally descriptive imagery. In the second inning, the story went, "Four good drives gave Brooklyn a pair for a foundation, and they put up a regular skyscraper before the whistle blew for the hired hands to quit work." As the Reds plunged into the cellar, the *Enquirer* tried a slight variation on its construction-site imagery, and pronounced their season dead and buried: "When it was all over the Reds dragged themselves out of the debris as happy as a squad of hoboes who had been chased out of town by a Vigilance

Committee."

In describing this latest 16-2 debacle, the *Enquirer* announced:

PITCHERS.
REDS NEED CAR LOAD.
THE SAME OLD STORY WITHOUT VARIATION.
BROOKLYNS THUMP PHILLIPS AND WIN IN A WALK.

But a bit lower down in the headline there appeared this ominous note:

CRESE HEISMAN'S DEBUT OCCURS THIS AFTERNOON.

McPhee had brought up another fresh face to suffer in this lost season.

On September 25, 21-year-old Christian Heisman took to the pitcher's box against Brooklyn. In the second inning, already trailing 4-0, young Heisman came up to bat against Wild Bill Donovan. One of Donovan's pitches went considerably awry, hit Heisman in the head, and knocked him unconscious. He had to be carried off the field. Brooklyn went on to win the game, 9-2. Young Heisman, recovering satisfactorily after the game but still in a state of shock, took the loss.

If only Doc could've been so lucky.

The benefits of competition

An idea of the cost of running a base ball team can be gained by the salaries fixed to some of the stars by the two warring leagues. For several years the salary limit has been $2,400 in the National, and the American paid $1,800 last season for a few men.

The following list shows what competition has done for the players:

NATIONAL LEAGUE. *Boston Team—Long, $2,000; DeMontreville, $2,400; Tenney, Lowe, $2,500; Dineen, $3,000 (a war-measure salary); Nichols, $2,700; Willis, $2,000. Brooklyn—Kelley, Keeler, Sheckard, Dahlen, Farrell, McGuire, $3,000; McJames, $3,000; Hughes, $2,500. Chicago—Doyle, $2,800; McCormick, $2,300. Cincinnati—Harley, $3,900 (including a big bonus); Beckley, $2,400; Rusie, $2,500. New York—Davis, $3,000; Buelow, $2,500. Philadelphia—McFarland, $2,850; Douglas, $2,700; Thomas, $2,700; Flick, $3,000; Delehanty [sic], $3,500. Pittsburgh—Wagner, $2,800; Clarke, $3,000. St. Louis—Burkett, $3,200; Heldrick, $2,800; Wallace, $2,800; Donovan, $2,800; Padden, $2,700.*

AMERICAN LEAGUE. *Boston—Stahl, $3,500; Criger, $3,800; Young, $3,000; Collins, $6,000. Baltimore—Donlin, $2,500; Williams, $2,900; McGinnity, $3,000. Chicago—Jones, $2,700; Mertes, $2,700; Griffith, $4,000; Callahan, $3,300; W. Sullivan, $2,800. Cleveland—Scott, $2,700; Bradley, $2,600; McCarthy, $2,500. Detroit—Gleason, $2,200; Barrett, $3,000. Milwaukee—Garvin, $2,500; Hawley, $3,000. Philadelphia—Lajoie, $4,000; Cross, $3,000; Frazier, $2,500; Bernard, $2,500. Washington—Carrick, $2,700; Mercer, $3,600.*

—Jack Carlson, from the Dayton *Herald*, May 20, 1901

The Matty–Alex Tie

A look at lifetime victories

Joseph M. Wayman

Old Pete: Grover Cleveland Alexander

Transcendental Graphics

Christy Mathewson's win on May 21, 1902 was credited to Dummy Taylor for years. As a result, Mathewson was credited with 372 wins, a mark broken by Grover Cleveland Alexander in 1930. It was Alexander's last victory and he thought it placed him atop the National League pitching heap.

In 1946 Mathewson officially was accorded the win that puts him, in most publications, in a lifetime tie with Alex.

Supposedly, Joe Reichler discovered the win for Mathewson in 1943, although *The Sporting News Baseball Register* 1940 edition gave Mathewson 14 wins for 1902. In any event, Reichler's recommendation for a records change was approved by National League President Ford Frick.

This wasn't actually a revision. Mathewson officially won the May 21, 1902 game, but the NL did not release its official pitching averages that season. Early statisticians accepted the unofficial *Reach Guide*'s pitching compilations, which listed Mathewson with 13 wins.

The game in question:

May 21, Time 1:40			R	H	E	Pitchers
New York	020 100 010		4	7	2	Taylor (6.1) Mathewson (W 2.2)
Pittsburgh	110 000 100		3	4	0	Tannehill (CG)

Mathewson relieved Taylor in the seventh, blew the lead, and watched the Giants recapture it for a victory.

Taylor had pitched well for six and a third inings and left the game ahead. In 1902, he would have been given the win by perhaps 80 percent of the official scorers. This day the scorer was in the other 20 per-

Joseph M. Wayman *is a lifelong baseball fan in retirement who continues this interest in publishing* Grandstand Baseball Journal.

cent, and Mathewson got the win.

We can verify the official record if we remember that a pitcher's fielding games equals his pitching games, and that in 1902 a pitcher's games were totaled from his *decisions* (wins, losses, ties, and protests), not from the games in which he appeared. Mathewson was credited with 34 official fielding games, which works out this way:

Official Decisions					
Fld Games	Dc	W	L	T	P
34	34	14	18	1	1

Mathewson had 14 *official* wins in 1902, even though he was credited with 13 until the mid-1940s.

The *Baseball Register* 1940 listed a 14-17 season for Mathewson, along with a revised lifetime 373-188 tally. This mistake in the loss column probably resulted from the discoverer of the May 21 win assuming that it had been wrongly counted as a loss. It never had been.

Here are some of the leading record sources which listed Mathewson's 1902 W-L tally, prior to Alexander's 1929 challenge.

Source	Year	Compiler	W	L
Official Record	1902	Nicholas E. Young	14 *	18
Sporting Life	1902	Harry R. Beringer	13	18
Reach Guide	1903	Ernest J. Lanigan	13	18
Spalding Guide	1903	Henry Chadwick	13	18
Balldom	1914	George L. Moreland	13	18
Spalding Guide	1917	John B. Foster	13	18
Who's Who In Baseball	1918	John J. Lawres	13	18
Bat Bag	1924	Al Munro Elias	13	18

*Derived record based on official figures.

The official record of 14-18 for Mathewson was not readily discernible. It had to be derived from Mathewson's "games" in the official fielding records. Mathewson's true won-lost record—using the scoring rules of his era, and properly retaining the eighteenth loss from 1902—is 373-187.

Unlike Mathewson's, Alexander's official lifetime W-L record of 373-208 has never been questioned. All the recognized record tomes, past and present, have accepted Alexander's year-by-year official records in the annual *Spalding Guides* for all his seasons, 1911-1930. And Alexander was well aware of the record he was chasing.

The New York *Times* lead headline for Alexander's August 10, 1929, second-game victory at Philadelphia was, "Alexander Wins 373rd Game, Sets Record." Ten days later, Alexander was sent home for "breaking training." He never won another big league game, though he lost three the following year for the Phillies. At the time, he—and everyone else—was secure in the knowledge that he was the all-time NL win leader.

Christy Mathewson

Triple Milestone Hitters

A new generation

Bill Gilbert

Each of the triple crown categories has a significant milestone that serves as a target for hitters. High-average hitters shoot for a .300 batting average while power hitters take aim at 30 home runs and 100 runs batted in. Players who hit for both average and power shoot for all three. In the 1988 *Baseball Abstract*, Bill James used the term "Hall of Fame season" to describe a year in which a player achieved the triple milestones of a .300 batting average, 30 home runs and 100 RBIs. This feat has been accomplished 212 times by 89 different players. Eleven players have done it five or more times and all are in the Hall of Fame.

Babe Ruth was the first player to achieve a triple milestone season in 1920 and he went on to do it twelve times, more than any other hitter. He was also the oldest to do it at the age of 38. Lou Gehrig is second with ten triple milestone seasons, and has the longest streak of consecutive seasons with nine. Jimmie Foxx is third with nine triple milestone seasons. Mel Ott, at age 20, was the youngest to do it (Ted Williams also did it at age 20, but was three months older). In 1987, at the age of 35, Dwight Evans became the oldest to do it for the first time.

In the past 75 years, there have been thirteen seasons when five or more players hit triple milestones.

These years generally fall into four periods. The first was 1929-1934, the most prolific period ever for hitters, when Hall-of-Famers Ruth, Gehrig, Foxx, Chuck Klein, Earl Averill, Ott, Al Simmons and Hack Wilson were putting up big numbers. In 1929 and 1930, there were a record ten players with triple milestones each year. The second prolific period for hitters was 1937-1940, when Hank Greenberg, Joe DiMaggio and Rudy York joined Foxx as repeat triple milestone hitters. The third was 1953-1955, when Stan Musial, Roy Campanella, Gil Hodges, Duke Snider, and Ted Kluszewski were in their prime and Willie Mays was beginning to make his mark. The fourth was 1959-1962, when Mays, Hank Aaron, Frank Robinson and Orlando Cepeda were regulars on the list.

Five players achieved triple milestones in 1970, suggesting the possible beginning of another period. However, it didn't turn out that way as the next six years produced a total of only four triple milestone seasons. The gap was extended to twenty-two years before there was another season in which five players reached triple milestones and it took an expansion year in 1993 to do it.

Is 1993 the beginning of another era of prolific triple milestone hitters? The evidence suggests that it is. Of the five players who achieved triple milestones in 1993 (Barry Bonds, Frank Thomas, Ken Griffey, Jr., Mike Piazza, and Juan Gonzalez), only Bonds was over the age of 25. In addition, five other players came close (John Olerud, Rafael Palmeiro, Albert Belle, Matt Williams, and Mo Vaughn) and all

Bill Gilbert *is retired after a 35-year career with Exxon in technical and managerial positions in Texas and Louisiana. A lifelong baseball fan, he spent fourteen years in Little League as a coach and administrator. Living thirty miles from the Astrodome, in Baytown, Texas, he attends about twenty games each year and spends part of his time writing for various baseball publications.*

are in their twenties.

The most convincing evidence can be found in the numbers from the shortened 1994 season. Coupled with diluted pitching and the incredible shrinking strike zone, hitters were putting up numbers that would have made 1929 and 1930 pale in comparison. When the strike began on August 12, three players had already achieved triple milestones (Jeff Bagwell .368-39-116, Albert Belle .357-36-101 and Frank Thomas .353-38-101). Thirteen others were on target to reach all three milestones and six more were close enough to have a chance. Injuries, slumps, and a return to more normal production levels would probably have caused some of these players to fall off this pace. However, it is likely that a record number of players would have achieved triple milestones in 1994. The question now is whether or not hitters have lost their edge after the longest off-season ever. An educated guess is that hitters will start a little slowly in 1995, but will pick up the pace as the season progresses, setting the stage for another offensive assault in 1996.

Players with Multiple .300 BA - 30 HR - 100 RBI Seasons

Player	No. of Seasons	Hall of Fame	Years
1. Babe Ruth	12	Yes	1920-21, 23-24, 26-33
2. Lou Gehrig	10	Yes	1927, 29-37
3. Jimmie Foxx	9	Yes	1929-30, 32-36, 38-39
4. Joe DiMaggio	7	Yes	1937-41, 48, 50
5. Ted Williams (R)	7	Yes	1939, 41-42, 46-47, 49, 51
6. Willie Mays	7	Yes	1954-55, 59, 61-63, 65
7. Hank Aaron	7	Yes	1957, 59, 61-63, 67, 71
8. Mel Ott	6	Yes	1929, 32, 34-36, 38
9. Stan Musial	6	Yes	1948-49, 51, 53-55
10. Hank Greenberg	5	Yes	1935, 37-40
11. Frank Robinson	5	Yes	1959, 61-62, 66, 69
12. Hack Wilson	4	Yes	1927-30
13. Chuck Klein	4	Yes	1929-32
14. Duke Snider	4	Yes	1950, 53-55
15. Ted Kluszewski	4	No	1953-56
16. Jim Rice	4	No	1977-79, 83
17. Rogers Hornsby	3	Yes	1922, 25, 29
18. Al Simmons	3	Yes	1929-30, 32
19. Earl Averill	3	Yes	1931-32, 34
20. Ralph Kiner	3	Yes	1947, 49, 51
21. Roy Campanella	3	Yes	1951, 53, 55
22. Mickey Mantle	3	Yes	1956, 61, 64
23. Orlando Cepeda	3	No	1961-62, 70
24. Billy Williams	3	Yes	1965, 70, 72
25. Eddie Murray	3	Active	1980, 82-83
26. Don Mattingly	3	Active	1985-87
27. Barry Bonds	3	Active	1990, 92-93
28. Frank Thomas	3	Active	1991, 93-94
29. Hal Trosky	2	No	1934, 36
30. Rudy York	2	No	1937, 40
31. Johnny Mize	2	Yes	1940, 47
32. Gil Hodges	2	No	1953-54
33. Eddie Mathews	2	Yes	1953, 59
34. Ernie Banks	2	Yes	1958-59
35. Dick Allen	2	No	1966, 72
36. Carl Yastrzemski	2	Yes	1967, 70
37. Greg Luzinski	2	No	1975, 77
38. Dave Parker	2	Inelig	1978, 85
39. Cecil Cooper	2	No	1982-83
40. Dale Murphy	2	Inelig	1983, 85
41. George Bell	2	Inelig	1986-87
42. Danny Tartabull	2	Active	1987, 91

(R) Rookie

Players with One .300 BA - 30 HR - 100 RBI Season

Player	Hall of Fame	Year
1. Ken Williams	No	1922
2. Jim Bottomley	Yes	1928
3. Lefty O'Doul	No	1929
4. Don Hurst	No	1929
5. Wally Berger (R)	No	1930
6. Goose Goslin	Yes	1930
7. Gabby Hartnett	Yes	1930
8. Babe Herman	No	1930
9. Ripper Collins	No	1934
10. Joe Medwick	Yes	1937
11. Bob Johnson	No	1938
12. Walker Cooper	No	1947
13. Walt Dropo (R)	No	1950
14. Del Ennis	No	1950
15. Gus Bell	No	1953
16. Al Rosen	No	1953
17. Wally Post	No	1955
18. Roy Sievers	No	1957
19. Bob Cerv	No	1958
20. Rocky Colavito	No	1958
21. Norm Cash	No	1961
22. Jim Gentile	No	1961
23. Dick Stuart	No	1961
24. Ron Santo	No	1964
25. Willie Stargell	Yes	1966
26. Joe Torre	No	1966
27. Willie McCovey	Yes	1969
28. Boog Powell	No	1969

29. Jim Hickman	No	1970
30. Tony Perez	No	1970
31. George Foster	No	1977
32. Fred Lynn	Inelig	1979
33. Dave Winfield	Active	1979
34. Reggie Jackson	Yes	1980
35. Ben Oglivie	No	1980
36. Pedro Guerrero	Inelig	1982
37. George Brett	Inelig	1985
38. Dwight Evans	Inelig	1987
39. Jose Canseco	Active	1988
40. Ryne Sandberg	Active	1990
41. Cal Ripken	Active	1991
42. Gary Sheffield	Active	1992
43. Juan Gonzalez	Active	1993
44. Ken Griffey, Jr.	Active	1993
45. Mike Piazza (R)	Active	1993
46. Jeff Bagwell	Active	1994
47. Albert Belle	Active	1994

Players with 4 triple milestone seasons not in the Hall of Fame.

Ted Kluszewski	1953-1956.
Jim Rice	1977-79, 1983.

Hall of Fame sluggers who never had a triple milestone season.

Player	Best Season
Johnny Bench	.293-45-148 in 1970.
Yogi Berra	.298-30-105 in 1956.
Roberto Clemente	.317-29-119 in 1966.
Al Kaline	.314-27-128 in 1956.
Harmon Killebrew	.288-46-122 in 1961.
Mike Schmidt	.316-31-91 in 1981.

Rookies with triple milestone seasons.

Wally Berger	.310-38-119 in 1930.
Ted Williams	.327-31-145 in 1939.
Walt Dropo	.322-34-144 in 1950.
Mike Piazza	.318-35-112 in 1993.

Three players on the same team to hit triple milestones.

1929 Philadelphia Phillies

Don Hurst	.304-31-125
Chuck Klein	.356-43-145
Lefty O'Doul	.398-32-122

1953 Brooklyn Dodgers

Roy Campanella	.312-41-142
Gil Hodges	.302-31-122
Duke Snider	.336-42-126

Players who hit each milestone only once—all in the same season.

Walt Dropo	.322-34-144 in 1950.
Bob Cerv	.305-38-104 in 1958.
Jim Hickman	.315-32-115 in 1970.

Player who hit additional milestones of 100 runs, 100 walks and 30 stolen bases.

Barry Bonds	.311-34-103-109-127-39 in 1992.

Triple Milestones 1994: Final Statistics

American League

	BA	HR	RBI
MADE IT	.300	30	100
Albert Belle	.357	36	101
Frank Thomas	.353	38	101
ON TARGET *	.300	21	70
Paul O'Neill	.359	21	83
Ken Griffey, Jr.	.323	40	90
Rafael Palmeiro	.319	23	76
Chili Davis	.311	26	84
Mo Vaughn	.310	26	82
CLOSE **	.285	19	65
Julio Franco	.319	20	98
Kirby Puckett	.317	20	112
Carlos Baerga	.314	19	80
Tim Salmon	.287	23	70

National League

	BA	HR	RBI
MADE IT	.300	30	100
Jeff Bagwell	.368	39	116
ON TARGET *	.300	21	70
Moises Alou	.339	22	78
Kevin Mitchell	.326	30	77
Andres Galarraga	.319	31	85
Mike Piazza	.319	24	92
Fred McGriff	.318	34	94
Barry Bonds	.312	37	81
Dante Bichette	.304	27	95
Sammy Sosa	.300	25	70
CLOSE **	.285	19	65
Larry Walker	.322	19	86
Bobby Bonilla	.290	20	67

*Players who were on target for .300-30-100 when strike started on 8/12.

** Players who were within .015 BA, 2 HR and 5 RBI of being on target when strike started.

The Pumpkin and Cabbage Tournament of 1866

High scoring and discord in upstate New York

Tony Kissel

It was a Woodstock-type festival for upstate New York baseball fans. It had controversy, illegal gambling, a Grand Tournament Ball, and an unbelievable 741 runs scored in just twelve games. For the steep price of $5, a Tournament "Season Ticket" allowed you to watch baseball from morning till dark from Monday, October 1, 1866, to Friday, October 5, 1866, at Auburn, New York's Driving Park.

At stake in this first baseball tournament ever held in Central New York were the bragging rights as the best team in upstate New York from Buffalo to Albany. Twelve teams met in a single-elimination series competing for coveted Gold and Silver Balls to be awarded to the two top clubs. Total attendance was at least 20,000.

On Monday morning, the Syracuse Arctics baseball club boarded the 6:45 AM train from Syracuse to arrive in time for their opening game at 9 AM against the Union Springs Frontenacs. The Auburn *Daily Advertiser* wrote, "Today the streets and hotels are enlivened with ball players and their friends, and every train adds to the crowd." The Arctics easily defeated Union Springs by a score of 36-18. Brown, of Syracuse, had a "perfect game," scoring six runs and making no outs.

After lunch, the Rochester Atlantics outhit the Macedons of Macedon to win by the score of 44-32. At 4 o'clock, the last game of the day had another Rochester team, the Excelsiors, facing the Hiawathas

of Utica. The Excelsiors showed little mercy to their opponents and led 37-5 after five innings, when the umpire stopped the game because of darkness.

The *Daily Advertiser* noted that "Greenbacks changed hands freely on the playing of the various clubs," and the paper's box scores listed only Runs Made and Outs Made for hitters, and Fly Balls Caught and Fly Balls Missed for the fielders.

Play heats up—On Tuesday morning, the hometown Auburns took the field at 9 against the Geneva Hobarts before 2,000 spectators. Auburn and Geneva scored 86 runs as both defenses gave their pitchers little support. Auburn held on to win, 56-30, and move into the second round. As the home team left the field to celebrate, the crowd had swelled to over 4,000 fans in anticipation of the next two games.

Although both clubs played well, the Pacifics of Rochester upset the Central Cities of Syracuse, 44-29. All but one Rochester Pacific player scored five runs or more during the game. Injuries played a factor in the feature game of the day between the two betting favorites. Durbin, of Niagara of Buffalo*, badly sprained his ankle, while Ford, of the Albany Knickerbockers, injured his hand in the sloppily played game. Niagara led all the way and won by a score of 29-18.

On Wednesday morning, the Syracuse Arctics gave the city of Rochester its only loss of the tournament, beating the Rochester Atlantics in a "pitcher's" battle, 27-19. Telford, for Syracuse, was perfect with

Tony Kissel *thanks Joe Overfield, John Schwartz, Erich DeMuran, and the Cayuga Museum in Auburn for their help.*

five runs scored and no outs made. At noon the Rochester Pacifics and Auburn squared off with betting heavy on both teams. Auburn led 10-4 after three innings much to the delight of the roaring crowd. The Pacifics took the lead for good in the fifth, and held on to defeat Auburn, 38-32. The *Daily Advertiser* blamed the defeat on Auburn's poor fielding.

The last game of the day between Rochester's Excelsiors and the Buffalo Niagaras was a hard-fought seven-inning contest. Niagara rallied to take the lead in the fifth only to have the Excelsiors tie it up at 27-27 in the seventh. The umpire decided to replay the game the next day because of darkness.

On Thursday morning the crowd was small when the Arctics of Syracuse and the Pacifics of Rochester took the field at 10. The Arctics were held to two runs after three innings, and when Rochester scored eight runs in the fourth to build its lead to 23-2, the game was all over. The Pacifics pounded out twelve runs in the last inning to win handily, 47-17. A close game followed with Niagara and the Rochester Excelsiors playing another see-saw battle. The Excelsiors jumped to a 7-0 lead, but then Niagara moved ahead 14-11, after five innings. When the Excelsiors scored ten runs in the sixth, it appeared the game was out of reach. The Niagaras, however, rallied with nine runs in the eighth to cut their deficit to three runs. When they held their opponents scoreless in the ninth, there was still hope for Niagara. Unfortunately, the Excelsiors held them to one run in their last at-bat to win a squeaker by the score of 28-26.

That evening, the Auburn streets and hotels were enlivened once more with the loud noises of enthusiastic ball players, their friends, and hundreds of spectators. At Markham Hall the Grand Tournament Ball was being held (tickets were $1), and the City Orchestra was providing the music. Pubs and taverns were packed with gamblers and revelers busy laying the odds for tomorrow's Grand Game for the Gold Ball.

Disputes off the field—Tournament officials were meanwhile conducting a secret meeting. Unhappy because the two finalists were both from Rochester, they decided to take steps to ensure attendance wouldn't suffer because of it. They voted prematurely to select the five individual players who would receive beautiful gold-mounted baseball bats made from ebony wood to reward them for their fine play. Two Auburn players, a Syracuse Central City outfielder, the Buffalo Niagaras pitcher, and an Albany

Knickerbocker would receive the awards. Officials then reviewed the rules for awarding the Gold and Silver Balls. In a complicated and flawed arrangement, the final game winner won the Gold Ball. However, the Silver Ball would be won by the team that had the best score against the Gold Ball winners. The team that lost the final game, if it hadn't already won the Silver Ball, would receive a third-place prize. Fourth Place would be awarded to the club that had the best score against the final game losers. Officials assumed all teams had been in agreement with this for weeks and understood the rules. When the meeting adjourned everyone was sworn to secrecy, but someone immediately leaked the news.

Later that evening the Rochester teams heard the news and called a meeting to decide what they should do. A niece of two of the players later offered a different version of the officials' earlier meeting. Rochester claimed new rules had been adopted which required the Pacifics to defeat the Excelsiors twice on Friday to win the Gold Ball. If the Excelsiors won, the Silver Ball would go to the Niagaras of Buffalo instead of to the Pacifics (unless it was a one-run game). The players had been under the impression that they had already won both balls. The players also considered the best player awards to be merely the final touch of infamy, and voted to send a list of demands to officials which, if not met, would result in their boycotting the finals. Parts of the letter read, "We have become rightfully entitled to the first and second prizes...unless the committee so award these prizes, both clubs go home, conscious of the fact that the Base Ball reputation of Rochester does not suffer by the lack of virtual possession of the trophies of success...we would question the justice of awarding the individual prizes before the tournament was concluded...we question also the justice of awarding a prize to a club who have won but one game and lost one (Niagara), in preference to a club who have won three games and lost none (the Pacifics)." When their bold request was finally signed and sealed, halfway into the night, the players then went to bed, not knowing whether they would be playing the next day.

Early Friday morning all was quiet in the city of Auburn as many slept late due to the previous night's festivities. Tournament officials received the players' letter early and, after their initial shock, hurried over to the Rochesters' hotel to try and persuade the teams to play. They refused all Rochester demands and claimed every team had known of the rules ahead of time, but did offer to reconsider their choices of the best players if anyone had a great game that day. This was the final insult to a proud group of players that had already beaten the best of Auburn, Buffalo, Syracuse, and Utica. Both Rochester clubs held fast to their positions, so the officials angrily left the meeting.

At 10, a throwing contest was held and H. Carr of the Union Springs Frontenacs won with a heave of 295 feet, 8 inches. A muffin match was played at forenoon and, "for awkwardness in getting around, the men chosen were quite remarkable."

Many spectators were now on the grounds and expecting a Gold Ball match to soon begin. Officials had to give them something for their money, so they had the Auburn and Buffalo teams stage an exhibition game that Auburn won by a score of 39-36.

Around 2:15 PM, two events occurred simultaneously. The chairman of the judges' committee announced to the throng that the Gold Ball would be saved for a later tournament, the Silver Ball would be given to the Buffalo Niagaras (who, with a record of 1-2-1, clearly didn't deserve it). Other teams could compete for third- and fourth-place prizes next week (none of them did), and individual prize winners were: Best Fielder to George Porter of the Central Cities of Syracuse; Best Catcher to Grover Hopkins of Auburn; Best Batter to Frank Wright of Auburn; Best Pitcher to Edgar Atwater of Niagara; and Best Baserunner to Grace of Albany.

Meanwhile, the Rochester ball players had emerged from their hotel and prepared to march down to the train depot. Each team in the tournament was expected to march in a parade down Genesee Street acknowledging the kranks. The two best teams were to carry the Gold and Silver balls aloft on their team poles, to display them to the crowd before taking them home. The Rochester Pacifics had attached a bright golden-orange pumpkin to their team's pole, with a piece of paper taped to it with the words "Auburn Gold Ball" written on it. The Rochester Excelsiors had attached a silver-blue cabbage to their team's pole, and taped a piece of paper to it with the words "Auburn Silver Ball" on it. Another player held aloft a brand new broom, splints up, with both teams' badges attached to it.

The Rochester teams marched down Genesee Street with "considerable feeling," and exchanged insults with people along the way. Their mock procession was noted in every major newspaper in Upstate New York, and was clearly the big story of the final day.

A very battered group of baseball players came home to Rochester. In addition to the assorted ankle sprains and broken fingers, catcher Sam Porter's mouth was cut severely by a thrown bat, and one eye was swollen shut thanks to a thrown ball. Farley Porter had a sprained ankle, badly cut-up hands, and a pulled hamstring that had caused Sullivan to have to run for him when he batted during the game on Thursday. A large crowd greeted the 6:45 p.m. train with the Rochester clubs on board. With the pumpkin still in tow (the cabbage didn't make it), the players were escorted to Congress Hall where supper was waiting for them. Later, everyone marched to the corner of Buffalo and State Streets, where a band played "Home, Sweet Home," and players and fans cheered one another.

Newspaper accounts were divided over the day's events. The Auburn *Daily Advertiser* predictably backed tournament officials, and insisted every team had known the rules beforehand, nothing had been changed, and officials had to select player prizes early because of a lack of time. The paper also noted that the tournament had lost money, and only a few unruly spirits on the Rochester clubs prevented the Final Game from being played. A Buffalo paper claimed to have discovered a plot whereby the Excelsiors would throw the Final Game to the Pacifics in order to get the Silver Ball, and thwart the committee's plans.

The Syracuse *Journal*, perhaps angered that the Syracuse Arctics received nothing for their efforts, claimed "considerable dissatisfaction is expressed at the action of the committee." The New York *World* observer stated "the honors were all carried off by Rochester, even if they had no balls to bring home." And the Rochester *Daily Democrat* printed its own selection of Best Players. Included were the Excelsiors' Sam Porter as Best Catcher, the Excelsiors' Sullivan as Best Baserunner, and the Pacifics' O. Hilton as Best Fielder. The paper added that there were bad feelings between the Auburn club and the Rochester teams, and accused officials from Auburn and Buffalo of conspiring against Rochester.

Epilogue—On July 3, 1867, the Niagaras of Buffalo captured the Auburn Gold Ball with a come-from-behind 25-24 victory over Auburn. Thus, for three short months, Buffalo owned both of the Auburn tournament's balls—which rightfully belonged to Rochester. On October 3 the Syracuse Central Cities defeated the Niagaras 38-27 and won both the championship of Western and Central New York, and the Auburn Gold Ball. One week later the Excelsiors of

Rochester beat the Niagaras before an "enormous crowd" and the teams dined together and patched up their differences.

In 1889 the well-traveled Auburn Gold Ball was used as the payment of a $170 bill at Syracuse's Globe Hotel. The gold-plated ball had been abducted several times since 1867.

In an 1899 article in the Syracuse *Sunday Herald*, Auburn players recollected that they had won the tournament of 1866, and all but the Pacifics had been "piemeat" for them. They insisted their club was better than any of Auburn's later professional teams. The players had clearly done well in their careers: a lawyer, a judge, a politician, two professors, a ship-building magnate, an iron merchant, a bookkeeper, and a postmaster who also owned an orange plantation.

Hester Hopkins Cochrane, daughter of Auburn player John Hopkins and the niece of Rochester players Sam and Farley Porter, wrote about the tournament and the players involved in the 1951 volume of *The Genesee Country Scrapbook* (Number 22), published in Rochester. Her relatives told her of their contempt for fielders who had to wear gloves on their hands to catch baseballs. They thought the catcher's chest protector and mask were unnecessary. They didn't like the modern low-scoring games dominated by pitchers and catchers, and believed fans in their day liked the high scores.

Ezra Sutton, third baseman for the Rochester Atlantics at only age 16, would go on to play major league ball from 1871 to 1888. His Atlantics teammate, shortstop Eugene Kimball, played major league ball in 1871. He is the man who made the first major league out, and he also hit into the first major league double play. The Rochester Pacifics shortstop, John McKelvey, played in the majors in 1875.

The Pumpkin and Cabbage Tournament was the first of several series played in the 1800s to select the best team in upstate New York. Although the Rochester Pacifics never dominated a series again, it deserved a better crown than the pumpkin chosen by the players. If the infamous Auburn Gold Ball still exists, maybe it is time finally to award the Rochester Baseball Association with the prize it won 130 years ago. As we look back now at The Grand Baseball Tournament of 1866, perhaps the words of a Syracuse reporter best reflect the feelings of the participants—"The system conferred rewards upon the conquered and insults upon the victors."

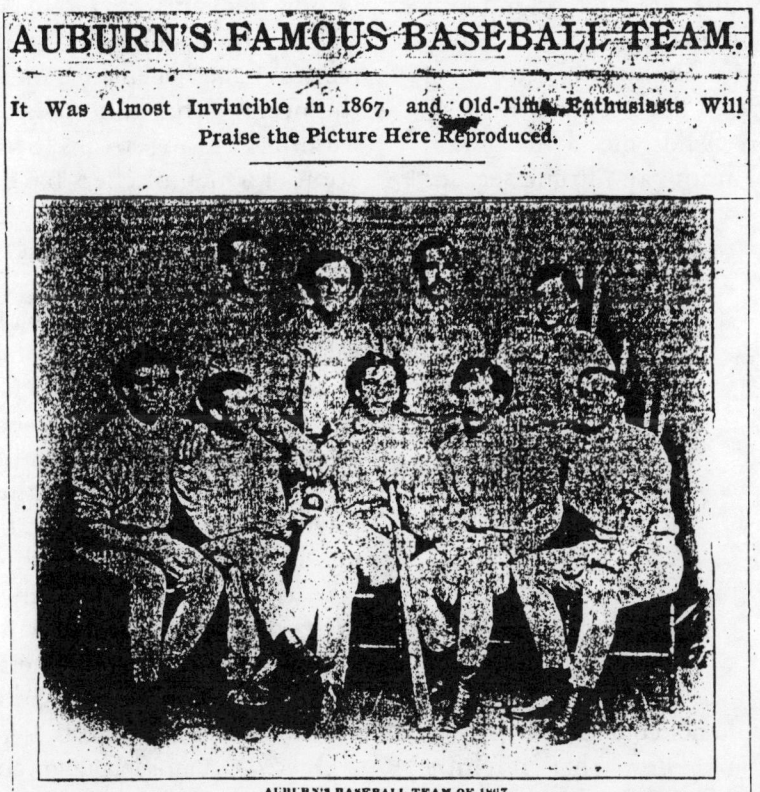

AUBURN'S FAMOUS BASEBALL TEAM.

It Was Almost Invincible in 1867, and Old-Time Enthusiasts Will Praise the Picture Here Reproduced.

AUBURN'S BASEBALL TEAM OF 1867.

Tony Kissel

We don't know who's who, but we do know that the Auburn players in this photo from the April 30, 1899 Syracuse Sunday Herald *are: Woolsey Hopkins, Grover Hopkins, Frank Wright, William Plunkett, Ed Woodin, Howard Freeman, John Hopkins, Tommy Towne, and Dick Kirby.*

The SABeRhagen Syndrome

Pitching streaks of a special kind

Michael McBride

Owners of Rotisserie League baseball franchises who have held the rights to Bret Saberhagen have undergone more mental anguish than Connie Mack when he tried to control Rube Waddell, or Michelangelo when he realized he'd forgotten to include the ball on the ceiling of the Sistine Chapel. Saberhagen had the habit of following seasons of agony with years of ecstasy. I have termed this tendency the SABeRhagen Syndrome. Until 1993, Saberhagen alternated winning and losing seasons throughout his career.

Table 1: SABeRhagen's W-L Record

Year	Wins	Losses
1984	10	11
1985	20	6
1986	7	12
1987	18	10
1988	14	16
1989	23	6
1990	5	9
1991	13	8
1992	3	5
Total	113	83

But this fluctuation should not come as a major surprise. Knowledgeable fans know that pitching (especially wins and losses) is a very unpredictable quantity and they recognize the importance of a

Michael McBride is a professor of political science at Whittier College and teaches a seminar on "The Literature of Baseball."

pitcher's ERA, the ratio of runners allowed to innings pitched, or other more exotic measures.

Nevertheless, Saberhagen's performance did lead me to wonder about pitchers' "winning streaks." That is, how frequently do pitchers put together streaks of winning (or losing) seasons in the course of their careers. Is Saberhagen an anomaly, or does he represent the norm? What follows is an analysis of pitchers' winning or losing streaks (by season), some consideration of which pitchers have had the most winning and losing seasons over their careers, and a brief look at Saberhagen's unique ability to avoid a streak of any kind whatsoever.

I should begin with some of the parameters which were used to generate the data, and I should note that in some cases where dozens of players compiled equivalent records the names have been omitted to protect the innocent (or guilty in the case of losing performances). I examined the records of every major league pitcher, in particular those who have pitched in ten or more seasons or who compiled five or more consecutive winning or losing records. (Ties, seasons with an equal number of wins and losses, served to stop a streak, counting as neither a win nor a loss.) I included every season regardless of the number of decisions. A 1-0 record is as good as going 12-4.

Over 700 major league pitchers (747) have pitched in ten or more seasons. Among this group, 191 have accumulated winning streaks of five or more years; nine of them actually accomplished the feat twice. An additional forty-two pitchers have compiled streaks of five or more in nine years or less for a total of 233 pitchers and 242 winning streaks.

The list of those with the longest streaks includes many of the game's greatest pitchers. Of the twenty-one pitchers with ten or more consecutive winning seasons, sixteen rank among *Total Baseball*'s top sixty in the Total Pitching Index category, fourteen in the top forty-five, and ten in the top twenty-five. Only Lew Burdette, Carl Erskine, and Jack Morris failed to rank among the top 136. This should not be too surprising. After all, winning games is one of the criteria we use for evaluating a pitcher's performance, although more statistically accurate measures may now be available.

The list of longest streaks does constitute a pitchers' "Who's Who." Grover Cleveland Alexander dominates the list with his record of nineteen consecutive winning seasons, five more than runner-up Whitey Ford. Only one of the eleven pitchers with more than ten consecutive winning seasons is not in the Hall of Fame. Of the ten pitchers with ten consecutive winning seasons, six are in Cooperstown, although Ruth is there primarily for his hitting. (Ironically, Ruth is the only pitcher in major league history to pitch in ten or more seasons and have a winning record in each of those years. He obviously benefits from including 1-0 records among the criteria.) Roger Clemens was approaching this record with nine winning seasons before his losing record in 1993.

The final column of Table 2 indicates the number of winning and losing seasons of the teams for which these men toiled during their streaks. Obviously most benefitted by playing for good clubs throughout their careers, but Alexander (five times), Gibson (four), Griffith (four), and especially Faber and Johnson (five each) had to overcome some adverse play on the part of their teammates.

Table 2: Consecutive winning seasons

	Consecutive Winning Seasons	Total Seasons	Team Record During Streak
Alexander, G.	19	20	14-5
Ford, W.	14	16	13-1
Gibson, B.	13	17	9-3-1
Feller, B.	13	16	11-2
Hubbell, C.	12	16	11-1
Marichal, J.	12	16	12-0
Mathewson, C.	12	17	12-0
Griffith, C.	12	21	8-4
Leever, S.	12	13	11-0
Spahn, W.	11	12	11-0
Ruffing, R.	11	22	11-0
Ruth, B.	10	10	9-1
Erskine, C.	10	12	10-0
Lemon, B.	10	13	10-0
Nichols, K.	10	15	10-0
Warneke, L.	10	15	9-1
Morris, J.	10	16	10-0
Burdette, L.	10	18	10-0
Faber, R.	10	20	5-4-1
Johnson, W.	10	21	5-5
Young, C.	10	22	8-2
15 Tied at 9			
25 Tied at 8			
37 Tied at 7			
47 Tied at 6			
97 Tied at 5			

Statistically, of course, the longer one's career, the greater the chances of compiling a streak. Therefore, it may be useful to look at the percentage of winning seasons compiled by those who pitched ten or more years. Ruth, with his 100 percent and Alexander top the list, but a few less well-known names appear. Still, most managers would be happy to include any of these people on their pitching staffs.

Table 3: Percent winning seasons

	W-L-T	Percent
Ruth, B.	10-0-0	100.0
Alexander, G.	19-1-0	95.0
Leever, S.	12-1-0	92.3
Chandler, S.	10-0-1	90.9
McGinnity, J.	9-0-1	90.0
Brazle, A.	9-1-0	90.0
Clemens, R.	9-1-0	90.0
Cuppy, N.	9-1-0	90.0
Kremer, R.	9-1-0	90.0
Richard, J.R.	9-1-0	90.0
Plank, E.	15-2-0	88.2
Hubbell, C.	14-1-1	87.5
Ford, W.	14-2-0	87.5
Coveleski, S.	12-2-0	85.7
Shocker, U.	11-0-2	84.6
Allen, J.	11-1-1	84.6
Palmer, J.	16-3-0	84.2
Feller, B.	15-2-1	83.3
Erskine, C.	10-1-1	83.3
Tudor, J.	10-1-1	83.3
Crowder, A.	9-2-0	81.8
Foutz, D.	9-0-2	81.8
Bridges, T.	13-2-1	81.3
Candelaria, J.	13-2-1	81.3
Marichal, J.	13-3-0	81.3

Putting together a significant number of winning records (consecutive or not) is no small achievement. To date only 106 pitchers have compiled ten or more winning seasons in their careers, twenty-three of them have fourteen or more.

Table 4: Most total winning seasons

	Winning Seasons	Total Seasons
Alexander, G.	19	20
Spahn, W.	17	21
Young, C.	17	22
Ryan, N.	17	26
Palmer, J.	16	19
Seaver, T.	16	20
Plank, E.	15	17
Feller, B.	15	18
Carlton, S.	15	23
Sutton, D.	15	23
Wynn, E.	15	23
Niekro, P.	15	24
John, T.	15	26
Ford, W.	14	16
Hubbell, C.	14	16
Harder, M.	14	20
Blyleven, B.	14	21
Johnson, W.	14	21
Pennock, H.	14	22
Perry, G.	14	22
Ruffing, R.	14	22
Quinn, J.	14	23
Kaat, J.	14	25
13 Tied at 13		
13 Tied at 12		
23 Tied at 11		
34 Tied at 10		

Once again the list of names is impressive, but in several cases longevity was a major factor. Twenty-two of the twenty-three did not compile winning records in eight or more seasons, with Jim Kaat topping the list at eleven.

A different perspective may be provided by looking at winning seasons versus the team records during those seasons. Here the efforts of Ted Lyons, Robin Roberts, Bert Blyleven, and Nolan Ryan appear more impressive. Table 5 ranks pitchers according to the percentage of winning seasons their teams had during the pitcher's winning years and includes anyone with twelve or more winning seasons. (I did not deduct the pitchers' records from their teams' records.)

Table 5: Winning seasons vs team records

	Winning Seasons	Team Record
Lyons, T.	13	5-7-1
Roberts, R.	12	5-6-1
Blyleven, B.	14	6-7-1
Ryan, N.	17	9-8-0
Niekro, P.	15	8-6-1
Johnson, W.	14	8-6-0
Faber, R.	13	7-5-1
Perry, G.	14	9-5-0
Kaat, J.	14	8-4-2
Donovan, B.	12	8-4-0
Griffith, C.	13	9-4-0
Young, C.	17	12-5-0
Quinn, J.	14	10-4
Gibson, B.	13	9-4-1
Alexander, G.	19	14-5-0
Seaver, T.	16	12-4-0
McDaniel, L.	12	9-3-0
Trucks, V.	12	9-3-0
Bridges, T.	13	10-3-0
Candelaria, J.	13	10-3-0
Fitzsimmons, F.	13	10-3-0
Harder, M.	14	11-3-0
Sutton, D.	15	12-3-0
Wynn, E.	15	12-3-0
Tiant, L.	13	10-2-1
Pennock, H.	14	11-2-1
Carlton, S.	15	12-2-1
Burdette, L.	13	11-2-0

Finally, since the data were available, I looked to see who got off to the fastest starts in their careers (that is, the most consecutive winning seasons) before running into a .500 season or worse. The top of the list is very similar to that in Table 1, with only Bob Gibson dropping out due to two losing seasons at the start of his career. Two dozen pitchers have begun with eight consecutive winning seasons and thirty-six others have started with from five to seven. In addition six others had an initial season of 0-0 followed by five or more winning seasons (including Hugh Casey who had eight).

Table 6: Fast starts (initial winning seasons)

Alexander, G.	19		Dean, D.	9
Ford, W.	14		Foutz, D.	9
Feller, B.	13		Shocker, U.	9
Hubbell, C.	12		Wiltse, H.	9
Marichal, J.	12		Gooden, D.	8
Erskine, C.	10		Brazle, A.	8
Faber, R.	10		Carruthers, B.	8

Nichols, K.	10		Coveleski, S.	8
Ruth, B.	10		Joss, A.	8
Young, C.	10		McGinnity, J.	8
Allen, J.	9		Palmer, J.	8
Clemens, R.	9		Raschi, V.	8
Cuppy, N.	9		Reulbach, E.	8

9 tied at 7

14 tied at 6 (includes 6 who had 1st season record of 0-0)

20 tied at 5 (Hugh Casey had 0-0 and then 8 W's)

We would expect players who compile winning records to stick around the major leagues for several years, barring injury or other problems. It is surprising, though, that a number of pitchers were able to extend their careers despite compiling extensive losing streaks, often at the beginning of their terms.

Twenty-five pitchers assembled losing streaks of seven or more seasons during their time in the Show. Thirty others had streaks of six seasons, and another 108 had five consecutive losing years. Seven of the thirty and twenty-one of the 108 had losing seasons every year they pitched. It is not surprising that they weren't allowed to shoot for more.

While we probably recognize most of the names of the "top" twenty-five (They were in the big leagues for at least seven years), they do not comprise an all-star staff. Only six won more than fifty games in their careers and, despite the fact that several had other seasons in which they had winning records, only three had a career winning percentage over .400. Probably the most ironic feature of the list is the presence of Charlie Robertson. The only man to pitch a regular-season perfect game from 1908 to 1964 (excluding Ernie Shore's relief of Babe Ruth in 1917), Robertson never had a winning season—a perfectly consistent loser who went on to compile a 49-80 record (.380) over eight years. In fact, no one with eight years or more in the majors was worse, since Milt Gaston, Ron Kline, and Bill Bailey all had at least *one* winning season. (Robertson has to share this honor with Pete Broberg, Socks Seibold, and Bill Hart.)

Table 7: Consecutive losing seasons

	Number	Total Seasons	Record
Bailey, Bill	10	11	33-75
Kline, Ron	10	17	71-115
Gaston, Milt	9	11	77-147
Seibold, Socks	8	8	48-86
Hart, Bill	8	8	66-120
Broberg, Pete	8	8	41-71
Robertson, Charlie	8	8	49-80

Fisher, Jack	8	11	69-118
Raffensberger, Ken	8	15	47-72
Judson, Howie	7	7	17-37
Pillette, Duane	7	8	38-66
Rasmussen, Eric	7	8	45-72
Willey, Carlton	7	8	29-51
Jefferson, Jesse	7	9	32-76
Littlefield, Dick	7	9	30-51
Camacho, Ernie	7	10	7-17
Ross, Buck	7	10	42-80
Beck, Boom Boom	7	12	28-62
Cunningham, Bert	7	12	79-118
Lockwood, Skip	7	12	31-61
Weiland, Bob	7	12	20-57
Benton, Larry	7	13	47-75
Wehmeier, Herm	7	13	58-80
Russell, Jack	7	15	46-98
Dietrich, Bill	7	16	43-59

30 tied at 6 (7 in 6 seasons)

108 tied at 5 (21 in 5 seasons)

Another example of remarkable staying power can be found in a list of players who pitched ten or more years without having more than one winning season. This list, unlike the others, includes several relief pitchers and may reflect the tendency to put some pitchers in only when their team has a lead, limiting their chances to win games.

Table 8: One or zero winning seasons*

	W-L-T
Bailey, Bill	1-10-0
Coleman, Joe	1-8-1
D'Acquisto, John	1-7-2
Fisher, Jack	1-9-1
Frazier, George	1-6-3
Hudson, Sid	1-10-1
Mingori, Steve	1-6-3
Murphy, Tom	1-8-3
Ortega, Phil	0-5-5
Ross, Buck	1-8-1
Ross, Gary	1-6-3
Smith, Eddie	1-7-2
Stanhouse, Don	1-5-4
Tiefenauer, Bobby	0-7-3

*minimum of 10 total seasons

This was not true, however, for Bill Bailey, whose 1-10 seasons' record and .299 career winning percentage are close to the worst for pitchers with ten or more years and 100+ decisions. (Jesse Jefferson with seven consecutive losing seasons and 100+ decisions did compile a slightly worse career record at 32-75 for .296.) Bailey also shares the record of ten consecutive losing seasons with Ron Kline, but Kline went on to have five consecutive winning seasons as well.

Bailey did not compile the most losing seasons. In fact, eight pitchers exceeded his total, led by Ken Raffensberger, Jack Russell, Bill Dietrich, and Tom Zachary. Overall, twenty pitchers reached ten losing seasons or more and another twenty totaled nine. Three of them, Tommy John (15-10), John Picus Quinn (14-9), and Nolan Ryan (17-9) probably do not really belong in the same class.

Table 9: Most losing seasons

	W-L-T		W-L-T
Raffensberger, Ken	1-12-1	Morgan, Mike	0-9-1
Russell, Jack	3-12-0	Fisher, Jack	1-9-1
Dietrich, Bill	3-12-1	Gaston, Milt	2-9-0
Zachary, Tom	7-12-0	Koslo, Dave	3-9-0
Cardwell, Don	2-11-1	Benton, Larry	3-9-1
Hamilton, Earl	3-11-0	Ruhle, Vern	3-9-1
Kline, Ron	5-11-1	Smith, Bob	4-9-0
Jones, Sad Sam	8-11-3	Hassler, Andy	5-9-0
Bailey, Bill	1-10-0	Ramos, Pedro	2-9-4
Hudson, Sid	1-10-1	Burris, Ray	4-9-2
Lockwood, Skip	2-10-0	Maul, Al	6-9-0
Ellsworth, Dick	2-10-1	Lee, Thornton	5-9-2
Roberts, Dave	3-10-0	Doak, Bill	6-9-1
Garver, Ned	3-10-1	Wyatt, Whit	6-9-1
Coffman, Dick	4-10-1	Drabowski, Moe	6-9-2
Friend, Bob	5-10-1	Fingers, Rollie	6-9-2
Slaton, Jim	5-10-1	MacFayden, Danny	7-9-1
Johnson, Si	4-10-3	Klippstein, Johnny	4-9-5
Mitchell, Clarence	8-10-0	Fryman, Woodie	7-9-2
John, Tommy	15-10-1	Quinn, Jack	14-9-0
		Ryan, Nolan	17-9-0

As these data show, some pitchers do achieve a degree of consistency during their careers. You would want to avoid the perfection of a Bill Bailey or Charlie Robertson, but you'd be well advised to hang onto a Grover Cleveland Alexander, Whitey Ford, or Roger Clemens. But the Alexanders may come along only once in a lifetime. While 247 pitchers with ten-plus years did have streaks of five or more consecutive seasons (188 winning, fifty-six losing, and three both), almost 500 of them did not, highlighting the unpredictability of a pitcher's performance from year to year. Which brings us back to Bret Saberhagen.

While most pitchers do not have extensive winning or losing streaks, it is even rarer for them to display the SABeRhagen Syndrome. Only twenty-five pitchers have begun their careers with streaks of five or more years alternating winning and losing seasons; only eleven of the twenty-five have extended the streak to six years, and only two of them to seven. Saberhagen, with his nine-year streak, stands alone, as unique in his pattern as Grover Cleveland Alexander with his remarkable nineteen-year winning streak. However, Saberhagen fans and owners can take heart, for three of those twenty-five went on to compile streaks of five or more winning seasons and two (Early Wynn and Gaylord Perry) went on to win 300 games and enter the Hall of Fame.

Table 10: Alternate winning and losing seasons at the beginning of a career*

	No.	1st Year		No.	1st Year
Saberhagen, Bret	9	1984	Capra, Buzz	5	1971
Perry, Gaylord	7	1962	Ehmke, Howard	5	1915
Bedrosian, Steve	6	1981	Filer, Tom	5	1982
Bosio, Chris	6	1986	Frohwirth, Todd	5	1987
Hogsett, Elon	6	1929	Heving, Joe	5	1930
Hutchings, Johnny	6	1940	Hiller, Frank	5	1946
King, Eric	6	1986	Kilroy, Matt	5	1886
Mahaffey, Art	6	1960	Merritt, Jim	5	1965
Romo, Vincente	6	1968	Mohorcic, Dale	5	1986
Simpson, Wayne	6	1970	Pearce, Jim	5	1949
Wynn, Early	6	1939	Reuschel, Rick	5	1972
Bankhead, Scott	5	1986	Timmerman, Tom	5	1969
Cox, Casey	5	1966			

*(or Losing and Winning Seasons)

Just another day at the ballpark

On May 11, 1923 Pete Schneider hit five home runs and a double, driving in fourteen runs, as Vernon (PCL) defeated Salt Lake City, 35-11. The home run and RBI totals are organized baseball records. Schneider, a lame-armed ex-pitcher for the Reds, was 6-for-8. Six other players hit home runs in the game, including Vernon outfielders Ping Bodie and Andy High, and first baseman Sam Leslie and outfielder Paul Strand for the home team.

Did the rarefied Utah atmosphere have anything to do with Schneider's record? Anecdotal evidence is impressive. Five days later the two teams again hit a total of eleven home runs in a 14-11 Vernon victory.

—Norman Macht

Dominant Pitchers: I

The Relative Control-Power Factor

Tony Blengino

The most common yardsticks of starting pitchers' performance can be very misleading. Won-lost records are heavily influenced by the strength of the pitcher's team, and ERAs are influenced by the pitcher's home ballpark, among other factors.

Two pitching statistics that are relatively unaffected by external stimuli are strikeout and walk totals. The relative control/power factor measures a pitcher's precision and dominance relative to his peers. The relative c/p factor is actually the sum of two sub-factors. The control factor measures a pitcher's strikeout/walk ratio against the average of other ERA title qualifiers in his league, while the power factor measures a strikeouts/nine innings ratio against them.

I am purposely using K/W ratio rather than W/9 IP ratio to measure control—both measure precision, but K/W ratio measures precision as it relates to dominance, which is more the focus of this study. Both factors are calculated by comparing the aforementioned ratios for all ERA title qualifiers in a given league to the average ratios for those qualifiers.

The two sub-factors are equal to the number of standard deviations above or below the average ratio. After the control and power factors have been calculated, they are simply added together, resulting in the relative c/p factor. In 1994, for instance, NL qualifi-

Tony Blengino is a Certified Public Accountant from Magnolia, New Jersey. He is a regular contributor to SABR publications and presenter at SABR conventions. He is co-author of two books to be published in the next year. Baseball's Top 100 is a look at the top 100 individual seasons in baseball history, and Future Stars is an analysis of current minor leaguers and their chances for major league success.

ers had a cumulative K/W ratio of 2.56 (with a standard deviation of 1.60), and a cumulative K/9 IP ratio of 6.31 (Std.Dev.= 1.42). Bret Saberhagen had a K/W ratio of 11.00 (+5.27 standard deviations), and a K/9 IP ratio of 7.26 (+0.66 Std.Dev.). His relative c/p factor of 5.93 led the NL in 1994. Randy Johnson led the AL with a +4.92 relative c/p factor (c=+1.78; p=+3.14). I have calculated relative c/p factors for all qualifying starting pitchers since 1901. By using relative performance, we can easily compare pitchers from different eras.

There are very few flukes on the list of relative c/p leaders. An analysis of W-L records of all qualifiers at various relative c/p factor levels shows a direct correlation between c/p factor and winning percentage. An analysis of relative c/p factors by pitchers' age shows that a pitcher's control develops as a pitcher matures, while his power deteriorates. A pitcher's relative c/p factor tends to peak around age 29. The c factor also peaks around that age, while the p factor gradually decreases after age 23. Using the database of pitchers' factors dating back to 1901, we can match a current pitcher to the most similar pitcher of a similar age in any era. This can help us predict which modern pitchers' careers will endure. Obviously, it was easy to predict greatness for Saberhagen and Roger Clemens in their early years—but this method also predicted long-term success for pitchers like Frank Viola and Bruce Hurst, despite mediocre W-L records and ERAs in their early years. It predicts long-term success for such pitchers as Pedro Martinez, Kevin Appier, Andy

Benes, Alex Fernandez and Jason Bere—but not for Ricky Bones, Jim Abbott or Bobby Jones. When projecting future success, a pitcher's age must be taken into consideration. The components of the c/p factor say as much about the pitcher as the factor itself. A young pitcher with a high p factor tends to be a better prospect than one with a high c factor, since control develops while power deteriorates over time.

The most dominant pitchers of all time—From my database of starting pitchers' relative c/p factors since 1901, I have compiled two lists of baseball's most dominant pitchers. The Career Value list includes the forty pitchers with the highest cumulative career c/p factors. These are derived by adding all of a pitcher's c/p factors from ERA title-qualifying seasons.

In contrast, the Peak Value list includes the 40 pitchers possessing the highest cumulative c/p factors over a consecutive three-year period. This list includes many of the pitchers on the Career Value list, but also many other pitchers who dominated for a relatively short period of time, but couldn't sustain the dominance for various reasons. Following is a thumbnail sketch of the top twenty pitchers on either list in alphabetical order. Tables listing more detailed career and peak c/p factor and other statistical information are also presented.

Grover Cleveland Alexander—Alexander ranks No. 14 on the Career Value list, and No. 21 on the Peak Value list. Another extreme control pitcher; only three others on Career Value list had lower career p factor (C. Young, Roberts, Derringer). His career winning percentage (.642) exceeded his teams' (.535) by .107—the largest margin of any pitcher in the study. In his peak period (1915-17) he went an amazing 94-35, 1.54. His relative ERA during his peak period was 182 (league average= 100), the second best in the study (behind Walter Johnson).

Chief Bender—Bender checks in at No. 20 on the Career Value list, and is unranked on the Peak Value list. Bender had the good fortune of playing for some awesome A's teams in the first fifth of the century. His .625 winning percentage (212-127) appears impressive, but is only .041 above his teams' winning percentage. This is a solid but unspectacular figure in this company, ranking only 21 among the career top 40. His 112 relative ERA also finishes back in the pack.

Bert Blyleven—No. 6 on the Career Value list, and

No. 20 on the Peak Value list. Amazingly, you don't hear his name mentioned very much when future Hall of Famers are discussed. He should be a first-ballot selection. Has the eighth highest c factor ever, and is one of only five pitchers with c and p factors above 20 (also Johnson, Vance, Grove, Seaver). His career relative ERA (117) is better than Hall of Famers Jenkins, Carlton, Roberts and Bender, among others. However, his career winning percentage exceeded his teams' by only .023—way down in Nolan Ryan territory (.022). To underscore Floyd Bannister's vulnerability to the gopher ball, Home Run Bert gave up only .78 HR/9 IP, well below Floyd's figure.

Tommy Bridges—No. 19 on the Career Value list, and unranked on the Peak Value list. This guy was truly a victim of his era. On the surface, he appears to be wild (1,672/1,192 career K/BB ratio), but in the context of his times, he had very good control. In the 1930's and early 1940's, it was common for AL hitters to walk more than they struck out. Also, his 3.57 ERA appears only OK on the surface, but he had a very high relative ERA of 126—fifteenth among the Career Value Top 40. The fourteen ahead of him are all either in the Hall of Fame or are named Roger Clemens. Bridges (194-138) is a slightly watered down version of Dazzy Vance.

Jim Bunning—No. 14 on the Career Value list, No. 30 on the Peak Value list. If Bunning had pitched for better teams in his career, or had his career started about five years later, causing him to peak in the pitcher-dominated late 60's rather than the hitting-dominated early 60's, he would have been in the Hall a long time ago. Both his relative ERA (114) and his W-L pct. relative to his teams' (+.030) are somewhat low in this company. In Bunning's peak period (1959-61) he was arguably the best in baseball.

Steve Carlton—No. 10 on the Career Value list, and No. 17 on the Peak Value list. No pitcher on these lists from the second half of the century won more games than his 329, and he was second to Ryan in whiffs (4,136). Like Ryan, Carlton peaked very late in his career. His peak period (1980-82) occurred between ages 35 and 37, and was truly awesome—60-24 for a .714 W-L pct., .159 higher than his teams', with a relative ERA of 143. He ruined his raw career numbers by hanging around about four years too long, during which he went an abysmal 16-37.

Roger Clemens—With his career still in full bloom,

he already ranks No. 17 on the Career Value list, and stands at No. 12 on the Peak Value list. His stats through 1994 are remarkably similar to Sandy Koufax's career numbers. Clemens is 172-93 (.649), 2.93, with 2,201 strikeouts in 2,394 innings. Koufax was 165-87 (.655), 2.76, with 2,396 strikeouts in 2,324 innings. However, there are three strong arguments in favor of Clemens when comparing the two. Though Koufax' career ERA is lower, Clemens' relative ERA of 146 is far better than Koufax' 131, and ranks behind only Lefty Grove and Walter Johnson among the Career Top 40. This is underscored by the second argument—Clemens has comparable career stats to Koufax's despite the fact that he has never faced an opposing pitcher in regular season play. Last, Clemens' Red Sox teams have a cumulative winning percentage of .512, giving him a .137 advantage—the best of all time. Koufax' W-L pct. exceeded that of his Dodger clubs by .094. If Clemens ages gracefully, as he should, a very strong argument will be able to be made that he was the greatest pitcher of the second half of the twentieth century—and maybe the greatest of all time.

David Cone—Ranks No. 15 on the Peak Value list, and should break into the Career Value list with a strong 1995 season. Unfortunately for Cone, he hit his peak just as the Mets were beginning to slip from theirs. During his peak seasons (1990-92) he went 41-31 for a .569 winning percentage, .074 better than the Mets, and recorded a 3.14 ERA (116 relative). His peak stats are actually quite unspectacular relative to this group. Predictably, Cone bounced back to win the 1994 AL Cy Young Award, as his power declined but his control improved, right in line with relative c/p theory.

Dizzy Dean—Ranks No. 28 on the Career Value list (despite only six qualifying seasons) and No. 18 on the Peak Value list. In a hitters' era, Dean was phenomenal before being felled by injury. His .644 winning percentage (150-83) exceeded his teams' by .088, tied for eighth among those on the career list. His relative ERA of 130 is tied for tenth among those on the peak list. Dean was equal parts power and control, and was on his way to becoming an all-time great when injured.

Bob Feller—Ranks No. 22 on the Career Value list, and No. 13 on the Peak Value list. Would rank much higher if the guts of his career weren't ripped out by his World War II military service. His career winning percentage of .621 (266-162) exceeded his teams' by .057, and he had a 3.25 career ERA (Relative= 122). Neither figure is in the extreme top echelon, but both are in Hall of Fame territory. He went 76-33 (.697) during his peak period (1939-41), .154 better than the Indians. This differential ranks him ninth among the Peak Value Top 40. Then he went off to war— probably preventing him from crashing the Top 10 on both lists.

Lefty Grove—Ranks No. 4 on the Career Value list, and No. 3 on the Peak Value list. What a pitcher. His amazing .680 career winning percentage (300-141) was the highest of anyone on the career list, and was .091 better than his teams' excellent .589 percentage. This is the fifth best overall differential, the third best among retired players (behind Alexander and Johnson). His career ERA of 3.06 took place within the context of the greatest hitters' era ever—his 148 relative ERA is the best of all time. During his peak period (1928-30), he went an amazing 72-19 (.791) with a 2.64 ERA—164 relative, the seventh best such mark ever. The greatest lefty ever, and probably just a shade behind Walter Johnson for the title of "Greatest Pitcher Ever."

Ron Guidry—Ranks No. 13 on the Career Value list, and No. 11 on the Peak Value list. In light of his relatively short career, such high rankings might seem surprising. He only won 170 games (losing only 91, for a .651 winning percentage), but relative to his league, he was awesome in every respect. His career relative ERA of 119 is better than those of Steve Carlton, Fergie Jenkins and Gaylord Perry, among others. His career winning percentage exceeded his teams' by .078, twelfth among the career top 40. His 6.61 c/p factor in 1981 was the highest since 1928.

Carl Hubbell—Ranks No. 11 on the Career Value list, and No. 19 on the Peak Value list. Recorded the eleventh highest career c factor. His career winning percentage of .622 (253-154) exceeded his teams' by a solid .067, fourteenth highest on the career list. His 130 career relative ERA (actual= 2.98) ranks tenth among those on the career list. Individual season factors would have been much higher if not for the existence of Dazzy Vance in his prime.

Fergie Jenkins—Ranks No. 7 on the Career Value list, and No. 9 on the Peak Value list. Had the fifth highest career c factor of all time, and the best one since Lefty Grove. Only pitcher in history of baseball to have over 3,000 strikeouts and fewer than 1,000 walks (997) for his career. Had a career ERA of 3.34, for a less than glittering relative ERA of 115. This was particularly due to his vulnerability to the gopher ball (.97 per nine innings), made even more remarkable by the relative scarcity of homers in the mid-to-late sixties. His .557 career winning percentage exceeded his teams' by a respectable .051. An amazingly consistent craftsman who missed only a handful of starts in his 18 consecutive seasons as an ERA qualifier (1966-83).

Randy Johnson—Ranks No. 16 on the Peak Value list, and is one or two solid seasons away from appearing on the Career Value list. His 1992-94 cumulative p factor of 9.90 is the third highest peak p factor of all time (behind Vance and Waddell)—he could challenge them with a big year in 1995. Johnson never gets to face an opposing pitcher, making his ungodly whiff totals even more amazing. His teams' winning percentage during his peak period was only .447, the worst on the list. His winning percentage over that span was .611, making him an excellent +.164 over time, sixth highest on the peak list. Could move even higher up the peak chart with a big 1995.

Walter Johnson—Ranks No. 1 on the Career Value List, and No. 5 on the Peak Value list. The best pitcher of all time. Period. Has the highest career c factor, and the third highest career p factor (behind Ryan and Vance). He recorded a .599 career winning percentage (417-279) despite pitching for mediocre clubs most of the time. His teams recorded a cumulative .501 winning percentage; his +.098 advantage ranks second among retired players, behind Alexander. His career ERA is an amazing 2.16; 147 relative to the league, second all time, behind Lefty Grove (148). He won 97 games in his peak period, and had a .724 winning percentage, .154 higher than his clubs'. He had an unbelievable 1.42 ERA in his peak period; an earth-shattering 219 relative to the league! By comparison, the next best relative ERA over a peak period was 182, by Alexander. His dominance may never be matched.

Sandy Koufax—Ranks No. 18 on the Career Value list (despite only eight qualifying seasons) and No. 7 on the Peak Value list. Only Lefty Grove and Christy Mathewson have better winning percentages among those on the career list. See the Clemens comment for discussion of the similarities between Koufax and the Rocket. Of course, Koufax got out of town before

his decline phase. His last six seasons were one extended peak period, with the last couple of seasons magnified by the increasing pitching dominance throughout baseball. The highest peak value of any pitcher since Grove, but could eventually be surpassed by Clemens as the best all-around pitcher in the second half of the twentieth century.

Christy Mathewson—Ranks No. 5 on the Career Value list, and No. 4 on the Peak Value list. Is at the front of the second tier of all time greats, just behind the Johnson-Grove level. Mathewson was the consummate control pitcher His career 40.89 c factor is the second highest ever, behind Walter Johnson, who had three more qualifying seasons. His .665 career winning percentage (373-188) is second to Grove among those on the career list, and was .082 better than his clubs'. His 2.13 career ERA was below both Johnson and Grove's, but his adjusted ERA was "only" 136, sixth best ever. He was 86-29 (.748) in his peak period (1907-09), and his peak period c factor of 12.32 is second only to Cy Young. Certainly one of the top five pitchers ever, and quite likely No. 3.

Nolan Ryan—Ranks No. 2 on the Career Value list, and No. 14 on the Peak Value list. Anyone with 5,714 career K's has to be near the top of the career list. What is surprising is his subpar relative ERA (112), by far the lowest among the career Top 10, and relative winning percentage (only .022 above his teams, also lowest among the career Top 10). Amazingly, his peak period occurred from ages 42-44! This sums up his career—he has done some incredible things which will never be equaled, but in no way does that make him one of the top ten pitchers in history. At no time in his career could he unequivocally have been called the best pitcher in baseball.

Tom Seaver—Ranks No. 8 on the Career Value list, and No. 10 on the Peak Value list. Ranks in the very top echelon of pitchers from the second half of the century, along with Koufax and Clemens. He had a career ERA of 2.86 (127 adjusted), and his career winning percentage of .603 (311-205) was .088 better than his teams', seventh among the career Top 40. His peak period extended from 1971-73, and his 162 adjusted ERA (2.23 actual) over that span ranks eighth among the peak Top 40.

Don Sutton—Ranks No. 12 on the Career Value list, and is unranked on the Peak Value list. Qualified for more ERA titles (22) than any pitcher on either list.

Had eleventh best c factor on career list, third best in last forty years. Won 20 games only once, and was never recognized as one of top two or three pitchers in baseball, even in his prime. Had a career 3.26 ERA—only 108 adjusted, well below all of the pitchers ranked ahead of him on the career list. His winning percentage (324-256; .559) only exceeded his clubs' by .026, also subpar. He is most comparable to Gaylord Perry. You can't argue with 324 wins.

Frank Tanana—Ranks No. 8 on the Peak Value list, and is unranked on the Career value list. No one seems to remember what an incredible pitcher he was as a youngster, routinely outpitching teammate Nolan Ryan. Between 1975-77, Tanana went 50-28 (.641) for teams that had a cumulative winning percentage of .458. This differential of .183 ranked him third among those on the peak list. His power dropped way off in 1978, and the reason became evident in 1979—major shoulder problems. A 240-game winner, with a .506 career winning percentage and 105 adjusted ERA (actual= 3.67).

Dazzy Vance—Ranks No. 3 on the Career value list, and No. 1 on the Peak Value list. Surprised? Consider this: Dazzy Vance had the first, second and fifth highest single-season c/p factors in 1924, 1925 and 1928. Only two NL pitchers had greater than 100 strikeouts in 1924 when Vance set the all-time c/p record (9.18)—and Vance struck out 262! And Vance didn't crack a big league rotation until age 31! His career mark of 197-140 seems relatively tame at first glance, but his .585 winning percentage exceeded that of his clubs by .086—Vance's teams had a .499 cumulative winning percentage; he is the only pitcher on the career list to pitch on teams with a cumulative losing record. His .702 peak period winning percentage exceeded his clubs' by .200, easily the highest mark of anyone on the peak list. Dazzy Vance utterly dominated hitters in an era when hitters utterly dominated pitchers. Had he either made the majors wight or ten years earlier, or pitched for better clubs, he would be right there with the all-time greats.

Rube Waddell—Ranks No. 9 on the Career Value list (despite losing a qualifying season to the 1901 cutoff), and No. 2 on the Peak Value list. Waddell was the first great power pitcher of the twentieth century. He recorded the third highest c/p factor ever, way back in 1902. Both his winning percentage (.574) and his teams' (.537) are exactly equal to Steve Carlton's corresponding figures. His 135 adjusted ERA (2.16 actual) ranks seventh among those on the career list. He was the chief competitor to Cy Young in the early 1900's, going 70-42 with a 155 adjusted ERA (2.01 actual) in his 1902-04 peak period. Like Dazzy Vance, he didn't win 200 games (193-143).

Cy Young—Ranks No. 16 on the Career Value list (despite losing 11 qualifying seasons to the 1901 cutoff), and No. 6 on the Peak Value list. Well, now I know why they named an award after this guy. His astronomical wins and losses totals (511-316) were largely a product of three-man rotations, but there is no denying his longevity (21 qualifying seasons) or his effectiveness. His .618 winning percentage exceeded his clubs' by .090, seventh all-time. His 138 career adjusted ERA ranks fifth behind Grove, Johnson, Clemens and Walsh among those on the career list. By a quirk, his "peak" period included his 1906 season, in which he went 13-21, 3.19, but had a 140/25 K/BB ratio, rendering his peak period stats somewhat meaningless. If his full career were included, he would likely move into the No. 4 spot on the career list. Relative to his peers, I doubt that he was as dominant as Johnson or Grove, but he is certainly in the next group, with Christy Mathewson.

NL Leaders
(1901-1994)

Year	Player	Rel. C/P Factor	Year	Player	Rel. C/P Factor	Year	Player	Rel. C/P Factor	Year	Player	Rel. C/P Factor
1901	Noodles Hahn	4.16	1925	Dazzy Vance	8.49	1948	Harry Brecheen	5.46	1971	Fergie Jenkins	6.23
1902	Deacon Phillippe	4.00	1926	Dazzy Vance	6.92	1949	Don Newcombe	4.02	1972	Steve Carlton	4.09
1903	C. Mathewson	5.2	1927	Dazzy Vance	7.29	1950	Larry Jansen	4.36	1973	Tom Seaver	5.45
1904	C. Mathewson	3.9	1928	Dazzy Vance	7.44	1951	Larry Jansen	3.69	1974	Tom Seaver	4.44
1905	C. Mathewson	5.1	1929	Dazzy Vance	5.70	1952	Warren Spahn	2.83	1975	Tom Seaver	3.96
1906	Deacon Phillippe	3.42	1930	Dazzy Vance	5.92	1953	Robin Roberts	4.15	1976	Tom Seaver	4.22
1907	C. Mathewson	5.1	1931	Dazzy Vance	4.77	1954	Robin Roberts	4.39	1977	Tom Seaver	3.54
1908	C. Mathewson	7.6	1932	Carl Hubbell	4.74	1955	Don Newcombe	4.16	1978	J.R. Richard	4.01
1909	C. Mathewson	4.8	1933	Carl Hubbell	1.66	1956	Robin Roberts	3.56	1979	J.R. Richard	6.13
1910	C. Mathewson	4.8	1934	Paul Dean	4.01	1957	Harvey Haddix	4.91	1980	Steve Carlton	5.20
1911	Rube Marquard	4.52	1935	Carl Hubbell	3.19	1958	Sam Jones	3.39	1981	F. Valenzuela	3.99
1912	C. Mathewson	4.0	1936	Dizzy Dean	5.61	1959	Don Drysdale	3.36	1982	Mario Soto	5.43
1913	Rube Marquard	3.22	1937	Dizzy Dean	4.49	1960	Don Drysdale	3.54	1983	Steve Carlton	4.28
1914	G.C. Alexander	4.24	1938	Carl Hubbell	5.24	1961	Sandy Koufax	4.58	1984	Dwight Gooden	6.13
1915	G.C. Alexander	5.57	1939	Paul Derringer	4.47	1962	Sandy Koufax	5.91	1985	Dennis Eckersley	4.51
1916	Dick Rudolph	2.68	1940	Luke Hamlin	4.06	1963	Sandy Koufax	5.31	1986	Mike Scott	5.56
1917	G.C. Alexander	4.68	1941	J.Vander Meer	4.85	1964	Sandy Koufax	4.20	1987	Nolan Ryan	6.13
1918	Hippo Vaughn	4.14	1942	J. Vander Meer	4.69	1965	Sandy Koufax	5.43	1988	Mike Scott	3.20
1919	G.C. Alexander	4.41	1943	Max Lanier	3.17	1966	Juan Marichal	3.49	1989	Pascual Perez	3.21
1920	Babe Adams	4.34	1944	K. Raffensberger	5.40	1967	Juan Marichal	3.10	1990	David Cone	4.93
1921	Babe Adams	4.06	1945	Ray Prim	5.14	1968	Bob Gibson	3.85	1991	David Cone	4.91
1922	Wilbur Cooper	3.92	1946	Mort Cooper	2.55	1969	Fergie Jenkins	3.31	1992	David Cone	3.51
1923	Dazzy Vance	6.50	1947	Ewell Blackwell	5.30	1970	Fergie Jenkins	5.41	1993	Jose Rijo	3.69
1924	Dazzy Vance	9.18							1994	Bret Saberhagen	5.93

AL Leaders
(1901-1994)

Year	Player	Rel. C/P Factor	Year	Player	Rel. C/P Factor	Year	Player	Rel. C/P Factor	Year	Player	Rel. C/P Factor
1901	Cy Young	6.59	1925	Walter Johnson	3.68	1948	Vic Raschi	3.26	1971	Vida Blue	4.44
1902	Rube Waddell	7.67	1926	Lefty Grove	6.03	1949	Mike Garcia	3.30	1972	Nolan Ryan	3.46
1903	Rube Waddell	5.87	1927	Garland Braxton	6.69	1950	Early Wynn	3.89	1973	Bert Blyleven	4.93
1904	Rube Waddell	5.36	1928	Lefty Grove	6.01	1951	Mickey McDermott	3.41	1974	Fergie Jenkins	5.40
1905	Cy Young	6.47	1929	Lefty Grove	5.59	1952	Bobby Shantz	3.87	1975	Frank Tanana	6.30
1906	Cy Young	4.95	1930	Lefty Grove	6.59	1953	Billy Pierce	4.00	1976	Frank Tanana	4.94
1907	Rube Waddell	5.85	1931	Lefty Grove	5.40	1954	Billy Pierce	3.48	1977	Frank Tanana	4.00
1908	Ed Walsh	3.93	1932	Lefty Grove	5.60	1955	Billy Pierce	4.18	1978	Ron Guidry	5.63
1909	Chief Bender	4.73	1933	Lefty Gomez	4.45	1956	Herb Score	4.37	1979	Ron Guidry	4.80
1910	Walter Johnson	5.50	1934	Schoolboy Rowe	4.49	1957	Connie Johnson	3.87	1980	Rudy May	5.31
1911	Smokey Joe Wood	5.15	1935	Johnny Allen	4.85	1958	Camilo Pascual	3.63	1981	Ron Guidry	6.61
1912	Walter Johnson	6.30	1936	Johnny Allen	4.72	1959	Jim Bunning	4.00	1982	Floyd Bannister	4.50
1913	Walter Johnson	7.11	1937	Lefty Gomez	5.01	1960	Jim Bunning	4.76	1983	LaMarr Hoyt	4.96
1914	Dutch Leonard	5.08	1938	Lefty Grove	4.07	1961	Juan Pizarro	3.85	1984	Mike Witt	2.97
1915	Walter Johnson	4.83	1939	Bob Feller	4.54	1962	Camilo Pascual	4.18	1985	Brett Saberhagen	4.30
1916	Walter Johnson	4.49	1940	Bob Feller	5.55	1963	Pedro Ramos	4.61	1986	Roger Clemens	4.11
1917	Walter Johnson	6.19	1941	Bobo Newsom	3.98	1964	Mickey Lolich	2.63	1987	Roger Clemens	3.55
1918	Walter Johnson	4.81	1942	Tiny Bonham	3.08	1965	Sonny Siebert	5.12	1988	Roger Clemens	6.46
1919	Walter Johnson	4.87	1943	Spud Chandler	3.89	1966	Sam McDowell	3.13	1989	Nolan Ryan	4.69
1920	Stan Coveleski	3.85	1944	Tex Hughson	5.15	1967	Jim Kaat	3.49	1990	Roger Clemens	4.69
1921	Dutch Leonard	4.37	1945	Hal Newhouser	4.10	1968	Luis Tiant	3.83	1991	Greg Swindell	4.20
1922	Urban Shocker	5.65	1946	Hal Newhouser	4.77	1969	Sam McDowell	4.25	1992	Roger Clemens	4.12
1923	Syl Johnson	4.81	1947	Tex Hughson	3.58	1970	Bob Johnson	3.26	1993	Randy Johnson	5.15
1924	Walter Johnson	5.90							1994	Randy Johnson	4.92

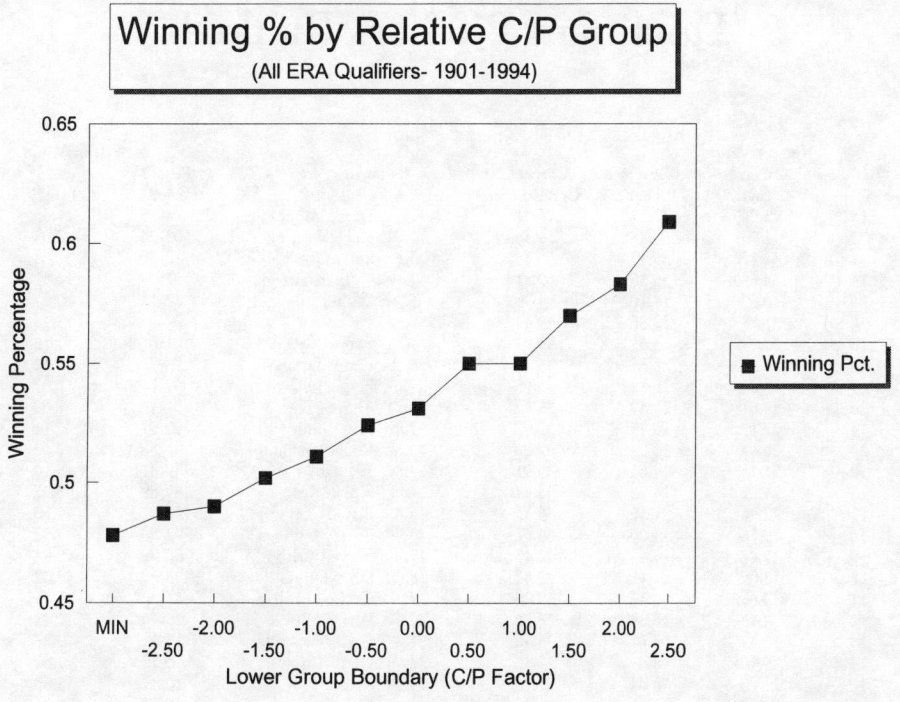

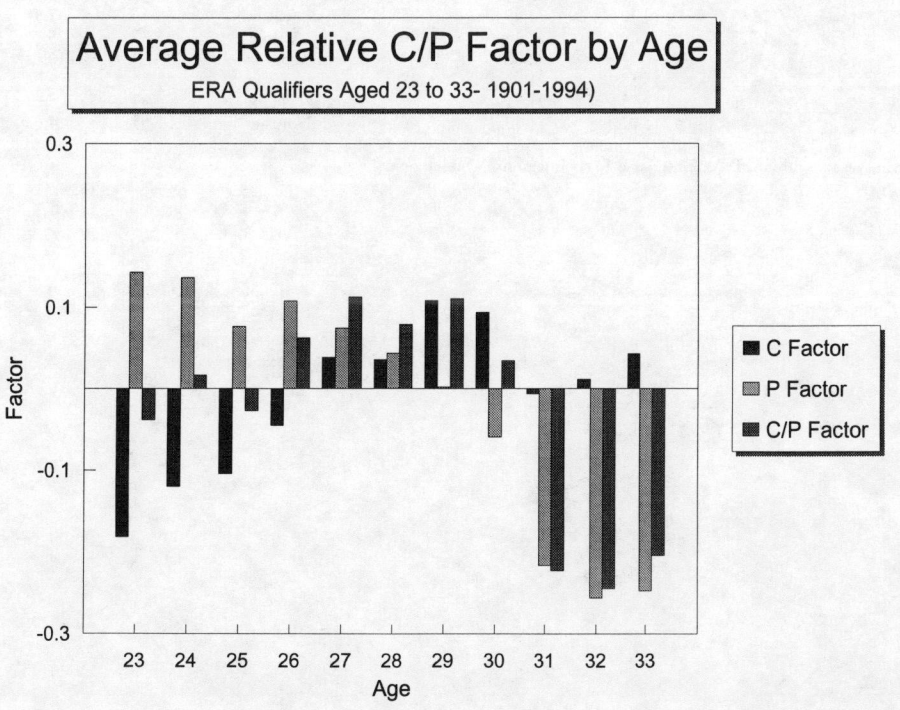

Dominant Pitchers Ranked

		Qualif. Seasons	Career Value Career C Fact.	Career P Fact	Career C/P Fact.
1.	Walter Johnson	18	43.94	32.57	76.51
2.	Nolan Ryan	20	11.03	58.33	69.36
3.	Dazzy Vance	11	32.72	35.43	68.15
4.	Lefty Grove	14	34.66	25.85	60.51
5.	C. Mathewson	15	40.89	14.10	54.99
6.	Bert Blyleven	18	28.58	20.86	49.44
7.	Fergie Jenkins	18	32.29	13.64	45.93
8.	Tom Seaver	19	21.15	20.35	41.50
9.	Rube Waddell @	9	13.04	28.12	41.16
10.	Steve Carlton	18	14.84	24.59	39.43
11.	Carl Hubbell	14	27.15	10.75	37.90
12.	Don Sutton	22	26.04	11.22	37.26
13.	Ron Guidry	10	21.28	14.63	35.91
14.	Jim Bunning	13	21.02	14.52	35.54
15.	G.C. Alexander	17	27.96	7.56	35.52
16.	Cy Young @	10	29.56	5.06	34.62
17.	Roger Clemens *	9	17.47	15.66	33.13
18.	Sandy Koufax	8	12.09	20.41	32.50
19.	Tommy Bridges	11	10.63	18.37	29.00
20.	Chief Bender	12	14.47	13.89	28.36
21.	Mickey Lolich	13	13.49	14.87	28.36
22.	Bob Feller	12	9.90	18.40	28.30
23.	Lefty Gomez	10	10.96	16.64	27.60
24.	Robin Roberts	15	29.08	-2.11	26.97
25.	Dennis Eckersley *	11	18.22	8.49	26.71
26.	Red Ruffing	18	12.93	13.34	26.27
27.	Gaylord Perry	20	18.21	7.74	25.95
28.	Dizzy Dean	6	13.40	12.26	25.66
29.	Harvey Haddix	9	14.20	10.23	24.43
30.	Billy Pierce	14	14.06	10.19	24.25
31.	Rube Marquard	13	11.24	12.92	24.16
32.	Hal Newhouser	11	8.04	15.92	23.96
33.	Eddie Plank	16	11.94	11.31	23.25
34.	Ed Walsh	7	14.14	9.10	23.24
35.	Paul Derringer	15	18.85	4.10	22.95
36.	Charlie Root	12	12.25	10.00	22.25
37.	Virgil Trucks	10	9.93	12.07	22.00
38.	Bob Gibson	14	6.36	15.58	21.94
39.	Dwight Gooden*	9	9.76	11.75	21.51
40.	Dutch Leonard	9	9.48	12.02	21.50

		Peak Period	Peak Value Peak C Fact.	Peak P Fact	Peak C/P Fact.
1.	Dazzy Vance	24-26	11.35	13.24	24.59
2.	Rube Waddell	02-04	7.01	11.90	18.91
3.	Lefty Grove	28-30	10.65	7.54	18.19
4.	C. Mathewson	07-09	12.32	5.26	17.58
5.	Walter Johnson	12-14	10.87	6.18	17.05
6.	Cy Young	04-06	13.98	2.67	16.65
7.	Sandy Koufax	61-63	7.13	8.67	15.80
8.	Frank Tanana	75-77	8.11	7.13	15.24
9.	Fergie Jenkins	69-71	11.07	3.88	14.95
10.	Tom Seaver	71-73	7.60	7.25	14.85
11.	Ron Guidry	79-81	7.11	7.09	14.20
12.	Roger Clemens *	86-88	7.60	6.51	14.11
13.	Bob Feller	39-41	5.10	8.98	14.08
14.	Nolan Ryan	87-89	3.97	9.68	13.65
15.	David Cone *	90-92	4.30	9.05	13.35
16.	Randy Johnson *	92-94	3.32	9.90	13.22
17.	Steve Carlton	80-82	5.94	7.26	13.20
18.	Dizzy Dean	35-37	8.02	5.15	13.17
19.	Carl Hubbell	31-33	8.77	4.17	12.94
20.	Bert Blyleven	73-75	7.42	5.48	12.90
21.	G.C. Alexander	15-17	9.32	3.37	12.69
22.	Ed Walsh	10-12	7.81	4.76	12.57
23.	Smokey Joe Wood	10-12	5.66	6.89	12.55
24.	Mike Scott	86-88	6.81	5.74	12.55
25.	Hal Newhouser	44-46	4.84	7.52	12.36
26.	J.R. Richard	77-79	3.56	8.69	12.25
27.	Deacon Phillippe	02-04	10.27	1.94	12.21
28.	Urban Shocker	22-24	9.28	2.93	12.21
29.	Lefty Gomez	32-34	5.56	6.61	12.17
30.	Jim Bunning	59-61	7.27	4.87	12.14
31.	Babe Adams	19-21	11.38	0.75	12.13
32.	Mario Soto	80-82	4.16	7.52	11.68
33.	Billy Pierce	53-55	5.72	5.95	11.67
34.	Johnny Vander Meer	41-43	2.48	8.95	11.43
35.	Schoolboy Rowe	34-36	7.51	3.86	11.37
36.	Johnny Allen	35-37	5.26	6.05	11.31
37.	Robin Roberts	52-54	10.12	1.06	11.18
38.	Dwight Gooden *	84-86	4.84	6.26	11.10
39.	Harvey Haddix	55-57	5.63	5.47	11.10
40.	Floyd Bannister	81-83	4.63	6.41	11.04

* Active

Totals do not include qualifying seasons prior to 1900; Young had 11 such seasons, Waddell one.

Dominant Pitchers: II

The Total Pitcher Index

Alan S. Kaufman and James C. Kaufman

There is no simple way to answer questions like, "Who was the best pitcher of all time?" or even, "Who was the best pitcher of the past generation?" Thorn and Palmer attempt to answer questions of that sort, and provide lists of pitchers in *Total Baseball* (third edition) rank-ordered on the basis of Total Pitcher Index (TPI). The TPI is a statistic that merges the esoteric concepts of Pitching Runs, Batting Runs and Fielding Runs, and divides the sum by the equally esoteric Runs Per Win factor. Their system indicates that Walter Johnson, Cy Young, and Pete Alexander rank 1-2-3 in all-time TPIs, with Tom Seaver, Bob Gibson and Jim Palmer pacing the past generation of pitchers. But you don't need to resort to complex statistics to rate the best pitchers of all time. Common sense suggests that a reasonable rating system is one that determines which pitchers were the most dominant relative to their peers throughout their careers.

To assess dominance, you can survey how well pitchers fared from year to year in the Cy Young balloting. That annual award rates pitchers on the basis of how their record stacks up against all other hurlers in their league, both in terms of the excellence of

Alan S. Kaufman and James C. Kaufman are the authors of The Worst Baseball Pitchers of All Time *(McFarland, 1993), an updated version of which was published in 1995 by Citadel Press. They have written for* Playboy, Baseball Digest, NINE, Baseball Quarterly Review, *and many other publications. Alan is the author of psychological tests and books that are used throughout the world and is a senior research scientist for PAR, Inc., in Odessa, Florida. James, an aspiring playwright, is a Teaching Fellow in the Department of Cognitive Psychology at Yale.*

their stats and their perceived value to their team. Pitchers who consistently rank among the leaders in the Cy Young balloting are objectively viewed as the most dominant of their era. The meaning of specific pitching accomplishments, such as winning 20 games or posting a 2.50 ERA, changes from decade to decade. But perceived dominance—ranking high year after year when compared to one's peers—has a constant meaning whether you are evaluating Christy Mathewson, Lefty Grove, or Roger Clemens.

The results of Cy Young balloting are, therefore, a sensible way to rank-order pitchers from the mid-1950s on, when the annual award was first instituted. To rank-order pitchers for the entire twentieth century, however, requires a little ingenuity. To accomplish this goal, we examined the results of four different approaches for awarding Cy Young trophies, or their equivalent, to pitchers who toiled before the Cy Young award was instituted. But we'll get to the hypothetical Cy Young ballots later in the article, when we attempt to determine the best pitchers of the century. For now, we'll focus on the most dominant pitchers of the past generation, as determined by their ranking in the actual Cy Young elections since 1956.

The Best Pitchers of the Past Generation—We looked at all of the election results from 1956 through 1994, and gave credit for pitchers who ranked first to fifth in each election (sometimes, of course, fewer than five pitchers earned votes). We gave each pitcher six points for coming in first in a Cy Young race, four for finishing second, three for finishing third, two for finishing fourth and one for finishing fifth. We ignored occasional ties in the voting, giving the full point amount to each pitcher (e. g., Cuellar and McLain each earned six points when they tied for the '69 AL award).

Chart 1 lists the most dominant pitchers since 1956, based on the Cy Young point system just described. Some pitchers whose careers started before 1956 are treated unfairly by the system, most notably Warren Spahn and Whitey Ford, but for the majority of hurlers from the past generation, this system provides a gauge of their relative dominance when they are compared to their peers.

Seaver heads the list by a small margin over Palmer and four-time winner Steve Carlton. Roger Clemens holds down third place thanks to second- and third-place finishes to buttress the three awards that he won. Fast-charging Greg Maddux, with three straight Cy Young awards in 1992, 1993, and tainted 1994, is tied with super-southpaws Sandy Koufax and Spahn for the fifth spot.

Although Seaver and Palmer trail Carlton four to three in terms of Cy Young trophies, they outranked Lefty by virtue of finishing among the top five during eight different seasons. Next in terms of year-to-year consistency are Carlton and Nolan Ryan, who ranked among the top five Cy Young finishers during six different seasons. Despite gaining Cy Young support in six seasons, Ryan is mired in a tie for thirteenth place in the accompanying chart because he finished second through fifth in Cy Young balloting but never cracked the winner's circle. Clemens, Spahn, Fergie Jenkins and Dan Quisenberry each finished among the top five in five different seasons.

Quiz, tied for tenth place on the list of hurlers, is the highest ranking relief pitcher, followed by Mike Marshall, Bruce Sutter and Rollie Fingers. Dennis Eckersley, tied with Marshall and others for sixteenth

Chart 1

Pitchers Ranking High in Cy Young Balloting, 1956-1994

	Pitcher	1st	2nd	3rd	4th	5th	Total Points
1.	Tom Seaver	3	2	1	1	1	32
2.	Jim Palmer	3	2	1	0	2	31
3.	Steve Carlton	4	0	1	1	0	29
4.	*Roger Clemens	3	1	1	0	0	25
5.	Sandy Koufax	3	0	1	0	0	21
	*Greg Maddux	3	0	1	0	0	21
	Warren Spahn	1	3	1	0	0	21
8.	Ferguson Jenkins	1	2	2	0	0	20
9.	Gaylord Perry	2	1	0	1	0	18
10.	Catfish Hunter	1	1	1	1	0	15
	Dan Quisenberry	0	2	2	0	1	15
	*Bret Saberhagen	2	0	1	0	0	15
13.	Ron Guidry	1	1	1	0	1	14
	Nolan Ryan	0	1	2	1	2	14
	*F. Valenzuela	1	1	1	0	1	14
16.	*Dennis Eckersley	1	1	0	1	0	13
	Bob Gibson	2	0	0	0	1	13
	*Tommy Glavine	1	1	1	0	0	13
	*Dwight Gooden	1	1	0	1	1	13
	*Orel Hershiser	1	0	1	2	0	13
	Mike Marshall	1	1	0	1	1	13
22.	Denny McLain	2	0	0	0	0	12
	*Dave Stewart	0	1	2	1	0	12
	Bruce Sutter	1	0	1	1	1	12
25.	*Rick Sutcliffe	1	1	0	0	1	11
26.	Tommy John	0	2	0	1	0	10
	Randy Jones	1	1	0	0	0	10
	*Jimmy Key	0	2	0	1	0	10
	*Jack McDowell	1	1	0	0	0	10
	Mike Scott	1	1	0	0	0	10
31.	Vida Blue	1	0	1	0	0	9
	*David Cone	1	0	1	0	0	9
	*Doug Drabek	1	0	0	1	1	9
	Rollie Fingers	1	0	1	0	0	9
	Whitey Ford	1	0	1	0	0	9
	*Jack Morris	0	0	2	1	1	9
	Jim Perry	1	0	1	0	0	9
	*Frank Viola	1	0	1	0	0	9
39.	Bert Blyleven	0	0	2	1	0	8
	Mike Cuellar	1	0	0	1	0	8
	Dave McNally	0	1	0	2	0	8
	Phil Niekro	0	1	1	0	1	8
	Don Sutton	0	0	1	1	3	8
	Pete Vuckovich	1	0	0	1	0	8
	Wilbur Wood	0	1	1	0	1	8
46.	Mickey Lolich	0	1	1	0	0	7
	Steve Rogers	0	1	0	1	1	7
	*Lee Smith	0	1	0	1	1	7

* = Active in 1994

Note: Total points are computed by alotting 6 points for finishing first, 4 points for second, 3 points for third, 2 points for fourth and 1 point for fifth-place.

place, earned points both as a starter and reliever. Quisenberry amassed most of his points during a sensational four-year stretch (1982-85) when he finished second twice and third twice. But for sustained dominance, no one can match Palmer's streak of winning three awards, finishing second once, third once and fifth once within a seven-year period (1972-78). For long-term consistency, however, Seaver is the champ. He earned votes in a record ten different Cy Young elections—the eight indicated in Chart 1 plus two in which he ranked seventh and eighth. He almost became the only pitcher to win awards in three different decades (he won in '69, '73 and '75, and finished a close second to Valenzuela in '81).

Palmer and Ryan each earned points in eight elections, followed by Jack Morris with seven. Like Ryan, Morris' ability to attract attention in so many elections did not rank him high in our chart because he never won the coveted award. Morris, who led the decade of the 1980s with 162 wins, was MVP of the 1991 World Series, and paced the 1992 World Champion Blue Jays with a 21-6 record, never finished higher than third in a Cy Young race.

Three-hundred game-winners Phil Niekro and Don Sutton also fell flat on the Cy Young ballot. Niekro earned votes in five elections spanning three decades, but ranked among the top five only three times. Sutton was among the top five finishers in five straight elections (1972-76)—something no one else has done—but his best finish was third in 1976. Niekro and Sutton each accumulated eight points, barely making our chart.

Contrasting with pitchers such as Morris, Niekro and Sutton, who earned relatively few points during long careers, are other hurlers who earned many points in a short space of time. In addition to Maddux's three straight Cy Youngs, he tacked on a third-place finish in 1989 (when he was 19-12 for the Cubs) to amass his twenty-one points during his first eight full seasons. Seaver earned seventeen points in his first eight years, Jenkins sixteen, Quisenberry fifteen, and Palmer and Fernando Valenzuela each earned fourteen. The only pitcher to accumulate more points in the first eight years is Rocket Roger with twenty-two. Both Maddux and Clemens stand a great chance of climbing to the top of the chart before they hang it up. So does Tommy Glavine, who has garnered one trophy and thirteen points during his first seven full seasons.

Overall, Koufax would have ranked higher in the chart and Spahn might have topped the list if awards had been given to both leagues before 1967. For two

of Spahn's second-place finishes, in 1958 and 1961, he was the highest ranking National League hurler. And had Cy Young awards been handed out a decade earlier, then Spahn's early career would probably have outstripped everyone else's; during his first eight full seasons (1946-53) Spahn won 21 to 23 games five times. Which brings us to the next goal of this article—an exploration of hypothetical Cy Young awards as a vehicle for ranking the best pitchers of the twentieth century. For that analysis, we used the same logic regarding dominance, but had to rely on both actual and hypothetical Cy Young votes.

The Best Pitchers of the 20th Century—To recreate Cy Young ballots from days gone by we examined the results of four different approaches for awarding the equivalent of Cy Young trophies to those who pitched before the Cy Young award was instituted in 1956 (and to those who hurled in the "other" league from 1956-1966, when only a single award was given). These approaches include:

(1) the results of balloting by SABR members, reported by Lyle Spatz in the 1988 *BRJ*;

(2) Thorn and Holway's annual Jim Creighton award, based on four of their stats (Wins-Above-League, Normalized ERA, Pitching Average, Overall On Base Average), as reported in their 1987 book *The Pitcher*;

(3) Bill Deane's selections for hypothetical Cy Young awards (reported in the 1993 *Total Baseball*, third edition), based on a variety of factors, including the SABR elections, MVP results, Pete Palmer's linear weights, and Deane's own intuitions and opinions; and

(4) our own hypothetical Cy Young award winners (1993 *BRJ*), based on a prediction system that was derived from consistencies in the voting patterns of sportswriters in the actual Cy Young elections.

These four systems are not entirely independent of each other (Deane, for example, relied to some extent on SABR elections), but they nonetheless offer an objective way to reach a consensus of the best pitchers in each league during each season before 1967, when Cy Young awards were given in each league for the first time.

Examination of the hypothetical Cy Young winners in the four systems yields the following results for the 122 mock elections for the years 1900-55 (111 elections) and 1956-66 (11 elections). Assigning each system one vote apiece produced the following distributions of votes in the 122 elections.

Vote	Frequency
4-0	47 (38.5%)
3-1	51 (41.8%)
2-2	10 (8.2%)
2-1-1	14 (11.5%)

As shown, about four out of ten "elections" selected a unanimous choice and about eight out of ten yielded a clear-cut choice (either 4-0 or 3-1). The remaining decisions either produced a tie for the trophy (2-2) or a split-decision winner (2-1-1). To integrate the results of the four systems, we assigned five points to each pitcher who won an election, whether by a clear-cut margin or by a split-decision. We gave four points to each pitcher who finished in a tie for first place (such as Koufax and Larry Jackson, who were each tabbed as the winner of the 1964 NL trophy by two of the four systems). We allotted three points to pitchers who finished second (the ones who earned the dissenting vote in the 3-1 decisions). And we gave two points for pitchers who tied for second place in the 2-1-1 outcomes.

In all cases, the four systems assumed primacy in the voting, even when the pitchers named did not fare well in MVP balloting (a relatively rare occurrence). However, we wanted to flesh out the number of pitchers receiving credit for outstanding seasons to make the comparisons a bit fairer among old-time and contemporary pitchers (since the latter had the benefit of finishing second or third in the actual elections). So, for example, King Carl Hubbell was the unanimous choice of the four systems in the 1936 NL Cy Young mock election, and he also won the NL MVP award that year. But Dizzy Dean finished second to Hubbell in the MVP vote and surely would have come in second in the Cy Young balloting as well. In 1939, Bucky Walters was the NL MVP and the Cy Young selection of all four systems. However, Paul Derringer finished third in the MVP race and Curt Davis was fifth; these men deserved to get some recognition in our Cy Young rankings, as did other hurlers in other seasons who were favorites of MVP voters.

MVP elections were held from 1911-14, 1922-29 and, by current rules, since 1931. We assigned pitchers who ranked highest in MVP elections (as long as they cracked the top dozen finishers) second-place, and sometimes third-place, finishes in seasons when the four systems produced unanimous winners; and we assigned pitchers third-place finishes in seasons in which two or more hurlers earned votes from the four systems. (We gave pitchers who got credit for a third-

place vote one point in our dominance system.) In the years when there were no MVP awards, we usually did not choose runners-up in the hypothetical Cy Young races. Occasionally we gave a second-place vote in a year when a pitcher was the unanimous choice of the four systems, but that was the exception. One such instance was in 1904 when the pennant-winning Giants' Iron Man McGinnity was the unanimous Cy Young choice based on his eye-popping 35-8 mark. We gave a second-place vote to his teammate, Christy Mathewson (33-12), who won ten more games than the next-best hurler (Jack Harper, 23-9).

Chart 2 shows the rankings of pitchers, past and present, based on a merger of actual and hypothetical Cy Young elections. We used the 5-4-3-2-1 rating system to determine point totals. The totals for more recent pitchers will differ from their totals in Chart 1 because different numbers of points are allotted for finishing first, second and third; fourth and fifth place finishes are excluded; ties in the balloting are treated differently; and so forth.

In addition to the results of the balloting, Chart 2 also indicates with a "√" pitchers enshrined in the Hall of Fame. Next to the √ is an indication of the number of times they were on the Hall of Fame ballot before election by the BBWAA or a notation ("Vet") to indicate that they were elected to the Hall by the Veteran's Committee or its equivalent.

Matty tops the chart, followed by Lefty Grove, Johnson, Spahn, and Alex. Bob Feller holds down the fifth spot in the list of the most dominant pitchers of the twentieth century, followed closely by a trio of recent stars, Palmer, Seaver, and Carlton. Clemens and Koufax tie for the tenth slot. Cy himself failed to rank among the top ten, but that was largely because we used 1900 as our cutoff point. He would have been the odds-on choice as the best pitcher in the NL in 1892 and '95, and would have been in a three-way dogfight with Kid Nichols and Frank Killen for the 1893 trophy.

Among the thirteen pitchers in Chart 2 who accumulated at least seventeen points, all eligible pitchers were elected to the Hall of Fame within the first four ballots, eight on the first ballot. If ten points is used as an arbitrary cutoff of dominance, then twenty-eight of thirty-three eligible hurlers were enshrined in the Hall of Fame. Exceptions are Bucky Walters, Billy Pierce, Mort Cooper, Wes Ferrell, and George Uhle.

The only pitchers with less than ten points to be elected to the Hall within ten years of eligibility are Early Wynn, Juan Marichal, Fingers (six), Herb

Chart 2

Real and Hypothetical Cy Young Rankings, 1904–1994

Pitcher	Hall of Fame	1st	Tied 1st	2nd	Tied 2nd	3rd	Total Points
1. Christy Mathewson	√-1st	8	0	1	0	1	44
2. Lefty Grove	√-4th	6	0	3	0	0	39
3. Walter Johnson	√-1st	6	1	1	0	0	37
4. Warren Spahn	√-1st	5	0	2	0	2	33
5. Pete Alexander	√-3rd	4	0	1	1	0	25
6. Bob Feller	√-1st	4	0	1	0	1	24
7. Jim Palmer	√-1st	3	0	2	0	1	22
Tom Seaver	√-1st	3	0	2	0	1	22
9. Steve Carlton	√-1st	4	0	0	0	1	21
10. *Roger Clemens	Not Elig.	3	0	1	0	1	19
Sandy Koufax	√-1st	3	1	0	0	0	19
12. Cy Young	√-2nd	3	0	1	0	0	18
13. Robin Roberts	√-4th	2	0	2	0	1	17
14. Dizzy Dean	√-9th	2	0	2	0	0	16
*Greg Maddux	Not Elig.	3	0	0	0	1	16
Hal Newhouser	√-Vet	3	0	0	0	1	16
17. Mordecai Brown	√-Vet	1	0	3	0	1	15
Carl Hubbell	√-3rd	2	1	0	0	1	15
Dazzy Vance	√-15th	2	0	1	1	0	15
Bucky Walters		3	0	0	0	0	15
21. Stan Coveleski	√-Vet	1	0	3	0	0	14
Burleigh Grimes	√-Vet	1	1	1	1	0	14
23. Whitey Ford	√-2nd	2	0	0	1	1	13
Lefty Gomez	√-Vet	2	0	1	0	0	13
Bob Lemon	√-12th	2	0	1	0	0	13
Joe McGinnity	√-Vet	2	0	1	0	0	13
Gaylord Perry	√-3rd	2	0	1	0	0	13
28. Ferguson Jenkins	√-3rd	1	0	1	1	2	12
Billy Pierce		0	1	1	2	1	12
Ed Walsh	√-Vet	1	1	0	1	1	12
31. Mort Cooper		2	0	0	0	1	11
*Bret Saberhagen	Not Elig.	2	0	0	0	1	11
33. Wes Ferrell		1	0	1	0	2	10
Bob Gibson	√-1st	2	0	0	0	0	10
Catfish Hunter	√-3rd	1	0	1	0	2	10
George Uhle		2	0	0	0	0	10
37. Jim Bunning		1	0	0	2	0	9
Jack Chesbro	√-Vet	1	1	0	0	0	9
Eddie Cicotte		1	1	0	0	0	9
*Tommy Glavine	Not Elig.	1	0	1	0	1	9
Ron Guidry		1	0	1	0	1	9
Pat Malone		1	1	0	0	0	9
Denny McLain		1	1	0	0	0	9
Don Newcombe		1	0	1	0	1	9
Jim Perry		1	0	1	0	1	9
Red Ruffing	√-15th	1	0	1	0	1	9
*F. Valenzuela	Not Elig.	1	0	1	0	1	9
Early Wynn	√-4th	1	0	1	0	1	9
49. Ewell Blackwell		1	0	1	0	0	8
Paul Derringer		0	0	2	0	2	8
Don Drysdale	√-10th	1	0	1	0	0	8
*Dennis Eckersley	Not Elig.	1	0	1	0	0	8
Red Faber	√-Vet	1	0	1	0	0	8
Ned Garver		1	0	1	0	0	8
*Dwight Gooden	Not Elig.	1	0	1	0	0	8
Randy Jones		1	0	1	0	0	8
Vern Law		1	0	1	0	0	8
Dolph Luque		1	0	1	0	0	8
Sal Maglie		1	0	1	0	0	8
Mike Marshall		1	0	1	0	0	8
*Jack McDowell	Not Elig.	1	0	1	0	0	8
Dan Quisenberry	Not Elig.	0	0	2	0	2	8
Johnny Sain		1	0	1	0	0	8
Mike Scott	Not Elig.	1	0	1	0	0	8
*Rick Sutcliffe	Not Elig.	1	0	1	0	0	8
Hippo Vaughn		1	0	1	0	0	8
Rube Waddell'	√-Vet	1	0	1	0	0	8
68. Addie Joss	√-Vet	0	1	1	0	0	7
Juan Marichal	√-3rd	0	0	2	0	1	7
Bruce Sutter		1	0	0	0	2	7

* = Active in 1994

Not Elig. = Not Eligible

Note: Total points are computed by giving 5 points for finishing first, 4 points for tying for first, 3 points for second, 2 points for tying for second, and 1 point for third. Hunter and Sutter were each given credit for a third-place finish when they actually finished fourth, but were within one point of the pitcher who came in third.

Hall of Famers not included in Chart 2: Chief Bender (Vet), Rollie Fingers (2nd), Jesse Haines (Vet), Waite Hoyt (Vet), Ted Lyons (10th), Rube Marquard (Vet), Herb Pennock (8th), Eddie Plank (Vet), Eppa Rixey (Vet) and Hoyt Wilhelm (8th).

Pennock (four) and Hoyt Wilhelm (one). Fingers and Wilhelm were relief pitchers, traditionally spurned by Cy Young voters, and Wynn and Marichal still managed to make Chart 2.

Of the dozen pitchers elected to Cooperstown on the first or second ballot, only Fingers earned fewer than ten points in our dominance system, and only Fingers, Ford, and Bob Gibson earned fewer than eighteen. Nolan Ryan, with a total of only five points, is conspicuously absent from Chart 2, and he is nearly a lock to be elected to the Hall on the first ballot.

Four relief pitchers ranked among the seventy most dominant pitchers of the twentieth century shown in Chart 2: Eckersley, Marshall, Quisenberry, and Sutter. Pierce, though ignored by Cooperstown, won three Jim Creighton awards in Thorn and Holway's *The Pitcher*, and Deane cited Pierce for two hypothetical Cy Young awards in *Total Baseball*. Pierce never did better than a tie for a Cy Young award (with Bob Porterfield in the AL in 1953) based on our voting system. He is the only pitcher in Chart 2 with nine or more points *not* to have won a single trophy outright.

The top dozen pitchers in the chart span all eras of baseball, from the 1890s (Young) to 1990s (Clemens), with representation given to the Dead Ball Era (Mathewson, Johnson, Alexander), the 1920s and '30s (Grove), the '40s and '50s (Spahn, Feller), the '60s (Koufax) and the '70s and '80s (Palmer, Seaver, Carlton).

As indicated in Chart 2, Matty would likely have made the top three in "Pitcher of the Year" elections during ten different seasons, with Grove and Spahn ranking high nine times and the Big Train eight times. And these number are conservative, especially for the old-timers. Mathewson was shut out of the rankings in 1914 when he posted a 24-13 mark, and Johnson earned no "votes" in 1910 when he won 25 games and led the AL in innings pitched (374), strikeouts (313) and complete games (38).

Nine pitchers in Chart 2 were active in 1994, although several are on the downside of their careers (Valenzuela, Eckersley, and Sutcliffe), and one (Dwight Gooden) has to overcome drug problems and a one-year suspension before posing any threat to the pitchers in the chart who have earned more than his eight points. In addition to Clemens and Maddux, Bret Saberhagen, Glavine, and Jack McDowell are all young enough and sufficiently in their prime to rank among the elite of the twentieth century before they retire.

We believe that the dominance system we developed for comparing pitchers of the past generation and for comparing pitchers across generations has merit, but any system will invariably benefit some hurlers while hurting others. We present this approach to offer one reasonably objective method of ranking pitchers, but recognize that all systems arouse controversy and arguments, and no system is without flaws. Ryan didn't make Chart 2 even though this tosser of seven no-hitters dominated batters for decades. Our system also excludes Eddie Plank (he earned three points), although Ty Cobb included the 327-game winner on his all-time pitching staff (along with Young, Mathewson, Johnson, Alexander, and Ed Walsh) in a 1942 *Sporting News* interview. Along this line, though, the TPI system advocated by *Total Baseball* ranks Feller and Koufax as the fortieth and seventy-eighth best pitchers of all time, with Rick Reuschel sandwiched in between, at forty-eighth) and Dave Stieb ranked ahead of both first-ballot Hall of Famers in the thirty-fifth slot.

GAME 3 Friday, September 30, 1955

```
New York   020  000  100 - 3   7   0
Brooklyn   220  200  20x - 8  11   1
```

NEW YORK (2-0)					
8/7 Cerv	13		k	k	k
5 McDougald	8		43	s	53
2 Berra	9		3^f	sx	43
9/8 Mantle	H		53	643p	53
3 Skowron	D		k	63	s
7/9 Howard	53		k	7	4^
4 Martin	k		53	53	6^
6 Rizzuto	se2		w	W	3^
1 Turley	53				
1 Morgan 2					
o Bauer 5	7				
1 Kucks 5					
o Carey 7	t"				
1 Sturdivant 7					

BROOKLYN (0-2)					
4 Gilliam	8	w'	S	7	w
6 Reese	W	w'	8	8	s'+
8 Snider	k	f32	W	s	7
2 Campanella	H'	4\	s'+	7	d
9 Furillo	8	d	7*	53	2^f
3 Hodges	8	53	63	7	6^f
5 JRobinson	S	4^	53	D	3^f
7 Amoros	P	i	w	s'x	
1 Podres	sx	k	34b	F16	

* fh'+

Pitchers: NEW YORK, Turley L (91xxx), Morgan (x86xx), Kucks (xx34x), Sturdivant (xxx47). BROOKLYN, Podres W.

Left on Base- NY 5, Bkl 11. T- 2:20. A- 34,209.

Ump-Honochick, Dascoli, Summers, Ballanfant, Donatelli, Flaherty.

Minor League Big Guns

A comparison of the top ten individual single-season home run records

Ernest J. Green

"*Taken together, the many meanings that can be given to, or extracted from, the numbers compel this conclusion: There is an irreducible indeterminacy in baseball judgments.*"
—*George Will*, Men at Work

Baseball has a way of taking numbers to a mythical level, especially round numbers. To hit .400 or to win 30 games in a season is to move into a magical realm populated by only the regal. One such number, 60 home runs in a season, has been so revered that surpassing it meant not acclaim but scorn and an asterisk. Even in the minor leagues that number retains its mystique, although it has been surpassed ten times. A comparison of those ten accomplishments is an exploration of baseball tradition and an examination of baseball logic and lore.

This article makes three types of comparisons. First, it compares the individual statistics of the hitters from various perspectives. Second, it contrasts the leagues and parks where the home runs were hit. Third, it considers the teams' seasons and historical locations to furnish a social psychological dimension to the achievements.

A Comparison of the Hitters—Minor league hitters from the highest classification to the lowest have exceeded 60 home runs in a season. The first was

Ernest J. Green is the author of The Diamonds of Dixie, *(Madison, 1995).*

Tony Lazzeri in 1925 and the last was Frosty Kennedy in 1956. The professional record was set by Joe Bauman with 72 in 1954.

Direct comparisons of individual achievements are difficult because the hitters played seasons of different lengths, ranging from Lazzeri's 200 games in the Pacific Coast League to Moose Clabaugh's 121 before he was called up to Brooklyn with 62 homers. Table 1 makes a more direct comparison by presenting efficiency numbers as home runs per game and home runs per at bat ratios.

Table 1

Home run per games and at bat ratios

Name	HRs	Games	HR/Game Ratio	HR/AB Ratio
Joe Bauman	72	138	1.92	6.92
Joe Hauser	69	153	2.22	8.26
Bob Crues	69	140	2.03	8.19
Dick Stuart	66	138	2.09	7.92
Bob Lennon	64	154	2.41	9.52
Joe Hauser	63	167	2.65	9.79
Moose Clabaugh	62	121	1.95	7.16
Ken Guettler	62	154	2.48	7.76
Tony Lazzeri	60	200	3.33	11.83
Frosty Kennedy	60	144	2.40	9.37

Joe Bauman's season overshadows those of the other hitters in more than total number of home runs. He had the best home run per game ratio (one for every 1.92 games) and the only home run at bat ratio under 7 (one home run for every 6.92 at bats). For comparison, Ruth hit a homer every 9.0 times at bat in 1927, his 60 home run year, and Roger Maris hit one every 9.67 at bats in 1961, when he hit 61.

Were the top minor league home run hitters free-swinging specialists who sacrificed other aspects of their offense to produce a big season? Not at all, as Table 2 shows. Numbers are not comparable for Lazzeri and Dick Stuart, who both played most of their careers in the major leagues, but of the remaining eight, two hit over .400 in their big years. Only Ken Guettler hit under .300 in his peak home run year, and he almost made it with a .293. Four had career batting averages of over .300 in the minors, and the lowest career batting average was a respectable .281 by Bob Lennon.

Table 2

Batting averages and home run totals of minor league big guns

Name	Big Year BA	Career BA	Career Home Runs[1]
Bauman	.400	.337	337
Hauser (1933)	.332	.299	399
Crues	.404	.337	232
Stuart	.298*	.265*	438*
Lennon	.345	.281	278
Hauser (1930)	.313	.299	399
Clabaugh	.376	.339	346
Guettler	.293	.289	330
Lazzeri	.355*	.297*	313*
Kennedy	.327	.342	228

*Played most of career in majors

Another measure of how powerful the big hitters were is slugging average. Table 3 shows once again that Joe Bauman's big season was by almost any measure the greatest offensive explosion ever in professional baseball. With 456 total bases in 498 at bats, he recorded the all-time professional slugging mark of .916. Three of the ten bettered Ruth's best slugging year, 1920, when he achieved an .847 slugging average.

Table 3

Slugging averages in peak home run years

Name	AB	Total Bases	SA
Bauman	498	456	.916
Hauser (1933)	570	429	.753
Crues	565	479	.848
Stuart	523	385	.736
Lennon	609	447	.733
Hauser (1930)	617	443	.718

Clabaugh	444	378	.851
Guettler	481	349	.726
Lazzeri	710	512	.721
Kennedy	562	402	.715

One possibility is that the big years were one-time flukes, caused by cozy parks (more on that later) or other special circumstances. Table 4, however, shows that big years were the norm for these hitters rather than the exception. Joe Hauser exceeded 60 home runs twice, in two different ball parks, with totals of 69 and 63. By assigning weights to the seasons in which each player hit from 20-29 (weight = 1) to 70+ (weight = 6) we can draw a rough comparative measure of career home run consistency.

Dick Stuart, Joe Hauser, and Joe Bauman outdistance the others by a considerable margin. What the scores do not reflect is that Hauser played in parts of nineteen seasons in the minors, while Bauman had only nine seasons of professional baseball. (See Table 5 for statistics on the other hitters). Stuart produced ten other seasons with more than 20 home runs, six at the major league level. His hitting prowess was fortunate, because the nickname Dr. Strangeglove was not unwarranted. With one exception, all the hitters had at least five seasons in which they exceeded 20 home runs. Tony Lazzeri, after his big home run year in the Pacific Coast League, went on to hit 178 home runs in the majors, but never again reached 20 in a single season.

Table 4

Number of seasons (major and minor league) with 20 or more home runs

Weights	(6)	(5)	(4)	(3)	(2)	(1)	
HR	70+	69-60	59-50	49-40	39-30	29-20	
Name							Score
Stuart	0	1	0	3	4	3	25
Hauser	0	2	0	1	3	4	22
Bauman	1	0	2	2	1	0	24
Guettler	0	1	0	1	2	4	16
Clabaugh	0	1	0	0	3	3	14
Crues	0	1	1	0	1	2	13
Kennedy	0	1	0	0	3	1	12
Lennon	0	1	0	0	1	3	10
Lazzeri	0	1	0	1	0	1	9

The ecology of big home run seasons—A popular explanation of minor league big home run seasons is that they were products of the dry air of the Southwest and the bandbox parks of the lower minors. This generalization contains a kernel of truth, but serves to conceal the real factors involved. Four of the big years were products of the Southwest (teams in New Mexico, Texas, Arizona, and Oklahoma). Salt Lake City, where Lazzeri hit 60 in 1925, is in a desert region, though not in the Southwest. Ken Guettler, playing for Shreveport in the Texas League in 1956, had about half of his games that year scheduled in southwestern-based Texas League cities. Overall, however, the Southwest had only six minor leagues, which was less than 25 percent of all leagues in minor league baseball in 1956, the last year for a 60+ season in the minors.

Table 5

Home Run Averages Per Season Over Career

Name	Seasons Played*	Average HR Per Season
Bauman	9	37.44
Kennedy	10	22.80
Guettler	15	22.00
Crues	11	21.09
Hauser	19	21.00
Clabaugh	17	20.35
Lennon	16	17.38

*Excludes full major league seasons; includes seasons split between majors and minors.

The problem with the Southwest as an explanation is that different characteristics of the area seem to cancel each other out. According to Robert Kemp Adair in *The Physics of Baseball*, a baseball will travel twenty extra feet with fifty-degree temperature increase. Assuming the Southwest is hotter than most other places where baseball is played, high home run outputs make sense. However, Adair also contends that the ball will travel slightly farther if humidity is high, since water vapor is lighter than air. Assuming that the Southwest is dryer than other areas where baseball is played, that works against big home run seasons.

A more likely explanation for high home run output in the Southwest is the effect of altitude on home run production. Adair's calculations show that a baseball will travel six feet extra for each one-inch drop in barometer, everything else being equal. Table 6 lists the elevation of *home* baseball parks for the ten big years. The mean elevation was 1,884.4 feet with four home ballparks at higher than 3,000 feet. In contrast, before 1993, Atlanta-Fulton County Stadium was major league baseball's highest at just about 1,000 feet above sea level. Since the real comparison is with other minor league cities, I took a 15 percent random sample of minor league cities in 1954, the year Joe

Bauman hit 72, and averaged the elevations. Minor league cities were playing at an average of 1,104.84 feet above sea level that year. The big guns clearly had advantages of thinner air in the location of their ballparks.

Table 6

Effects of Altitude on Home Run Production

Name	Location of Home Ball Park	Altitude
Bauman	Roswell, NM	3,573 ft.
Hauser	Minneapolis, MN	840 ft.
Crues	Amarillo, TX	3,672 ft.
Stuart	Lincoln, NE	1,176 ft.
Lennon	Nashville, TN	550 ft.
Hauser	Baltimore, MD	445 ft.
Clabaugh	Tyler, TX	558 ft.
Guettler	Shreveport, LA	206 ft.
Lazzeri	Salt Lake City, UT	4,390 ft.
Kennedy	Plainview, TX	3,434 ft.

Baseball, unlike other sports, is not played on fields of identical dimensions. Ballparks have varied in distances to outfield fences, heights of fences, and even slopes of playing fields. The variations are often the first explanations we consider when we try to explain exceptional home run output.

A compilation of ballpark advantages would have to take into account not only home fields, but the dimensions of parks in the other cities where hitters play half their games. Too many variables exist to make a systematic comparison possible, but some general observations are instructive. Two of the home parks were so freakish that the home run totals could be considered tainted, but eccentric playing fields have always been one of the minors' charms, and have existed so often that "standard" is almost meaningless.

In 1933, when Joe Hauser set the professional record for home runs in a season (later broken by Joe Bauman), fifty of his 69 home runs were hit at home. The home field was Nicollet Park in Minneapolis, which was a lopsided 334-432-279 from left to center to right. The right field "power alley," used often by the lefthanded hitting Hauser, was only 328 feet. Before 1935, the right field fence was 25 feet high, but that height couldn't contain the fly balls hit by Hauser. Hauser hit 399 minor league home runs in his career, and 208 of them were hit while playing for Minneapolis. In 1930, however, playing at Terrapin Park for the Baltimore Orioles, Joe hit 63 home runs.

The layout there was a little more conventional: right field ran 310 feet down the line.

Another suspicious mark was the Southern Association record of 64, set by Bob Lennon for Nashville in 1954. Lennon, a lefthander, played in the infamous Sulphur Dell. The odd-shaped park was in a depression near the city dump (outfielders, closest to the dump's odors, referred to the park as "Suffer Hell") and the right field fence was only 262 feet away from home plate. After 1931 a 30-foot screen was added to the 16-foot wooden fence, which sat on a shelf, or ridge, so that right fielders had to run up, down, and across a hill to catch flies, but to no avail. Lazy pop flies still disappeared over everything. Aside from the one big season, Lennon never managed more than 31 home runs in a year. His second highest output was in 1955, but in all fairness he did hit them somewhere other than Sulphur Dell. His home park in 1955 was Nicolett Field, in Minneapolis.

Bob Crues tied Hauser's record in 1948, playing for Amarillo in the West Texas-New Mexico League. His total included eight grand slams, and he hit .404 with an incredible 254 runs batted in. The year before Crues had hit 52 home runs for Amarillo, but his non-Amarillo seasons never produced more than 32 home runs. Home runs fairly flew out of the park at Amarillo in the last glory days of the minors: 208 in 1947; 214 in 1948; 216 in 1952; 210 in 1953, and 207 in 1955.

The other big hitters had more conventional home ball parks, though each had its quirks. Dick Stuart may have been able to take advantage of a short (380 feet) center field fence at Sherman Field in Lincoln, Nebraska, but had 330-foot foul lines to contend with.

Ken Guettler's 62 home runs for Shreveport in 1956 gain in respectability when considering the home park. Spar Stadium was 320 feet down the left field line and Guettler was righthanded. But Spar was never known as a hitter's park, and aside from that one exceptional mark, never showed up in home run records.

As usual, Joe Bauman's record looks even more impressive when considering his ballpark circumstances. The lefthander aimed at a fence 329 feet down the line when playing at home in the redundantly named Park Field. The only bandbox park in the Longhorn League in the 1950s was at Big Springs, Texas, according to Joe, and he couldn't buy a home run there. In fact, as he closed in on the record in 1954, they pitched around him for an entire series at Big Springs. Joe's record breaking 70th, and his 71st and 72nd, were hit at Artesia, New Mexico. In Artesia's strange-looking, metal fenced park, right field was 360 feet down the line, and the wind, Joe said, "always blew in against you."

Social and psychological factors—When the minor leaguers hit their 60+ home runs, media attention and the pressures it entails was minimal. Also missing was the tension that could have been converted into motivation and excitement. While we usually evalu-

Sulphur Dell, Nashville, in 1908.

National Baseball Library, Cooperstown, NY

ate home run production as an individual achievement, evidence of a group factor is suggested by team standings in the big years. The leagues that hosted the teams involved averaged eight teams per circuit. Given a random finishing place, only one or two of the big hitters' teams would have finished in second place, or any other standing. Yet, as Table 7 shows, six of the teams (60 percent) finished in second place, and another in third place, which landed them in the playoffs.

Table 7

Final Standings of Teams in Big Home Run Years

Name	Team Standing	Games Behind	League	Class	Teams in League
Bauman	2nd	5*	Longhorn	C	8
Hauser (1933)	2nd	15-1/2*	Amer. Assoc.	AA	8
Crues	2nd	4†	West.Tex.-NM	C	8
Stuart	2nd	2-1/2†	Western	A	8
Lennon	7th	30	Southern Ass.	AA	8
Hauser (1930)	2nd	8#	International	AA	8
Clabaugh	3rd	11-1/2#	East Texas	D	6
Guettler	7th	27	Texas	AA	8
Lazzeri	2nd	12-1/2#	Pacific Coast	AA	8
Kennedy	5th	15	Southwestern	B	10

*Made post-season playoffs

†Won post-season playoffs

#League did not hold post-season playoffs

Winning was as important as player development in the minor leagues of the pre-1960 decades. A pennant race generated local excitement, and the chase may have provided the incentive for extraordinary effort and increased home run production. As remarkable as the high number of second-place finishes is the absence of pennant winning teams. Perhaps complacency accompanies first place the same way that hopelessness settles in on a second division club.

After 1920, 60+ home runs were hit in every decade through the 1950s. The output was not randomly distributed, however. 60 percent of the big years came between 1948 and 1956. The number of minor leagues, and thus the total number of minor league players, peaked in the late 1940s. By 1954, the numbers had shrunk by a third, yet half the big home years occurred between 1954 and 1956. Why should the decay of the minor leagues be correlated with home run records?

The post-WWII expansion to a record number of minor leagues and teams was short-lived. Television, air-conditioning, and other factors caused a rapid shrinkage of the minors in the early 1950s. Since no major league expansion occurred in those years, the minors were left with a large talent pool from which to choose, and the fifties had the cream of a talented crop. However, this would have been as true for pitchers as power hitters.

Hitters were helped more by the fact that ballparks began to deteriorate and were not modernized to keep pace with stronger, more athletic players. Parks like Nicollet and Sulphur Dell, which must have given starting pitchers nightmares the night before their next start, were still around. Batted balls were still cutting the thin air of southwestern leagues which were about to disappear. The mid-1950s were a last hurrah for the minor leagues, and a select few big hitters went out in a blaze of miniature glory.

Table 8

Total Minor Leagues in Existence in Years in which 60+ Home Runs Were Hit

Name	Yr	No. Minor Leagues
Lazzeri	1925	25
Clabaugh	1926	28
Hauser	1930	23
Hauser	1933	14
Crues	1948	58
Bauman	1954	36
Lennon	1954	36
Stuart	1956	28
Guettler	1956	28
Kennedy	1956	28

The '50s also produced the last generation of players like Joe Bauman and Ken Guettler, who played their entire careers in the minors. The average age of players during the season in which 60 or more home runs were hit was 28. The player development focus in today's minors means that a player is old at 25, and either moves up or moves out. If 60 home runs are exceeded again, it will be at the major league level unless some drastic alteration of the system occurs.

George Will's comment about the indeterminacy of baseball judgments, with which this paper began, is ultimately true. In making baseball comparisons, there is always another variable that could have been considered, or a competing interpretation of existing data that could have been employed. This can be frustrating, but it never stops discussion among students of the game. Asking questions is more fun than having the satisfaction of conclusive answers.

Hitting Hard to All Fields

The life of Bobby Brown

Talmage Boston

As a New York Yankee in the late DiMaggio–early Mantle era, Bobby Brown sprayed line drives, an appropriate style of hitting for a man whose life has turned out to be a line drive of constant achievement in many directions. The ballplayer, cardiologist, and former American League President is the only American athlete enshrined in three separate college Halls of Fame (Stanford, UCLA and Tulane). In a society needing role models, there is none better than Dr. Brown.

Childhood and Amateur Career: 1924-1946—Baseball likes to promote the image of the game's impact on fathers and sons—playing catch and going to ball games together as the baseball bat gets passed from one generation to the next. The image fits the relationship between Bobby Brown and his dad Bill, a perfect baseball father if there ever was one.

Bill Brown played the game well enough as a young man to compete at the semipro level and to think about making the big leagues. Knowing that the money in baseball during this century's early decades didn't compare with what a successful executive could make, Bill reluctantly abandoned the game for a career in business.

His son Bobby started swinging a bat at age five with his father as mentor and coach. When Bobby

turned nine, Bill tied a ball to a rope and then hung it from the ceiling of their basement, where the youngster could practice hitting a moving target during cold New Jersey winters. By the time he was eleven, Bobby found himself playing with high school boys. At thirteen, while starring in New Jersey American Legion ball, he attracted New York Yankee scouts who immediately noticed his perfect left-handed swing.

When Bobby turned fifteen, his father took a job on the West Coast, and the young hitting star began playing year-round in the San Francisco area. Attending the DiMaggio brothers' high school, Brown played shortstop and hit .583 as a junior, playing against future Yankee teammates Jerry Coleman and Charlie Silvera. Bobby's average dipped to .360 during his senior year, probably because of his dual duties as both team captain and president of the student body.

When minor leaguers came home to the Bay Area after the end of their seasons, Brown honed his skills by playing with them in pickup games. He always hit well against these pros, and his major league dreams seemed realistic.

As important as baseball was in the Brown family, the game was never allowed to interfere with Bobby's higher education. In college Brown played for three schools. In the spring of '43 at Stanford, he hit .460, gained All-Conference honors, learned he didn't want to become a chemical engineer, and decided to be a doctor.

Talmage Boston is a Dallas civil trial attorney whose articles on baseball have appeared in Elysian Fields Quarterly, *the* Dallas Morning News, *and the* Forth Worth Star Telegram. *His first book, entitled* 1939: Baseball's Pivotal Year, *was published by The Summit Group in 1994.*

When his World War II military service began in the summer of 1943, Bobby had to transfer to UCLA where he completed his premed studies while participating in the Navy's V-12 officer training program. In the spring of '44, he hit .444 for the Bruins, was elected team captain on the league championship team, and was again named All-Conference. Finally, he went to Tulane for medical school in the spring of '45, where, with one year of college eligibility left, he hit almost .500, leading the team to a 22-6 record.

When the baseball season ended at Tulane, fifteen of the sixteen major league teams were eager to sign the hard-hitting infielder. Bobby's father served as negotiator, and he accepted the Yankee offer of $52,000 paid over three years, the second-highest bonus ever received by a young player at that time. When Tulane's medical school dean heard about the bonus, he asked Brown if the Yankees would like to endow a chair.

Life in the Pros: 1946-1954—Brown's minor league career began and ended in 1946 at Newark in the International League. Playing with the famed Bears, he roomed with Yogi Berra, led the league in base hits, and batted .341 for the season, second only to Jackie Robinson's .349. For his spectacular play, Garden State sportswriters named Brown the New Jersey Athlete of the Year.

The Yankees called up Brown, Berra, Frank Colman, and Vic Raschi at the end of the '46 season. In an era when eighty percent of major league players did not attend any college, Yankee veterans at first resented the handsome rookie third baseman, whom the press had already started calling "The Golden Boy." They nicknamed Brown "Quack."

In the last week of the '46 season, with the Red Sox having wrapped up the American League pennant, Bobby and Yogi each got to appear in seven games with Brown hitting .333 (8 for 24) while Berra hit .346 (8 for 22).

At spring training in '47, Brown battled popular Billy Johnson to a stalemate for the third base position. Two weeks after Opening Day, Boston's Mel Parnell hit Bobby with a pitch on the hand, breaking a finger. By the time it healed, Johnson's hot hitting and consistent fielding had cemented his position in the starting lineup, limiting Bobby's role to pinch-hitting. Faced with a sporadic playing role for the first time in his life, Brown made the most of it, leading the American League in pinch-hits with 9 in 27 chances, and finishing the year with an even .300 batting average.

Bobby Brown's favorite moment as a player came in the 1947 World Series, when his hitting performance earned him the nickname "The Wand." Yankee manager Bucky Harris gave Brown four pinch-hit chances to bat against the Dodgers, and Bobby went 3 for 3 with a walk, driving in three runs. In Game Seven, after hitting a double in the fourth inning to drive in a run, Brown stood on second base, heard the roar of the crowd, knew that his team was going to be the world champions, and looked into the stands in time to see his father sail a favorite hat into the sky. Bobby Brown could smile, knowing he had fulfilled the dream of his personal hero and greatest fan.

In 1948, Brown played more than he had as a rookie, again hit .300, but still couldn't break into the starting lineup on a consistent basis.

Casey Stengel arrived on the Yankee Stadium scene in 1949 and led the team to the pennant on the season's last day. Stengel, the great platooner, split the third base duties between lefty-swinger Brown and the right-handed Johnson.

Bobby had his most productive season in 1949, knocking in 61 runs in 104 games. In the postseason, Brown proved his '47 heroics were no fluke by going 6 for 12 in the '49 Fall Classic, hitting the Series' key blow—a triple with the bases loaded to break open Game Four. The hit was made particularly sweet in light of the Dodgers' decision to walk Joe DiMaggio intentionally to get to Brown.

When the '49 season ended, Bobby returned to Tulane to resume his medical school studies as he had done the previous three years. That fall, his sister introduced the World Series star to Sara French, a Sophie Newcomb College homecoming queen from Dallas' Highland Park. She became Mrs. Bobby Brown two years later.

The Yankees repeated as Series champions in 1950, with Brown and Johnson platooning at third throughout the year. Stengel knew that Brown seemed to play his best baseball in the postseason, and handed him the starting position in the World Series against the Whiz Kid Phillies. In Game One, Brown doubled and scored the game's only run. In Game Three, his eighth inning ground ball smash became the Series' most important play, as Philadelphia shortstop Granny Hamner booted it, allowing the tying run to score. In Game Four, Brown hit a triple to knock in a key run.

After three Fall Classics, Brown's post-season batting average stood at a cool .481. More significant than his Series performances, after the close of the '50 season Brown became the first major leaguer ever to earn his M.D. as an active player.

Brown's last season as a full-time player turned out to be 1951. The Yankees traded Johnson to the Cardinals early in the year to make room for rookie Gil McDougald. Stengel platooned Brown and the right-handed hitting McDougald at the hot corner throughout the year. McDougald was voted Rookie of the Year, and his hitting and fielding slightly surpassed the young doctor's.

Stengel continued to play his two third basemen evenly in the '51 Series against the Willie Mays–Bobby Thomson Giants, with Brown having another great Series going five-for-fourteen (.357). Bobby's average would have been even better if the umpires hadn't missed a call when Willie Mays caught Brown's smash on the rebound off the outfield wall. Because the centerfielder's back was to the field, the umps' view was blocked. It appeared that the acrobatic Mays had caught the ball over his shoulder on the fly.

Sitting in the outfield bleachers, Bobby's father witnessed Mays' "catch" and almost jumped onto the field. When the game ended, a calmer Bill Brown gave Bobby the greatest compliment of his life. "My son is not the greatest ballplayer in the world, but he is the best son."

The Korean War disrupted Brown's career from 1952 to 1954, allowing him to play in only 29 games in '52, none in '53, and 28 in '54. During the war, Brown received a Treasury Department Medal for Bravery serving as a battalion surgeon in an Army M.A.S.H. unit, and later was assigned to the Tokyo Army Hospital.

Upon receiving his honorable discharge, Brown returned to the Yankees at the end of the '54 campaign for a few last swings, but his skills had eroded. He was making only $19,500 a year as a player, and it seemed time to become a full-time physician.

Although he was never an everyday player during his career, he hit .279 over parts of eight seasons and was a legitimate World Series star. He performed in four of them, never hit below .333 in any of them, and played a major role in the Yankees winning all four. His .439 Series batting average is the highest in baseball history for anyone with forty or more at bats. His .707 slugging percentage is fourth highest in Series history, trailing only Reggie Jackson, Babe Ruth, and Lou Gehrig.

In his recent autobiography, Tommy Henrich described Bobby Brown, the player: "He couldn't run, field, or throw, but with a million dollars on the line, he wouldn't choke up at the plate. In every pressure situation, Bobby was always the one in charge at the plate. The pitcher was the one in trouble, not Bobby. You can't teach that attitude, and you can't practice it. Either you have the attitude of a champion up there with men on base and the pennant or World Series hanging in the balance, or you don't. Bobby did."

Brown's hitting came naturally, but he improved it with constant practice. Teammate Irv Noren told author Dom Forker that when the Yankees were on the road, Brown "would call up the visiting team before the game to find out if he could come to hit. For an hour-and-a-half he would hit. He wanted it."

Bobby's fielding has been maligned, and the criticism was deserved when he arrived in the majors. When Casey Stengel first saw Bobby play third base, the Ol' Perfessor remarked, "Brown looks like he's been a hitter for twelve years and a fielder for one." Teammate Gene Woodling joked to his med student teammate, "Bobby, if I ever get sick, don't you dare show up. You have such bad hands I never want you operating on me." Knowing his weakness, Brown worked hard to become a creditable fielder. By 1950, he had a better fielding average than Billy Johnson.

Beginning in 1948 and continuing through 1950, the Yankees allowed Brown to miss spring training to complete his medical school semesters at Tulane. When he was finally in a position to go to St. Petersburg, along came the Korean War.

Upon joining the team each season on Opening Day, Brown split his focus between baseball and medicine by studying constantly between games. Berra remembered, "At the ballpark, Bobby'd have his medical books with him and he'd have the team doctor give him tests." To Brown, studying while playing was natural. He had always done it.

The Doctor: 1954-1984—After retiring as a player in 1954, Brown spent three years as a resident in internal medicine in San Francisco, then went to Tulane for a one-year cardiology fellowship in 1957. Medical school friend Albert Goggans persuaded Bobby to join him in a cardiology practice in Fort Worth in 1958, and they remained partners for twenty-six years.

Brown practiced cardiology with the same intensity he had as a hitter in World Series competition, and the pressures were comparable. Bobby told Bruce Chadwick in a 1982 interview, "I learned in baseball how to respond to enormous pressure. As a doctor I find myself in the same pressure-filled situations." Brown described his cardiology practice as "a twenty-four hour a day specialty that's fraught with daily emergencies of an extreme nature. The hours are long and the stress is great."

During his Fort Worth years, in addition to practicing cardiology and raising a family, Brown somehow found time to chair Fort Worth's Park Board, sit on the board of a major bank, and serve as one of the massive Amon Carter Foundation's three trustees.

The Baseball Executive: 1974, 1984-1994—During his twenty-six year career in medicine, Bobby Brown took one six-month break in 1974 to become president of the Texas Rangers for his friend Brad Corbett, who then owned the team. At the close of the '74 season, he returned to his practice.

In 1983, major league owners searched for a replacement to succeed Bowie Kuhn as baseball commissioner. To Brown's surprise, they called him to interview for the position. He became a finalist, and owners and league executives were committed to finding a place for Brown in the game. American League President Lee MacPhail decided to retire in 1984, and pushed through his personal choice of Bobby Brown to succeed him. MacPhail based his choice on the facts that Brown "had all the attributes necessary. He knew how the game worked, both on the field and in the front office. I also knew he could get along with many people, and that's important, because he has to deal with the owners of teams who are usually top businessmen who think their way is the best."

For Bobby Brown, the decision to leave cardiology to return to full-time baseball was not difficult. He told author Tom Horton in a 1993 interview, "A cardiologist sees and experiences a great deal of bleak time in a patient's life and I decided it was time for me to leave, so I did. Becoming American League president was a once in a lifetime opportunity. When it knocked, I knew it was the only knock."

Upon becoming American League president, Brown announced his goals for the job. In no particular order, he wanted (1) to get more young kids playing the game, (2) to have baseball become more integral in the inner city, (3) to wage a campaign against the players' use of smokeless tobacco, and (4) to assist owners in gaining control of expenses, thereby permitting economic survival for each team.

White Sox owner Jerry Reinsdorf spoke for the other owners in his evaluation of Brown. "Everybody likes him. He's a true gentleman. He's a low key individual who doesn't cause confrontations, and keeps the league running very smoothly."

Commissioner Giamatti once told the New York *Times* about the fun and chemistry he had sharing his baseball duties with Bobby Brown:

> Last fall after the World Series, the rules committee met. Everybody in the room, with the exception of myself, had spent his life in major league baseball. The conversation got long and interesting when we started talking about the strike zone—all these baseball people standing up trying to figure out just where the armpits are exactly. Then, because people thought the American public was not ready to hear on television "the nipple zone," we decided to define the strike zone as the middle of the chest.
>
> Dr. Brown was marvelous. Every time someone would propose an anatomically inoffensive term, like the breastbone, he'd explain that wasn't where we wanted the strike zone to be. So we ended up with "mid-chest to the knees," first to avoid the specious argument about where armpits are, and second, by lowering the strike zone we hope...to get umpires to focus on the high pitch more.

Bobby Brown has now retired, leaving the American League presidency during 1994 in time to avoid the strike that demoralized everyone involved with the game. Never content to observe life from the sidelines, he has already re-engaged in Fort Worth community service, joining the board of the Southwestern Medical Foundation, remaining a trustee of the Amon Carter Foundation, and speaking to a variety of groups to share the lessons he has learned from his unique career. Most important, he and his best friend and former cardiology partner, Dr. Albert Goggans, are now leading a $750,000 capital fundraising drive to benefit All Saints Hospital in Fort Worth.

The three successful careers of Bobby Brown are a testimony to his philosophy. "There's more to life than being an athlete. If you think otherwise, you miss a lot and spend many days looking back. I never had to do that. Life has taught me to do the very best I can every single day."

Which Yankee Teams Were Best?

Not the Babe's

Russell O. Wright

Afavorite topic among fans is selecting the best teams in the history of a franchise. "Best" is primarily a matter of opinion, but the "most successful" teams can be selected by the numbers. Applying such numbers to the Yankees, the most successful franchise of all, yields the surprising result that the Yankees of the Babe Ruth era rank last among their most successful teams. This is shown by the following data taken from my book *The Best of Teams, The Worst of Teams*.

Table 1. Pennant/World Series winners

American League

1903-35			1936-64			1965-94		
Team	Pen	Series	Team	Pen	Series	Team	Pen	Series
A's	8	5	Yankees	22	16	A's	6	4
Yankees	7	4	Tigers	2	1	Orioles	6	3
Red Sox	6	5*	Indians	2	1	Yankees	4	2
Tigers	5	1	Red Sox	1	0	Twins	3	2
White Sox	3	2	White Sox	1	0	Red Sox	3	0
Senators	3	1	Browns	1	0	Blue Jays	2	2
Indians	1	1				Tigers	2	2
						Royals	2	1
						Brewers	1	0
Total	33	19	Total	29	18	Total	29	16

* No World Series in 1904

National League

1903-35			1936-64			1965-94		
Team	Pen	Series	Team	Pen	Series	Team	Pen	Series
Giants	11	4	Dodgers	9	3	Dodgers	7	3
Cubs	8	2	Cards	5	4	Reds	5	3
Cards	5	3	Giants	5	1	Cards	5	2
Pirates	4	2	Reds	3	1	Mets	3	2
Dodgers	2	0	Braves	3	1	Phillies	3	1
Reds	1	1	Cubs	2	0	Pirates	2	2
Braves	1	1	Pirates	1	1	Braves	2	0
Phillies	1	0	Phillies	1	0	Giants	1	0
						Padres	1	0
Total	33	13	Total	29	11	Total	29	13

Peak Yankees World Series Domination 1927-53

American League			National League		
Team	Pen	Series	Team	Pen	Series
Yankees	16	15	Cards	8	5
Tigers	4	2	Dodgers	5	0
A's	3	2	Cubs	5	0
Indians	1	1	Giants	4	1
Red Sox	1	0	Reds	2	1
Twins	1	0	Braves	1	0
Orioles	1	0	Phillies	1	0
			Pirates	1	0
Total AL	27	20	Total NL	27	7

Table 1 puts the best Yankees teams in perspective. The Yankees did not win a pennant until 1921, and during the thirty-three seasons from 1903-35 they

Russell O. Wright *is the author of* The Best of Teams, the Worst of Teams, *and* The Evolution of Baseball, *both published by McFarland.*

were only one of five top teams. The Giants, Cubs, and A's won more pennants and the A's and Red Sox had five World Series wins while the Giants and Yankees had four. The American League won nineteen World Series titles or 59 percent (with no World Series in 1904 there was a total of only thirty-two played from 1903-35).

During the twenty-nine seasons from 1936-64, the Yankees dominated baseball. They won twenty-two of twenty-nine pennants (76 percent), and they won their World Series sixteen times (73 percent). No other American League team won more than two pennants in this period, and two (the A's and the Senators/Twins) didn't win any. Every National League team won at least one pennant, the Dodgers winning nine or 31 percent of the available pennants, almost twice as many as the second-place Cards and Giants. But the Dodgers won the World Series only three times while the Cards won in four of their five World Series chances. The National League overall only won 38 percent of the World Series titles due to the domination of the Yankees.

In the thirty seasons from 1965-94, the Yankees were just another good team. They won four pennants and the World Series twice, but the Dodgers, Orioles, A's, Reds, and Cards won more pennants (the Dodgers leading with seven). The A's led with four World Series wins while the Dodgers, Orioles, and Reds had three each and six teams tied the Yankees at two. The American League lead over the National League in World Series wins was 57 percent to 46 percent (due to the strike there were no pennants and no World Series in 1994).

The most successful Yankee teams played between 1936 and 1964, when Babe Ruth was gone and Lou Gehrig was near the end of his career (Table 2). Over a shorter time frame, the Yankees won fourteen of the sixteen available pennants from 1949-64 (88 percent), their peak period for winning pennants. The peak for the Yankees in the World Series was from 1927-53, when they won fifteen of the sixteen World Series they played in (94 percent). Their only loss during that time was to the Cards in 1942. From 1927-53, the Cards won five of the eight World Series they played in, but the rest of the National League won only two of nineteen (11 percent), most of those losses coming at the hands of the Yankees.

Table 2. Best Yankees teams overview

Pennants:1921, 22, 23, 26, 27, 28, 1932, 36, 37, 38, 39, 1941, 42, 43, 47, 49, 1950, 51, 52, 53, 55, 56, 57, 58, 1960, 61, 62, 63, 64, 1976, 77, 78, 1981

Won Series: 23, 27, 28, 1932, 36, 37, 38, 39, 1941, 43, 47, 49, 1950, 51, 52, 53, 56, 58, 61, 62, 77, 78

Period	1920-34	1935-49	1950-64
Years	15	15	15
Div. Titles	-	-	-
Pennants	7	9	13
Won Series	4	8	8
Avg. Finish	2.0	1.8	1.2
Games Behind	2.4	-5.0	-3.9
Winning %	.611	.621	.624
Key Players	**Ruth**	**DiMaggio**	**Mantle**
(Hall of	**Gehrig**	**Dickey**	**Berra**
Fame in	**Combs**	Henrich	Bauer
Bold)	B.Meusel	Keller	Howard
	Lazzeri	Gordon	McDougald
	Hoyt	**Ruffing**	**Ford**
	Pennock	Gomez	Turley
	Shawkey	Chandler	Reynolds
	Pipgras	Murphy	Lopat

Period	1921-28	1936-43	1949-56	1957-64	1974-81
Years	8	8	8	8	8
Div. Titles	-	-	-	-	5 (1980)
Pennants	6	7	7	7	4
Won Series	3	6	6	3	2
Avg. Finish	1.9	1.3	1.1	1.3	2.0
Games Behind	-1.9	-12.1	-2.9	-4.4	1.6
Winning %	.611	.652	.637	.612	.581
Key Players	**Ruth**	**DiMaggio**	**Mantle**	**Mantle**	**Jackson**
(Hall of	**Gehrig**	**Gehrig**	**Berra**	**Berra**	Nettles
Fame in	**Combs**	**Dickey**	**Rizzuto**	Maris	Munson
Bold)	B.Meusel	Gordon	Bauer	Howard	Chambliss
	Pipp	Keller	McDougald	Skowron	Piniella
	Hoyt	**Ruffing**	**Ford**	Rich'son	**Hunter**
	Pennock	Gomez	Reynolds	**Ford**	Guidry
	Shawkey	Chandler	Lopat	Terry	Gossage
	Bush	Murphy	Raschi	Turley	Lyle

Table 2 shows the pennants and World Series won by the Yankees and the years in which they were won; the best fifteen-year and eight-year periods; the key statistics for those periods, and the key players for those periods.

The key statistics show division titles (1969 and after), pennants, and World Series won in the period; the average finish in the standings; the average number of games behind (a negative number means games ahead); and the average winning percentage (all averages are for the years in the period). Key players in the period who were later elected to the Hall of Fame are shown in bold type.

The forty-five seasons from 1920-64 for the Yankees are divided evenly into fifteen-year periods. The period from 1950-64 was the most successful with thirteen pennants and eight World Series wins. The average finish from 1950-64 was the best at 1.2 and the winning percentage was the best at .624. The 1935-49 teams, however, had the best games-behind average, finishing 5.0 games ahead on average. Thus the most successful Yankee teams over fifteen-year periods were those headed by Mickey Mantle, Yogi Berra, and Whitey Ford.

Eight-year periods show that the 1936-43 and 1949-56 teams were equally successful in pennants and World Series won. The 1949-56 teams had the best average finish at 1.1 (finishing first seven of the eight years), but the 1936-43 teams had the best winning percentage at .652 and a huge lead in average games behind of -12.1, meaning that on average they finished 12.1 games ahead each season. Thus, over eight-year periods the teams of DiMaggio, Gehrig, Dickey, Ruffing, and Gomez probably edge out the Mantle, Berra, and Ford combination.

As shown in my book *The Evolution of Baseball*, the 1927 and 1939 Yankees were the most dominant franchise teams for a single season. The 1936-37-38 Yankees were not far behind the 1939 team, and that explains the domination of the 1936-43 Yankees that resulted in the amazing average-games-behind figure of -12.1. These were Yankee teams that overwhelmed the opposition.

Of the five teams listed for eight-year periods, the famous Yankees of Ruth, Gehrig, Combs, Hoyt, and Pennock rank only fourth. The 1974-81 teams rank a distant fifth [the "(1980)" on the table means the 1974-81 teams won a division title in 1980 but no pennant].

Among teams that don't make the list, the 1983-87 Yankees averaged .561, but never won the division. The 1994 Yankees won the division with a .619 average at the time of the strike, but they had no opportunity to win a pennant or Series title and were only in the second year of a comeback. Thus, even though these two sets of teams might make another franchise list, they can't make the best teams list for the Yankees.

Table 3. Best Yankees teams

Pennant: 1921, 22, 23, 26, 27, 28, 1932, 36, 37, 38, 39, 1941, 42, 43, 47

Series: 1923, 27, 28, 1932, 36, 37, 38, 39, 1941, 43, 47

Period	1920-24	1926-30	1935-39	1940-44
Years	5	5	5	5
Div. Titles	-	-	-	-
Pennants	3	3	4	3
Won Series	1	2	4	2
Avg. Finish	1.6	1.6	1.2	1.8
Games Behind	-3.3	1.9	-11.2	-6.3
Winning %	.620	.618	.656	.614
Key Players	**Ruth**	**Ruth**	**DiMaggio**	**DiMaggio**
(Hall of	Pipp	**Gehrig**	**Gehrig**	**Dickey**
Fame in	B.Meusel	**Combs**	**Dickey**	Gordon
Bold)	Schang	B.Meusel	Rolfe	Keller
	Ward	Lazzeri	Crosetti	Henrich
	Hoyt	**Hoyt**	**Ruffing**	**Ruffing**
	Shawkey	**Pennock**	Gomez	Bonham
	Mays	Pipgras	Pearson	Chandler
	Bush	Moore	Murphy	Murphy

Pennant: 1949, 1950, 51, 52, 53, 55, 56, 57, 58, 1960, 61, 62, 63, 64, 1976, 77, 78, 1981

Series: 1949, 1950, 51, 52, 53, 56, 58, 61, 62, 77, 78

Period	1949-53	1954-58	1960-64	1976-80
Years	5	5	5	5
Div. Titles	-	-	-	4 (1980)
Pennants	5	4	5	3
Won Series	5	2	2	2
Avg. Finish	1.0	1.2	1.0	1.6
Games Behind	-3.9	-4.4	-6.5	-0.7
Winning %	.635	.631	.630	.607
Key Players	**DiMaggio**	**Mantle**	**Mantle**	Jackson
(Hall of	**Berra**	**Berra**	Maris	Nettles
Fame in	**Mantle**	Skowron	Skowron	Munson
Bold)	**Rizzuto**	McDougald	Howard	Chambliss
	Bauer	Bauer	Boyer	Randolph
	Woodling	**Ford**	Rich'son	Guidry
	Raschi	Turley	Kubek	Figueroa
	Reynolds	Grim	**Ford**	Gossage
	Lopat	Larsen	Terry	Lyle

Table 3 shows the best Yankees teams by five-year periods. The other data shown is as explained in Table 2. Five-year periods are the best for determining most successful "teams" because over the shorter period it is more nearly true that there was only one basic team.

The peak five-year winning percentage period for the Yankees was 1935-39, but the most successful teams in terms of pennants and World Series wins came in 1949-53, which was the next best five-year winning percentage period.

The 1949-53 Yankees won five straight pennants (for a perfect average finish of 1.0), and five straight World Series titles. It's the major league record for success. The 1960-64 Yankees won five straight pennants, but won the World Series only twice. The 1935-39 team won four straight pennants and World Series titles from 1936-39, and had the best games-behind record of all the teams to go with its best winning percentage record.

When the Yankee teams are grouped together in five-year periods such as they are here, the 1927 Yankees—arguably the best team of all time in terms of dominating its opposition—fall into a very ordinary five-year period. The 1926-30 Yankees have a relatively unimpressive record because they were far behind the Philadelphia A's in 1929-30. The 1926-30 Yankees rank only sixth in winning percentage among the eight teams shown here. What's more, their games-behind record is the worst of all the Yankee teams shown. The 1926-30 Yankees are the only group to fail to record a negative games-behind mark,

i.e, they failed to lead all other teams on an average basis over the five-year period chosen. The 1926-30 Yankees do tie the 1935-39 Yankees for most Hall of Fame players—five—on the list of key players for the period. But they are far behind the 1935-39 Yankees in all other respects. Since the 1920-24 Yankees rank only fourth in winning percentage, sixth in games behind, and last in World Series wins, the conclusion is inescapable that the two sets of teams associated with Babe Ruth were probably the least successful Yankee teams of all in terms of results over five-year periods. Only the 1976-80 teams are comparable.

The Yankees of 1976-80 reflect the more competitive nature of their time with the lowest winning percentage of all the teams listed. But they still were dominant in their period with four division titles (including the 1980 title shown in parenthesis that did not result in a pennant) and three pennants won.

The most successful Yankee teams on a five-year basis were clearly the DiMaggio, Berra, Mantle, Raschi, and Reynolds Yankees of 1949-53 followed by the DiMaggio, Gehrig, Dickey, Ruffing, and Gomez Yankees of 1935-39. This essentially confirms the longer term results of Table 2, and makes Joe DiMaggio the only Yankee star to play on the franchise's two most successful teams.

GAME 4 Saturday, October 1, 1955
New York   110 102 000 - 5 9 0
Brooklyn   001 330 10x - 8 14 0

NEW YORK (2-1)

8 Noren	k	7	s	8	3\
5 McDougald	H	63	k	8	9
9 Mantle	k	k	s	13	13
2 Berra	8	sx	wx	7	
3 Collins	W	Ws	f46	43	
7 Howard	13b	f15	S	53	
4 Martin	43+	s'+x	D'	8	
6 Rizzuto	s's	543p	3^f	w	
1 Larson	8	63			
1 Kucks 5					
o ERobinson 6 s'					
r RColeman 6					
1 Morgan 7					
o Skowron 8	8				
1 Sturdivant 8					

BROOKLYN (1-2)

4 Gilliam	63	d'	Ws	43	s
6 Reese	3^	9	S+	s+x	23b
8 Snider	3-	43	H"	f36	i
2 Campanella	8	H	d	S	8
9 Furillo	k	S	k	s+	4^
3 Hodges	s	H'	13+	s"	
5 JRobinson	9	53	5\	8	
7 Amoros	W	13	s	43	
1 Erskine	6^f				
1 Bessent 4	k				
1 Labine 5	k	63			

Pitchers: NEW YORK, Larsen L (991xx), Kucks (xx6xx), RColeman (xx26x), Morgan (xxx3x), Sturdivant (xxxx5). BROOKLYN, Erskine (95xxx), Bessent (x44xx), Labine W (xx593).
Left on Base- NY 7, Bkl 9. T- 2:57.A- 36,242.
Ump-Dascoli, Summers, Ballanfant, Honochick, Donatelli, Flaherty.

1969: Carew Steals Home

Seven thefts tied what was then thought to be the record

Ron Marshall

Hall of Famer Rod Carew captured seven batting titles during his illustrious career, his first coming in 1969. In only his third season in the major leagues the 23-year-old native of Panama fashioned a robust .332 average to easily outdistance his nearest competitors. The 1969 season was a banner year for Carew and the Minnesota Twins. Paced by the play of Carew and teammates Harmon Killebrew, Tony Oliva, Cesar Tovar, and Jim Perry, the Twins won the American League Western Division title in the first year of divisional play.

In addition to his contributions to the Twins offensive attack, Carew thrilled the baseball world that spring with an assault on the major league record for steals of home in a season. Well before the midway point of the season Carew had stolen home six times, placing him only one behind the then recognized major league record of seven set by Pete Reiser in 1946. (In 1991 the SABR ad hoc committee on Steals of Home established the now accepted record of eight steals of home by Ty Cobb in 1912.) After adding another steal of home a month later, Carew's attempt to break Reiser's mark was thwarted with two unsuccessful attempts in September.

Carew's propensity for pilfering the plate was developed not by chance but rather by design. The Twins manager was the fiery Billy Martin, who had ascended to his first managerial post after a brief tenure on the Twins coaching staff. Minnesota's rookie pilot was determined that his team would be more aggressive on the bases.

As part of his new philosophy Martin took Carew aside during spring training and began instructing him in the fine art of stealing home. "That spring Billy worked with me for hours on stealing home," recalled Rod in his autobiography *Carew*. "He suggested I take a slow walking lead in which you come to a stop…that walking lead was essential: you'd have momentum already started toward home. We had it timed to the split second. If a pitcher wound up instead of pitching from a stretch…we determined that I ought to make it home safely."

Number One—Rod successfully swiped home twice in two tries during spring training and did not wait for long to unveil his newly perfected skill. On April 9 in Kansas City, Carew led off the fifth inning with a double off Royals starter Roger Nelson. Two outs later Carew was stationed at third with Graig Nettles at bat. Nelson, nicknamed "Spider" because of his long arms, went into a full windup on his first offering to Nettles. Carew flashed a sign to Nettles to indicate his intention to steal and took off after Nelson started his next delivery. A startled Nelson threw high to the plate and Carew slid in with his first career steal of home.

Number Two—Ten days later in Minneapolis, Carew again occupied third with two out with the Twins

Ron Marshall is a sports historian and a SABR member since 1985. He is assistant audio-visual archivist at the Sports Museum of New England. He thanks Ted Hathaway and Dave Smith for their help with this article.

trailing the California Angels, 5-4. As the ageless knuckleballer Hoyt Wilhelm pitched to Harmon Killebrew, Carew noted the inordinate amount of time Wilhelm's knuckler took to arrive at home plate. Rod signaled his intention to Killebrew and took off on Wilhelm's next offering. Apparently the Killer missed the sign because he prepared to swing at the pitch. At the last second Harmon aborted his swing, thus avoiding imminent disaster. Carew cruised in easily with the game-tying run and his second steal of home.

Number Three—Carew made amends to Harmon on his next dash home two weeks later against the Seattle Pilots. The Twins had pushed across three runs in the fifth inning to increase their lead to 4-0, and had the bases loaded with two outs and lefty swinger Rich Reese at bat. With the third baseman playing well away from the bag and Pilot hurler Darrell Brandon not heeding Carew's presence, all three runners broke simultaneously. Rod's hook slide neatly avoided the tag of Seattle catcher Larry Haney, and the Twins had pulled off a rare triple steal. It would be the first of three the Twins would successfully execute in 1969. The play gave Killebrew his first stolen base in two years. It also marked the second time Carew had stolen home with a lefthand batter in the box, flying in the face of standard baseball logic. "I've always maintained that you can steal home with a lefthand hitter at the plate," crowed an ecstatic Billy Martin.

Number Four—The Twins' penchant for grand larceny reached a peak on May 18 in a game against the Detroit Tigers. Southpaw Mickey Lolich had been staked to a 2-0 lead in the bottom of the third inning. Then Cesar Tovar and Carew executed a double steal to put runners on second and third. Tovar stole home

Rod Carew eyes his next move.

Transcendental Graphics

on Lolich's next delivery while, incredibly, Carew remained stationed at second. Two pitches later Carew swiped third and, in an audacious display of daring, stole home on the next pitch.

The Twins duo's romp around the bases set or tied several records, not the least of which was two steals of home in the same inning. Rod became one of the few men in baseball history to steal his way around the bases in an inning. The feat had not been accomplished in over twenty-eight years.

Number Five—The Twins pulled off their second successful triple steal of the season on June 4 against New York. Taking advantage of the Yankees' rookie catcher John Ellis, Carew stole home on Yankee reliever Lindy McDaniel's first pitch to Twins shortstop Leo Cardenas in the bottom of the eighth inning. "We were anticipating he would run," recalled Yankee Manager Ralph Houk. "Ellis just didn't come out quite far enough with the ball to get him."

Number Six—Carew netted his next steal of home on June 16 against the California Angels. He and teammate Tony Oliva successfully executed double steals on consecutive pitches from a beleaguered Tom Murphy in the first inning. It marked the only time Carew attempted to steal home when there were no outs.

Number Seven—With the entire league now alerted to his antics it became increasingly difficult for Rod to find a good opportunity to steal home. Finally, a month later a lapse in concentration by Chicago's rookie lefthander Jerry Nyman gave Carew the chance he needed. Nyman walked Twins outfielder Charlie Manuel with the bases loaded in the bottom of the third inning to force home a run and give the

Twins a 5-2 lead.

Nyman focused his attention on the next batter, Twins catcher John Roseboro, and forgot about the current occupant of third base. He went into a full windup. "I made up my mind that I would go on the first pitch if he wound up," recalled Carew. "I was really surprised to see him wind up."

Despite a good jump the ensuing play at the plate would have been extremely close had White Sox catcher Don Pavletich held the ball. "I really think he might have had me," mused Carew. "We had him all the way, too," sighed Pavletich. "But I took my eye off the ball when I saw him coming."

Final attempts—Now tied with Reiser for what was then thought to be the all-time record, Carew spent the next 2-1/2 months trying for the tie-breaker. On September 10 in Chicago a then youthful Tommy John cut down Carew in his bid to tie Reiser. This time Pavletich held the ball, and after nine consecutive successful steals of home (counting the two in spring training) Carew was finally caught.

With the 1969 season winding to a close and opportunities to break Reiser's mark dwindling, Rod's final attempt ended in disappointment and controversy. On September 26 in Seattle's Sick's Stadium before approximately 6,500 fans Carew found himself on third base with two outs and Minnesota ahead 3-1. Getting a good jump on Pilot righthander Skip Lockwood, Carew broke for the plate.

Mike Lamey, then with the Minneapolis *Star*, describes what transpired: "His hook slide knocked home plate umpire Jim Honochick off his feet. When Honochick regained his feet he called Carew out for not touching the plate, although Rod's slide mark showed he tipped the corner."

In absolute disgust, Carew slammed his helmet to the ground, which prompted an ejection from Honochick. Apparently Carew's reaction was well warranted. The next day Seattle catcher Jerry McNertney confided to Carew that he had been amazed at the call. McNertney admitted that even though he couldn't confirm Carew had touched the plate, he was sure he had never tagged Carew as he slid past him. "I think the umpire's (Honochick's) vision was blocked, so he automatically gave me the thumb," sighed Carew.

If not for this probably blown call Carew would now be tied with Cobb instead of receiving no recognition in the record books. This seems particularly unfair since it has been documented that at least six of Cobb's eight steals of home in 1912 were on the back end of double steal attempts (with the ball thrown through to second). In contrast, none of Carew's steals of home were achieved in this fashion, but were "straight" steals of home, in which he went with the pitch and the ball was never thrown down.

Carew would go on to steal home ten more times in his career to finish with seventeen career steals of home. Along the way Rod managed to collect 3,053 hits in compiling a .328 lifetime batting average. Carew's remarkable achievements were properly acknowledged with his election to the Hall of Fame in 1991. Yet if it were not for one errant umpire's call one more record might have been added to an already record-setting career.

Rod Carew's Attempted Steals of Home: 1969

Date	Opponent	Pitcher	Catcher	Inning	Outs	Score	Runners	Umpire	Batter	Result
4/9	at Kansas City	Nelson	Campanis	5	2	2-2	3rd	Stewart	Nettles*	Safe
4/19	California	Wilhelm	Egan	7	2	4-5	3rd	Denkinger	Killebrew	Safe
4/30	Seattle	Brandon	Haney	5	2	4-0	1st,2nd,3rd	Honochick	Reese*	Safe
5/18	Detroit	Lolich	Freehan	3	2	1-2	3rd	Barnett	Cardenas	Safe
6/4	New York	McDaniel	Ellis	8	2	3-2	1st,2nd,3rd	Goetz	Cardenas	Safe
6/16	California	Murphy	Azcue	1	0	1-0	2nd,3rd	Rice	Killebrew	Safe
7/16	Chicago	Nyman	Pavletich	2	2	5-2	1st,2nd,3rd	Stewart	Roseboro*	Safe
9/10	at Chicago	John	Pavletich	3	2	0-1	1st,2nd,3rd	Goetz	Cardenas	Out
9/26	at Seattle	Lockwood	McNertney	3	2	3-1	2nd,3rd	Honochick	Tovar	Out

*Indicates lefthanded batter

Note: Twins score given first

Pinch-Hitting Pitchers

A survey of a once-special breed of player

Gene Noll

The role of today's pitcher in professional baseball is almost exclusively defensive. The pitchers—especially in the American League—are a compartmentalized group of people, totally insulated from the offense. They are further separated into such specialized roles as "starters," "swingmen," "closers," "setup men," and "middle relievers," to name a few. Few even last beyond a limited amount of innings when performing their roles, often falling prey to the manager's "pitch count." As a result of such selective use, the pitcher is virtually eliminated from the offensive part of the game.[1]

Time was, however, when the pitcher was used more extensively. An elite group of men used to be called upon to both pitch on scheduled days and to come off the bench and contribute to the offense as a hitter on their days off. These were versatile players who were comfortable and effective in both roles, some of whom were used ahead of nonpitching substitutes.

Early professional baseball—In the early days of baseball, substitute batters were not allowed. Substitutes were rarely used at all, except in case of injury. Rosters were small and a pitcher was expected to throw the entire nine innings, even if he was losing badly. By the 1880s the schedule had increased to 140 games in both the National League and the American Association. Consequently, one or two additional pitchers were added to club rosters.

Pitchers were expected to contribute when not used on the mound. Pitchers who could hit were often used in the field and a few even had long "second" careers playing other positions when they lost their effectiveness as hurlers. Two examples are John Montgomery Ward and William "Kid" Gleason. Ward started out as a pitcher, but was hurt and became ineffective. He then went on to a productive career as a shortstop. Gleason, who started as a pitcher with the Philadelphia Phillies in the late 1880s, became ineffective when the distance from the mound to the plate was increased to sixty feet, six inches in 1894. He later became a solid second baseman, compiling a .261 lifetime average over thirteen seasons. Both men also became effective managers, showing a resourcefulness rarely seen in baseball.

A quick survey of Hall of Fame pitchers during this time reveals an era of the "iron men." Hoss Radbourn played 128 games as an infielder-outfielder, John Clarkson played thirty-three games outside the pitcher's box, Kid Nichols played twenty-six games in the infield and outfield, and Amos Rusie, one of the first pinch hitters, played twenty-two games away from the mound.

The Pioneers—Substitutions were first legalized for the 1889 season, when each team was allowed to designate one player who could replace a starter at the

---

Gene Noll is an analyst with the federal government who lives in Arlington, Virginia when he's not on the road playing fastpitch softball.

beginning of an inning. Since the managers almost always selected a pitcher as the sub, many of the 1889 pinch hitters were pitchers, who then went in to pitch. One year later, two subs could be designated and inserted into the lineup at any time. In 1891, teams were allowed an unlimited number of substitutions. Pinch hitters were not used frequently by club managers at first, however, and would take another twenty years to be implemented more extensively. One reason for the infrequent use of pinch hitters was that most clubs carried only three pitchers and one or two substitute position players during the 1890s.

A few players did substitute hit, and many were pitchers. The first player to substitute hit was rookie Bobby Lowe, who did it with the Boston National Leaguers on May 1, 1891. Lowe made his first appearance in a major league uniform an inauspicious one by popping out to short in the eighth inning against Monte Ward's Brooklyn Bridegrooms. Lowe then went in to pitch in the ninth and gave up two runs in a game where the outcome had long been out of doubt, the Bridegrooms winning 13 to 6. Lowe, who enjoyed a long major league career, and who was also the first to hit four home runs in a game, never pitched again.[2]

Seven pinch-hit at bats were recorded in each league in 1891, but not one appearance resulted in a hit.[3] That would not occur until June 7, 1892, when catcher John Joseph Doyle of the Cleveland Spiders singled and moved the runner from first to third.[4] It would be another year before a pitcher would have a successful pinch hit. Kid Gleason got it on July 28, 1893. Gleason, then with the St. Louis Browns, singled for pitcher Albert Clarkson in the eighth inning with the bases empty. He did not advance. St. Louis later came from behind in the ninth to win 5-4 against the Cleveland Spiders.[5]

The first successful pinch-hit home run by a pitcher was by Jack Stivetts in 1894. A lifetime .297 hitter, Stivetts was used frequently away from the mound. Playing for Boston in 1894, he came off the bench on June 28 to hit for Kid Nichols in the ninth inning against St. Louis and delivered a three-run homer with two out, tying the game. He stayed in to pitch the tenth, and Boston scored two runs, holding off St. Louis 12-10, Stivetts obtaining the win.[6]

Despite the limited use of pinch hitters, a few pioneers did emerge during this period. Besides Stivetts were Al Orth, Frank Kitson, George "Win" Mercer, Jim "Nixey" Callahan, and Mike O'Neill. Orth, an effective hurler who compiled a 204-189 record, was also one of the more prolific pinch hitters of his era.

He was able to accumulate seventy-eight pinch at bats and seventeen pinch hits during his fifteen-year career. Like a lot of hurlers during this period, he also played seventy-three games as an infielder-outfielder. Kitson, who pitched right but hit left, and who won twenty-two games with Baltimore in 1899, also once led the senior circuit with three pinch hits in 1902. Mercer, who played almost as many games in the field as he did on the mound, was one of the first league leaders in pinch hits with two in 1895. O'Neill, who played for five seasons at the beginning of the century, is best remembered as the first pitcher to hit a grand slam pinch-hit home run, in 1902 while playing for the St. Louis Cardinals. Callahan, who played fourteen seasons in the major leagues, also accumulated forty-eight pinch at bats and a .250 lifetime pinch-hit average.

The Heyday—The nineteen-teens saw an evolutionary change in the use of players. Major league rosters had increased to seventeen or eighteen players in the early 1900s and to twenty-one or twenty-two players by the mid "teens." American League rosters, however, had twenty-five-player limits by the late teens. Managers could use more players. Pitchers were still used off the bench as pinch hitters. George Mullin, a former ace pitcher with Detroit during the era of Ty Cobb, was the first pitcher to pinch hit in a World Series. In the 1909 Series against Pittsburgh, he flew out in the ninth inning of Game Five. A lifetime 228-196 pitcher, Mullin was also 20-101 lifetime as a pinch hitter.

Between 1911 and 1926, pitchers were used as pinch hitters in World Series nine times. One of the best of the era was Jack Bentley, who played mostly for John McGraw's Giants during the 1920s. He was once tabbed as "the next Babe Ruth" because he hit .351 in 1922 and compiled a 41-6 pitching record while playing for the minor league Baltimore Orioles in the early 1920s. Though his career was hardly Ruthian, Bentley is among the top pinch-hitting pitchers lifetime, compiling a .301 average. He also went 2-4 lifetime pinch hitting in World Series competition. Clarence Mitchell, a lefthander, was the first pitcher to get a pinch hit in World Series competition, singling for Brooklyn in the 1920 Series against Cleveland. He accumulated thirty-one pinch hits lifetime.

Walter "Dutch" Ruether, who pitched between 1917 and 1927, is the only pitcher to pinch hit for three different teams in World Series competition.[7] His thirty-four pinch hits and 145 at bats lifetime rank him fifth all-time among pitchers in both categories.

George Uhle, who won 200 games lifetime between 1919 and 1936 was also a top pinch hitter. A lifetime .288 hitter, Uhle also was an effective player off the bench going 44-169 lifetime, ranking third among pitchers in both categories. Another pitcher of note during this era was Ray Caldwell. A versatile player, Caldwell was used in the outfield for forty-six games and at first base for six during his major league career. He also led his league in pinch-hit at bats with thirty-three in 1915. His 36-154 record ranks him fourth behind Uhle. Another pitcher of note during this period was Fred Heimach. His major league career lasted from 1920 to 1933, mostly with the Philadelphia Athletics. He compiled a remarkable .384 pinch-hit mark during his career, collecting twenty hits in fifty-two appearances.

The 1920s and 1930s were the heyday of pinch hitting pitchers. The best was Red Lucas. His 114 hits and 437 at bats lifetime rank him first by far among pitchers. These marks were also the best among pinch hitters until Smoky Burgess, one of the first pinch-hitting specialists, broke the mark. He still ranks sixth overall lifetime in both categories. In addition, he also led his league four times in pinch hits, the most of any pitcher.

Lucas was not without competition, however. Wes Ferrell, who played mostly for the Red Sox and Cleveland during his career, also compiled a .601 winning percentage. He hit nine home runs during the 1931 season, a record for pitchers. His thirty-eight home runs lifetime also rank him first among pitchers. It is little wonder that he was used 139 times as a pinch hitter during his career, collecting thirty-one hits.

Red Lucas, pinch-hitting pitcher extraordinaire.

Transcendental Graphics

Hall of Famer Red Ruffing and Lynwood "Schoolboy" Rowe also deserve special mention. Ruffing, whose career with the Red Sox and Yankees spanned from the mid-1920s to the postwar years, is the pitcher closest to Red Lucas. As a member of some of the Yankees' best teams, Ruffing was also used as a pinch hitter in three World Series, going 0-3 lifetime. His fifty-eight hits and 228 at bats rank him second all-time among pitchers.

Schoolboy Rowe, mainly known for his pitching prowess with Detroit in the mid-1930s, also was an effective pinch hitter, especially toward the end of his career, when he finished up with the Phillies. He collected fifteen hits in 1943, tying him with Lucas for the most hits in a season by a pitcher. Lynn Nelson, a mediocre pitcher at best who played seven seasons between 1930 and 1940, is most noted for having three pinch-hit homers during his major league career, ranking him second among pitchers.

Decline and fall—The postwar years saw a marked decline in the use of pinch-hitting pitchers. An evolutionary change in rosters coincided with this change. All major league clubs by the late 1930s were allowed to keep twenty-five players on a roster. As a result, more clubs carried more pitchers as relief specialists and more importantly, more reserve fielders. Many of these reserve players were used as pinch-hitting specialists by resourceful managers thus further removing decent hitting pitchers from the offense.

A few pitchers did emerge, however, most notably Bob Lemon, Mickey McDermott and Don Newcombe. McDermott, a versatile player who also played a few games in the outfield for the Kansas City Athletics, was 25-127 lifetime, ranking him ninth and tenth on the lists on the next page. Newcombe, who is the only man to win the Rookie of the Year, MVP, and Cy Young awards, was also able to accumulate eighty-seven pinch-hit appearances during his career. He also played first base in Japan after his major league career ended. Hall of Famer Lemon started his career as a weak-hitting third baseman who threw hard and converted to pitching. Ironically, his pinch-hitting average was higher than his overall average. He compiled thirty-one hits in 109 pinch at bats during his career. The 1960s was the last era of effective pinch-hitting pitchers. The most notable was Gary Peters. In fact, he was the last pitcher used extensively as a pinch hitter. His sixteen for 66 lifetime mark does not qualify him for the all-time list, but his four lifetime pinch-hit homers are the most of any pitcher. Ironically, Peters' last year was in 1972, on the eve of the AL's designated-hitter rule.

The elimination of the pitcher from the offense could make these pitchers' pinch hitting records unbreakable. Unless Organized Baseball imposes a fundamental rule change, these records could well be the ones that remain through the generations.

Endnotes:

1. Ironically, the last pitcher to be used as a pinch hitter in World Series competition was Minnesota Twins reliever Rick Aguilera, who was used in the 12th inning of Game Three against Atlanta. Manager Tom Kelly had exhausted his bench and was forced to use Aguilera to hit for pitcher Bob Guthrie, who did not have a single major league at bat. Aguilera flew out but stayed in to pitch and lost the game in the bottom of the 12th. It was his only plate appearance of the Series.

2. Boston *Globe* V-39, #122, p. 12. Also Philadelphia *Record*, May 2, 1891. Lowe pinch hit for Hall of Fame pitcher, John Clarkson.

3. A total of seven players made pinch-hit appearances for both major leagues in 1891. In the National League they were: Bob Caruthers of Brooklyn, Amos Rusie of New York, and Frank "Piggie" Ward of Pittsburgh. In the American Association they were: Ben Sanders of Philadelphia, Jack Stivetts of St. Louis, and Calvin Griffith, who played for St. Louis and Boston. Stivetts led all in number of appearances with two.

4. Cleveland *Plain Dealer*, V-50, #160 June 8, 1892, p. 5. Also New York *Times* June 8 1892, V-41, #12726, p. 6.

5. Cleveland *Plain Dealer*, V-51, #210, July 29, 1893, p. 5.

6. Boston *Globe*, V-45, #180, June 29, 1894, p. 2. Also, Davids, L. Robert, *Great Hitting Pitchers*, (SABR Press, 1979), p. 46.

7. Ruether pinch hit for Cincinnati in 1919, Washington in 1925, and the Yankees twice in 1926. He had no hits in four World Series pinch-hit appearances.

Lifetime leaders

	Name	AB			Name	Hits
1.	Red Lucas	437		1.	Red Lucas	114
2.	Red Ruffing	228		2.	Red Ruffing	58
3.	George Uhle	169		3.	George Uhle	44
4.	Ray Caldwell	154		4.	Ray Caldwell	36
5.	Dutch Reuther	145		5.	Dutch Ruether	34
6.	Wes Ferrell	139		6.	Wes Ferrell	31
7.	Clarence Mitchell	134		6.	Bob Lemon	31
7.	Chubby Dean	134		6.	Clarence Mitchell	31
9.	Mickey McDermott	127		9.	Chubby Dean	30
10.	Walter Johnson	110		10.	Jack Bentley	25
				10.	Mickey McDermott	25

Season leaders

	Name	AB	Year	Team
1.	Red Lucas	*60	1931	Cincinnati
2.	Schoolboy Rowe	*49	1943	Phillies
3.	Red Lucas	42	1929	Cincinnati
3.	Lucas	42	1932	Cincinnati
5.	Lucas	41	1933	Cincinnati
6.	Lucas	*39	1930	Cincinnati
7.	Lynn Nelson	*38	1937	Athletics
7.	Mickey McDermott	38	1955	Washington
9.	Lucas	*37	1937	Pittsburgh
10.	Lucas	34	1934	Pittsburgh
11.	Early Wynn	32	1948	Washington
11.	Jean Dubuc	32	1914	Detroit

	Name	Hits	Year	Team
1.	Red Lucas	*15	1931	Cincinnati
1.	Schoolboy Rowe	*15	1943	Phillies
3.	Lucas	*14	1930	Cincinnati
4.	Lucas	*13	1929	Cincinnati
4.	Lucas	13	1933	Cincinnati
5.	George Uhle	*11	1924	Cleveland
5.	Ralph Winegarner	11	1935	Cleveland
7.	Erv Brame	10	1929	Pittsburgh
7.	Lucas	10	1932	Cincinnati
7.	Jack Bentley	*10	1923	Giants
10.	Bentley	*9	1925	Giants
10.	Benn Karr	9	1920	Red Sox
10.	Wes Ferrell	9	1935	Red Sox
10.	Ray Caldwell	9	2915	New York Yankees
10.	Lucas	*9	1936	Pittsburgh
10.	Lynn Nelson	*9	1937	Athletics

*Led league

Czech Baseball

Emerging from the cold

Ted Kapnick

More than five years after 1989's Velvet Revolution peacefully overthrew the Communist government in Czechoslovakia, a sport usually associated with the West continues to grow and develop in a land dominated by hockey rinks and soccer fields. Baseball in the Czech Republic (the former Czechoslovakia split into two republics, Czech and Slovak, on January 1, 1993), while increasing in popularity before the '89 revolution, now stands ready to explode as a major sport in the former Communist land.

Since 1990, the number of players in the Czech Republic has grown from 2,000 to 5,000, an astonishing 150 percent increase. And the future of the game is indeed bright, as eighty percent of these 5,000 participants are under eighteen years old.

"The kids are eager to play, and we trust the popularity of the game will continue to grow in the schools and throughout the country," says Jan Bagin, until recently executive director of the Czech Baseball Association, an organization that runs all baseball-related activities in the Republic, including overseeing 45 clubs covering all age groups, from ten year olds to seniors. A member of SABR for the past eleven years, Bagin feels baseball's popularity has soared since it became an Olympic medal sport in 1992 at the Barcelona summer games.

"Having baseball in the Olympics is the most important factor in the growth of the game here. It shows that the game isn't just an American or Japanese game, but a worldwide one as well," says Bagin, 40, who has been associated with baseball in Czechoslovakia and now in the Czech Republic since 1975 as a player, coach, and administrator.

Beginnings—Baseball's beginnings in Czechoslovakia date to 1919, when the game was introduced in the western Bohemian town of Plzen, just one year after the creation of the country out of the ashes of the First World War. (Before the war, the Czech lands and Slovakia were part of the Austro-Hungarian Empire.) An American organization, the YMCA, organized the first real exhibition game played in Czechoslovakia, in May, 1920 in Plzen.

Despite a promising start, the sport didn't catch on, and baseball wasn't played in Czechoslovakia again until 1948. The rise to power of the Communist Party that same year wiped out all things remotely Western, including baseball. For the next fifteen years the crack of the bat wasn't heard throughout the country. Then, in 1963, a baseball/softball committee was established, which led to an exhibition game being played with a Cuban team the following year. As baseball is popular in Communist Cuba, it followed that the Communist government in Czechoslovakia would again allow the sport to be played.

By 1965, Czechs established first contacts with the Confederation of European Baseball Associations (CEBA). Three years later university students in Prague began playing the game on a regular basis.

Ted Kapnick is a teacher of English living in Prague.

Forming an unofficial league, the students received badly needed equipment, instruction, and technical know-how from the American and Cuban embassies. By the early seventies, the pioneering students, mostly of Czech and not Slovak origin, had spread the game throughout the Czech part of Czechoslovakia. Thus, baseball took off in Prague and other Czech towns, and to this day, the sport is much more developed in the Czech Republic than in Slovakia. Official league play in the Czech lands began with the 1978 season, and by the mid-eighties, Czech teams could travel abroad once or twice a year to compete in tournaments.

One such event occurred in 1987, when the Czech Senior National Team made its first trip to the then Soviet Union. One year later the seniors participated for the first time in the European Championships B Pool competition. As baseball still wasn't an "official" sport in the Slovak part of the country, the team was comprised only of Czechs. In 1989, the year of the Velvet Revolution, the first Czech Junior National Team took part in the European championships.

Equipment and diamonds—Bagin remembers those years before the momentous events of '89, when it was impossible to order baseball equipment from Western countries. Most Czechs were fielding grounders with used gloves from friends abroad, or inferior Cuban products. But there was a way according to Bagin to obtain cherished Rawlings baseballs or Spalding gloves: trickery.

"We had to change our Czech money on the black market into Western currencies, then smuggle the money out in gloves or bats when we traveled to a tournament. It depended on how smart you were. The authorities never controlled sport equipment on entering the country, so you could buy whatever you wanted and bring it back," explains Bagin sitting in his office on Strahov, a sports complex situated on a hill near Prague's historic castle.

Trips were infrequent, though. American, Japanese and other Western products didn't really make their way to Prague until after the revolution. Nowadays, Western sporting goods companies compete to win the Czech Baseball Association's favor, vying to be the official supplier of the Association's baseballs, bats and other equipment. Recently, Rawlings baseballs became the official ball used by budding and seasoned Czech players. And Easton's European affiliation signed a three-year contract in 1992 to supply bats and various other equipment according to the Association's needs.

But while equipment and interest aren't a problem, finding the funds and a suitable site for a quality baseball field has always been a huge concern. Until now.

Wedged between railroad tracks and rows of leafy green trees in south central Prague, the new National Baseball Center will eventually comprise two senior and two Little League diamonds, with enough seating for 1,500 at each senior field. Slated to be finished by mid-1997, the complex's first full-sized field was completed this spring. The $880,000 facility will be built by a mixture of public and private funds, and will feature a clubhouse and, in the long run, lights.

"It'll be the best baseball complex in Central Europe when finished," says Bagin, who this summer resigned his position with the Baseball Association to take a similar position with the National Baseball Center.

One other quality field exists in Prague, but only one decent diamond exists outside the capital. Most clubs play on converted soccer fields, with some grass in the outfield and an all dirt infield, and this lack of facilities continues to plague the development of the sport in the Republic.

Competition—Having a decent place to play is an ongoing problem, but an organization does exist to help in other areas. Major League Baseball International (MLBI), affiliated with Major League Baseball, exists to increase baseball's popularity worldwide. It conducts clinics and seminars each winter. Over about three days, Major League coaches convey their knowledge and expertise to eager baseball hungry coaches, players and administrators in countries like the Czech Republic and others yearning to promote and develop the sport.

MLBI's Envoy Program is another big part of the organization's efforts to expand and develop baseball as a global sport. The International Baseball Association, and the European Amateur Baseball Confederation (CEB) are assisting MLBI with the program, which is sponsored by Mizuno, Easton and Rawlings.

"Our goal is to provide topflight instruction to developing baseball programs around the world," says Steve Baker, MLBI vice president for game development. The program completed its fourth summer in 1994, sending forty instructors to twenty-two countries, including six to the Czech Republic.

John Whitman, a coach at Antioch High School in northern California, taught Czech kids two years ago as part of the Envoy Program. He helped coach the Czech National Cadet Team at the 1993 European

Championships in Trieste, Italy, where the thirteen-to fifteen-year-olds captured the bronze medal. It was the first time a baseball team from the Czech Republic or the former Czechoslovakia had won a medal in international play. The result marked a tremendous turnaround from 1992, when the cadets finished seventh at the championships. Improving even further, the Cadets this summer registered the Republic's best result ever, with a silver medal.

Not having an Envoy coach didn't hamper the Republic's juvenile squad, as it brought home the Czech Republic's second baseball medal in 1994, taking a bronze in France at the European championships. This summer, with the championship held in Prague, they were third again. In Holland at last summer's European championships, the junior national team finished a strong fourth, duplicating its showing at the 1993 championships.

Jim Jones, in the Republic as part of the Envoy Program, managed the team in Oostrehout, Holland, as he did the previous summer in Spain. Jones, with twenty years of college coaching experience, just completed his fifth consecutive summer teaching kids in Czechoslovakia, and now the Czech Republic, about baseball skills and strategy. Two twenty-year-olds from the junior national team, pitcher-infielder Josef Srbecky and catcher-outfielder Matej Miksousky, have honed their skills under Jones' guidance to the point that the Atlanta Braves scouted the pair at several European Junior Championships.

While the juniors and other national teams are making progress, the Czech Republic's seniors wound up a disappointing fifth at the European Championships B Pool competition last summer in Slovenia. Much work lies ahead if the country's seniors are eventually to qualify for the Olympics. The winner of the B pool automatically advances to the A pool championships, where perennial powers Italy and Holland await. Coveted Olympic berths go to the top two finishers in the A pool.

While the Czechs aren't quite on par with the Italians or Dutch, the bronze medals won by the cadets and juveniles, along with strong showings by the juniors, bode well for the future. To prepare for that future, the Czech juniors and cadets traveled to the U.S. to learn and improve their skills. While the juniors participated in the annual International Baseball Festival in northern New Jersey the past two summers, the cadets took to the air to California to compete at last summer's RBI World Series in Los Angeles. The juniors' fine performance during their first-ever trip to the U.S. in 1993 impressed the tournament's organizers, who invited the juniors back to play in last summer's festival.

Prague Baseball Week—Back in the Czech Republic, three clubs have dominated the country's top league, Extraliga. Technika Brno, Sokol Krc Praha, and Kovo Praha between them have captured most of the league's titles since play began seventeen years ago. That isn't surprising, as baseball's hot spots in the republic are the major cities of Prague, Brno and Ostrava.

As baseball continues to grow inside the country, teams from Europe and the U.S. regularly make trips to the Czech Republic to compete against the Republic's best. While it began during Communist times, Prague Baseball Week, staged this year at the new National Baseball Center, now attracts Western sponsors and teams without restrictions. Having just completed its fourteenth year, the annual international tournament held in late June regularly lures top competition and many baseball enthusiasts.

The event features teams from the U.S., Holland, Italy, Germany, and both the Czech and Slovak Republics. Using Prague's excellent public transportation, fans flock to see the sport they love. Many wear American major league caps and T-shirts, and trade American baseball cards, but most aren't really familiar with the teams or players. Prague Baseball Week receives some media attention in the republic, and a half-hour highlights show is broadcast on Czech National TV following the end of the tournament, but the country's many newspapers still focus on tennis, hockey, and soccer

Bagin's work never ends, even if the action on the field ceases in mid-October. He is constantly busy promoting the game, often traveling around Europe and the U.S. in search of support and assistance for Czech baseball.

The future of Czech baseball lies with younsters, and Bagin knows it. A program to teach baseball in the schools throughout the country occupies the executive director and his one-person staff during most of the off-season. "We look to the schools to increase the amount of participants in the game. The goal is to get kids involved early and to get them involved with the clubs later," says Bagin, who is pushing for an exhibition of baseball photos from around the world to tour Czech cities. "We want to increase the popularity of the game in our country, and to show the people the beauty of the game," says Bagin. "We want to let people in the Republic know baseball is growing throughout the world."

The 1910 White Sox

Hard times on the South Side

Ted Farmer

Making the case for the 1910 White Sox as the worst hitting team of all time is easy. Their collective .211 team batting average (the worst major league mark of the twentieth century), .261 slugging average, and seven total home runs places them in elite company. Their futility extends far beyond mere statistics, however, and a close examination of the team's season reveals a struggle far beyond the norm for a weak ball club.

A full two months before the start of the season, an incident occurred that would prove to be a bad omen. While on a hunting trip, club owner Charles Comiskey and American League President Ban Johnson were involved in a train wreck near Frankfort, Kentucky. Although the Old Roman escaped uninjured, the stage was set for a tumultuous spring training.

Following the 1909 season Comiskey decided that 1910 would be the last year that his White Sox would train in California, where they had worked out since 1908. The "White Sox Special," a train that included a large entourage of reporters, fans—and Ban Johnson—pulled out in late February. Despite a new manager, several rookies, and question marks at many positions, Comiskey guaranteed a pennant as the team left on the long journey to the Coast. He had no

way of knowing what lay ahead.

Shortly after leaving Denver on February 27, a spreading switch at a siding derailed the rear car of the seven-car Special. The car hopped the tracks to the right. Had it gone to the left, it would have toppled into the icy waters of Palmer Lake, possibly pulling other cars with it. As it was, no one was injured and the train continued westward, only to be delayed for several days in Ogden, Utah by severe flooding.

When the team finally arrived in San Francisco on March 10, it was presumed that their bad luck was behind them and they settled in for an adventurous spring training itinerary that included stops in Texas, Oklahoma, Arizona, and New Mexico.

On March 11 the worst earthquake in northern California since the great quake of 1906 rattled the area. Once again none of the White Sox were injured, a short-lived bit of good luck.

The following day, starting catcher Billy Sullivan, who had managed the club in 1909, stepped on a rusty nail. Sullivan neglected to go to the doctor, instead relying upon turpentine that had been suggested by a pharmacist. Blood poisoning set in and Sullivan almost lost his leg. He eventually made a full recovery, but he would be out of the lineup until July 1.

Raw material—New skipper Hugh Duffy had been brought in after an extensive search. Duffy had reason for concern as he considered his new team. Rookies Rollie Zeider, Lena Blackburne, and John "Shano"

Ted Farmer *is a historian who lives in Blacksburg, Virginia.*

Collins were talented, but whether or not they were ready for the majors remained to be seen. Charlie Mullen, Vic Holm, and Chester Waite were also in their first camp; their contributions in 1910 would range from negligible to non-existent. Perhaps the most promising youngster in California that spring was a big, powerful first baseman. Arnold "Chick" Gandil would make his impact on Chicago a few years later.

In contrast to the rookies, Duffy saw aging veterans up and down the lineup. Freddy Parent and Billy Sullivan were both 35, Patsy Dougherty was 33, and Fred Payne and Lee Tannehill were 29. All of their careers were nearly over.

Early inklings—In one of the first spring training games, Zeider and Bruno Block were injured. Zeider would be diagnosed with typhoid fever a few days later. Freddy Parent developed a case of the "grip;" Chester Waite came down with smallpox. Billy Purtell was bothered by an ear infection and Bobby Messenger suffered from tonsillitis. Since the Sox had split into two teams, injuries had a disruptive impact on their exhibition games. On March 13, Duffy had to insert himself into the lineup.

As the two Sox squads continued on their respective swings through California, they were beset by more injuries. Almost none of the regular players went unscathed. Even more troubling was the fact that the Pale Hose were, more often than not, being beaten by the minor league teams that faced them. Most disturbing was the manner in which they were losing; hits and runs were rare, nearly all of the Sox were in severe batting slumps. This prompted I. E. Sanborn of the Chicago *Daily Tribune*, who was all too familiar with weak-hitting Chicago teams, to write, "it is the same old bunch of sweet pitchers and sour apple batters."

Indeed, the pitching staff, one of the best in the majors, was the only strong aspect of the club. Despite an impressive finish in spring training, little was expected from the everyday lineup. Most observers anticipated a second division finish.

The Chisox' hitting woes evidenced themselves early. In their fourth game they became the victims of the year's first no-hitter, falling 1-0 to Cleveland's Addie Joss.

On May 4, Duffy benched Ed Hahn, whose hot bat during spring training had been one of the few bright spots on the team. Hahn began the season by going 6 for 53 (.113). He would never play another major league game. This was the first in a seemingly endless string of moves and transactions, desperate attempts to get production out of a lineup that struggled for every hit, run, and base. Throughout the year, Duffy shuffled his lineup like a deck of cards.

By June 11 the team had reached the crisis level. Although still in the early stages of the season, they had already been no-hit once, one-hit twice and two-hit three times! With their best hitter, Patsy Dougherty, mired in an 18 for 96 slump, the Sox acquired outfielder George Browne on waivers from Washington. Browne was brought in, Sanborn wrote, "to brace up the team's batting, which gives promise of shrinking to the vanishing point unless something desperate is done." Purchasing Browne was a definite sign of desperation. He was hitting just .182 with the Senators.

The slump continues—Normally, the acquisition of a .182 hitter would be no reason for joy. But this was no normal team. After posting a .197 batting average in April, the team batted a slightly better .198 for May before going into a serious slump at the beginning of June. The team was hitting just .156 for the month of June on the day Browne was acquired. Furthermore, they had not yet hit a home run and regulars such as Blackburne, Collins, and Payne were all under the .200 mark. Of the twenty-one regulars who played at least ten games for Chicago that year, eleven were destined to bat under .200.

Obviously, batting slumps and hitless streaks were rampant throughout the lineup. Performances such as 19 for 109 (Purtell), 4 for 60 (Parent), and 4 for 45 (Gandil) were common throughout the season. During one stretch that extended from July 2 through August 4, cleanup hitter Dougherty went 33 games without an extra-base hit.

The outfield for Chicago was an especially weak aspect of the team. Eighteen men saw duty in the outer grasses of the field. Combined they drove in 112 runs. Sam Crawford of Detroit drove in 120 in 1910.

Nowhere, however, was production more limited than behind the plate. A trio that consisted of Fred Payne, Bruno Block, and Billy Sullivan came to bat 551 times. Their collective average was .206, with ten doubles, six triples and no home runs.

No amount of platooning, batting order shuffling, or acquisitions managed to change the team's fortunes. Glimmers of hope faded as quickly as they appeared. On June 18, Red Kelly, the former captain of the Notre Dame team, made his debut. Kelly rapped two singles in four at-bats and secured a starting position in the outfield. He proceeded to go 7 for

45 in fourteen games over the next two months. Those proved to be the only games of his major league career.

Time and again the team received excellent pitching efforts from Ed Walsh, Doc White, Frank Lange, and Fred Olmstead, only to lose by scores of 1-0 and 2-1.

It was hoped that the July 1 opening of the new White Sox stadium, Comiskey Park, would give Duffy's men an uplift. It did nothing of the sort. Called "the baseball palace of the world" and built at a cost of $750,000, the park boasted of a complete lighting system and clubhouses that contained hot and cold baths, showers, and rubbing tables. In the first game in their new park, the Sox were, fittingly, shutout 2-0 by St. Louis.

If one can point to a single game, however, that typifies the White Sox' season, it may be the game of August 4. On that day, Ed Walsh held the Athletics to no runs and six hits over 16 innings. However, Jack Coombs pitched a 3-hit shutout for Philadelphia, striking out 18 White Sox. The game was called because of darkness.

At this point in the season seven of the eleven hitters at the bottom of the American League statistics were White Sox. Almost unbelievably, Ty Cobb had more hits (136) than the three leading Sox hitters combined (Dougherty, Tannehill, and Browne 132).

On August 11, with an eye on the future (and, perhaps attendance figures for the rest of the season), the White Sox became the beneficiaries of what would later be called "one of the queerest baseball deals ever recorded." In exchange for veteran pitcher Frank Smith, whose best days were behind him, and light-hitting third baseman Billy Purtell, Chicago received second baseman Amby McConnell and hard-hitting third sacker Harry Lord from Boston. Lord, who had fallen out of favor with the Red Sox management, became the White Sox' one consistent threat at the plate. He batted .297 the rest of the year in a Chicago uniform and would hit .321 in 1911. McConnell instantly moved into the starting job at second, and the newcomers usually batted 1-2 in the order.

The rest of the season saw some improvement. Team average peaked with a September showing of .229, and the team played over .500 baseball.

When the dust had settled, the team's record stood at 68-85, 35-1/2 games behind the champion A's. Had it not been for the brilliant pitching staff (2.01 ERA, 785 strikeouts, 23 shutouts), the team would surely have finished in the cellar. As it was, they were sixth.

How bad?—Compared to other weak teams throughout history (1899 Spiders, 1906 Pilgrims, 1909 Senators, 1942 White Sox, to name a few), the offensive numbers for the 1910 White Sox are the worst of all, by any measure.

The combination of rookies and veterans, none of whom was an offensive threat, had been a recipe for disaster. Although this makes the lack of offensive production somewhat explainable, the final numbers are still difficult to believe. No Chicago player finished in the top ten in the American League in batting average, hits, slugging average, home runs, triples, doubles, or runs scored.

As a team, the Sox finished last in batting average, slugging average, home runs, and doubles. It would be 21 years before another American League team accomplished this feat (ironically, the 1931 White Sox). In addition, they were next to last in triples and runs scored, and the disparity between the team batting average of .211 and that of the league, .243, is the second greatest difference in American League history. The team had been shut out in 25 games and had managed to score just one run in 28 others. They failed to get an extra-base hit in 72 contests, and their total of 180 is the second lowest in the history of the American League. Their longest hitting streak was made by Patsy Dougherty: eight games.

Following the season, the rebuilding process began. Ping Bodie and Matty McIntyre, two solid hitters, were acquired, and the 1911 White Sox batted .269. Eventually, strong batsmen such as Eddie Collins, Buck Weaver, and Joe Jackson were brought in and would form the nucleus of the powerhouse White Sox teams of the latter part of the decade.

Charles Comiskey had always been known to favor low-scoring contests and scientific baseball. Perhaps his 1910 team changed the Old Roman's philosophy.

Streaks

Statistics vs. serendipity

Neal Moran

In a 1993 *BRJ* article, "No Hitter Lollapaloosas," I observed that the statistical probability of Johnny Vander Meer pulling off two no-hitters in a row in 1938 was 0.0096 percent or 10,332 to 1. In a 1994 *BRJ* article, "The DiMaggio Streak: How Big a Deal Was It?" Charles Blahaus calculates that the probability of DiMaggio hitting in 56 straight games in 1941 was 0.13 percent.

How do these probabilities compare with other famous streaks? Consider the following examples: Bobby Lowe's four home runs in a row in 1894, Carl Hubbell's twenty-four-game winning streak in 1936-37, the 1916 New York Giants' twenty-six-game winning streak, and Walt Dropo's twelve hits in a row in 1950. Their probabilities are summarized in the table below.

	Probability That Year	Career
Bobby Lowe's 4 Home Runs	.0003	.0001
Walt Dropo's 12 Straight Hits	.0001	.0006
Carl Hubbell's 24 Straight Wins	.00805	.0043
Johnny Vander Meer's 2 No-Hitters	.000096	.0004
Joe DiMaggio's 56-Game Hit Streak	.0013	.0024
1916 NY Giants' 26 Straight Wins	.00003	N/A

Among players, Vander Meer's 1938 season still wins the lollapaloosa sweepstakes. DiMaggio's fifty-six-game hitting streak was really more difficult than a simple probability analysis would indicate, because there would be some instances where he'd have five at bats and other times only two. Applying an *average* number of at bats for each of the fifty-six games significantly increases his chances. It would be more accurate to string together the probabilities of getting a hit in each individual game, taking the number of plate appearances into account. Still more accurate would be a series of simulated 1941 seasons based on DiMaggio's overall batting stats. Rerun the simulation about a zillion times and see how often a fifty-six-game hitting streak comes up. Anyone with the programming skills and the computer resources to do this is welcome to try.

Among teams, the 1916 Giants, who won twenty-six straight games and finished *fourth* were the kings of the lollapaloosas. Pulling off that streak in a season where they only won eighty-six games had odds of 29,660 to 1. Unbelievably, they also had a seventeen-game winning streak that season.

Some further questions also come up. How improbable was this streak in the context of the ballplayer's overall career, rather than just his particular season? Also, how improbable would such a streak be for the "average" player that season? Finally, what were the chances that some other great player could have pulled off such a streak during his career?

If the year of the streak was fairly typical of the player's overall career, using career totals significantly increases the probability of the streak. The player will

---

Neal Moran is a capital markets specialist and a lifelong Phillies fan.

have a lot more opportunities to pull it off. For example, Walt Dropo, a .270 career hitter, hit just six points higher (.276) the year of his streak. As a result, it was six times more likely that he would get twelve straight hits *sometime* in his career than in that particular season. On the other hand, Bobby Lowe had only seventy homers in his career, but seventeen in 1894. If he'd had a string of average seasons instead of bunching up his power numbers in 1893 and 1894, the four consecutive homers would be far less probable.

The streak can contaminate the statistics if it is large relative to seasonal totals. The fact that Carl Hubbell won twenty-four straight games in 1936-37 gave him a high winning percentage during those years, which in turn increases the probability that he would win a lot of games in a row. As good as Hubbell was, we had no reason to expect ahead of time that he would win 77 percent of his decisions during those two years. That's why consecutive game streaks aren't suited for this analysis. With the benefit of hindsight, we can see that a "typical" season for Lou Gehrig or Cal Ripken meant playing every game. That tells us nothing about what our expectations should have been for such a streak ahead of time.

It's one thing to view a streak in the context of a player's overall season or career. What are the chances that a "typical" player that year would have pulled off such a feat?

	Probability
4 Home Runs in 1894	.000006
56-Game Hitting Streak in 1941	.000089
12 Straight Hits in 1952	.000617
2 No-Hitters in 1938 (35 starts)	.0000018
24 Straight Wins (62 decisions)	.0000023

All of the streaks would be highly improbable for an average player. In some cases, though, the improbability has likely been exaggerated. Bobby Lowe's four home runs has been touted as extraordinary because they occurred in the dead ball era. In fact, there were over 600 homers hit in the National League that season. It wasn't like doing it in 1961, but they weren't the hitless wonders either. (For reference, the 1906 White Sox hit only seven homers all season and still won the World Series.)

Another way to look at these streaks is to assess the likelihood of someone else pulling off the same feat. The odds that Ty Cobb would hit in fifty-six straight games *sometime* in his career are about 37 to 1. The odds that he would have had twelve consecutive hits are about 15 to 1 (47 to 1 if walks break the streak). Babe Ruth's career statistics indicate that he had a pretty good chance (about 5 to 1) of hitting four straight homers. Contrast that with the "called shot." On average, Ruth hit a homer once every 14.6 plate appearances, so calling a home run at random, with one try, would have been nearly three times less likely than hitting four homers in a row sometime in his career. And that doesn't even consider whether challenging the opposing pitcher significantly increases the probability of getting plunked in the head.

Lefty Grove's extraordinary career record gave him a 30 to 1 chance of winning twenty-four straight at some point. Nolan Ryan had a 147 to 1 chance of pitching two straight no-hitters during his career. The 1906 Chicago Cubs had about a 13 to 1 chance of winning twenty-six straight during the season, but they still managed to lose to the Hitless Wonders in the World Series.

A final way to look at a streak is probably the most obvious: how close have others actually come to matching it? A lot of players have hit four homers in a game, including Ed Delahanty, also in the 1890s. Pinky Higgins in 1938 also had twelve straight hits. A few pitchers have come close to winning twenty-four straight. In 1947 Ewell Blackwell took a second straight no-hitter into the ninth and lost it with one out. Howard Ehmke combined a no-hitter and a one-hitter fifteen years *before* Vander Meer's feat. (Anthony Young's remarkable twenty-seven consecutive losses may be the most remarkable streak—and triumph of hope over experience—of all. But that's for another time.) No one has come all that close to DiMaggio's fifty-six, even if Pete Rose made a good run at it.

Eye-catchers in the Microfilm

1904: Headline: "Giants Not A Misnomer." Average height of McGraw's team is 5'10-1/2", average weight 171.

1907: Against the Giants, Fred Clarke slides home, is blocked by Roger Bresnahan's new shin guards, fails to score. Umpire ignores his complaint. Visits Harry Pulliam, NL president. "It was not exactly a protest, but Clarke asked the NL executive to rule on the legality of the new-fangled means of protection." (They're okay, but it will be several years before all catchers wear them.)

1909: The Detroit Tigers used 2,460 balls during the season.

—A.D. Suehsdorf

Managers and Close Games

"Push-button Joe" McCarthy and the D-Score

Bob Boynton

An analysis of American and National League seasons from 1901 through 1992 yields a surprisingly simple formula which relates a team's seasonal winning percentage to runs scored and allowed:

$$Pct = 500 + 100\,[(R\text{-}OR)/G],$$

where R stands for a team's run production, OR is that of its opponents, G is the number of games played, and Pct is the team's winning percentage (based on 1000, *sans* decimal). For example, if a team scores one run per game more than its opponents, it will finish with a winning percentage in the neighborhood of 600. As shown in Figure 1, data points scatter around the line generated by the formula, indicating that some teams do worse and others better than what the formula predicts. This difference will be called D. If, as in the example just mentioned, a team were to score an average of one run per game more than its opponents while finishing the season at 630, then D would be 30. D-scores are negative if the team's winning percentage is less than what the formula predicts. Ideally, D-scores should factor out a team's absolute performance. For example, a score of 30 could also result from a 410 season if the formula predicts only 380.

To finish the season with a positive D-score, a team must win more than its share of relatively close games. For example, suppose that the home team were to lose the first game of a three-game series 7-1 but win the next two 1-0 and 5-2. Despite scoring only seven runs compared to its opponent's nine, the home team would have a winning record for the series. This outcome would contribute positively to the team's winning percentage while subtracting two from the R-OR total which would help to lower the predicted winning percentage at the end of the season. Both factors contribute toward raising the D-score.

39 Long-Term Managers Examined—Winning or losing close games depends to some extent upon the kinds of conspicuous managerial decisions that fans like to second-guess. Realistically, however, there is so much randomness in baseball that such short-term evaluations are nearly meaningless. On a winning day, a manager is more lucky than good if a chosen relief pitcher gets a crucial double-play grounder, a pinch hitter bloops a game-winning single, or a late-inning defensive replacement saves the day with a spectacular catch. Such events do not certify managerial genius unless they are part of an extended pattern in which such tactical successes outnumber the inevitable failures. To make a meaningful analysis, a manager's record must be investigated over the long haul, for which a full season is perhaps a minimum requirement. The analysis to follow emphasizes the lifetime records of those thirty-nine men who managed in the major leagues for ten or more full seasons during the years from 1901 through 1992. Tables and

Bob Boynton, who discovered SABR shortly before he became an emeritus professor in 1991, is currently secretary of the San Diego Ted Williams Chapter and has attended the last six national conventions.

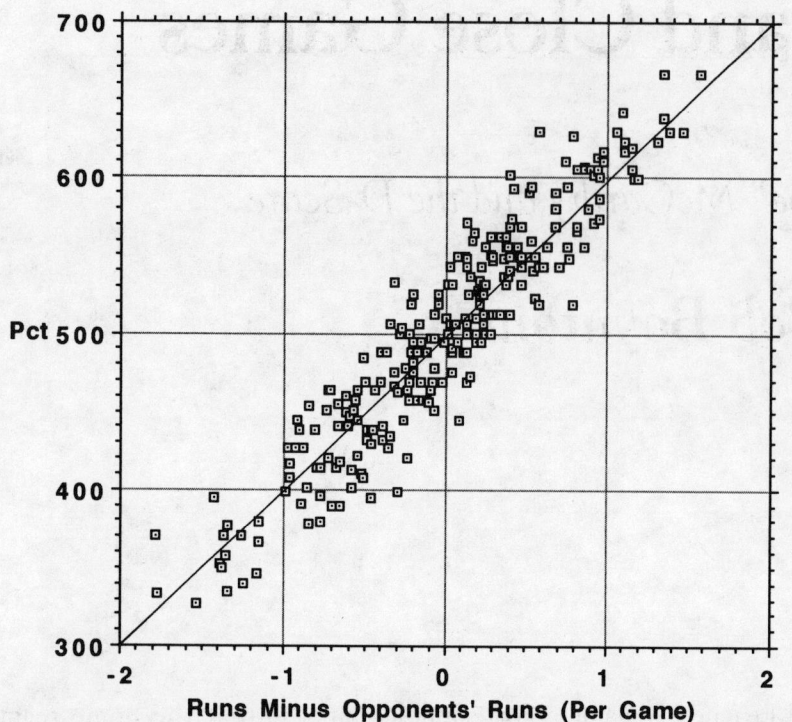

Figure 1. Relation between winning percentage and per-game average run differential for all major league team-seasons in the decade of the 70s. Data for all other eras from 1901 through 1992 also have this general appearance, with correlations that range from .84 (in the 80s) to .94 (in the 20s), with a mean of .90. The line represents the formula described in the text. Team-seasons above the line yield positive D-scores; those below the line, negative ones.

are positive (twenty-seven of forty, averaging 4.2). This is not unexpected for a select group culled from the pool of more than 400 men who have managed in the big leagues for at least part of a season during the twentieth century.

The Anomalous Record of Joe McCarthy—Not surprisingly, there is a positive relation between D-scores and winning percentage. The exception — and it is a huge one—is Joe McCarthy. His data point lies totally out of the distribution at the upper left in Figure 2. (If McCarthy is excluded, the correlation between winning percentage and average D-score is .51. With him, it plunges to .28.)

McCarthy's location in Figure 2 confirms that he achieved the highest lifetime winning percentage of any manager. But it also reveals that he accomplished this despite turning in the lowest average D-score. There is no intention here to minimize McCarthy's success in the all-impor-

graphs have been updated to include the 1993 season, during which a fortieth manager (Joe Torre) completed his tenth full season. (Analyses of group data do not generally include the 1993 season.) The 1994 strike season has not been considered.

In Figure 2, each manager's name refers to a nearby data point whose vertical position depends upon his career winning percentage. The horizontal location is based upon the mean value of all full-season D-scores for his career. (The corresponding numerical values are in Table 1.) Most of the average D-scores

Figure 2. The name of each manager is positioned near a data point that represents the career-average D-score of his team's (or teams') full seasons (horizontal) and his career winning percentage (vertical). It is argued that the anomalous location of Joe McCarthy validates his characterization by Jimmy Dykes as a "push-button manager." Numerical data are listed in the appendix. Data are complete through the 1993 season.

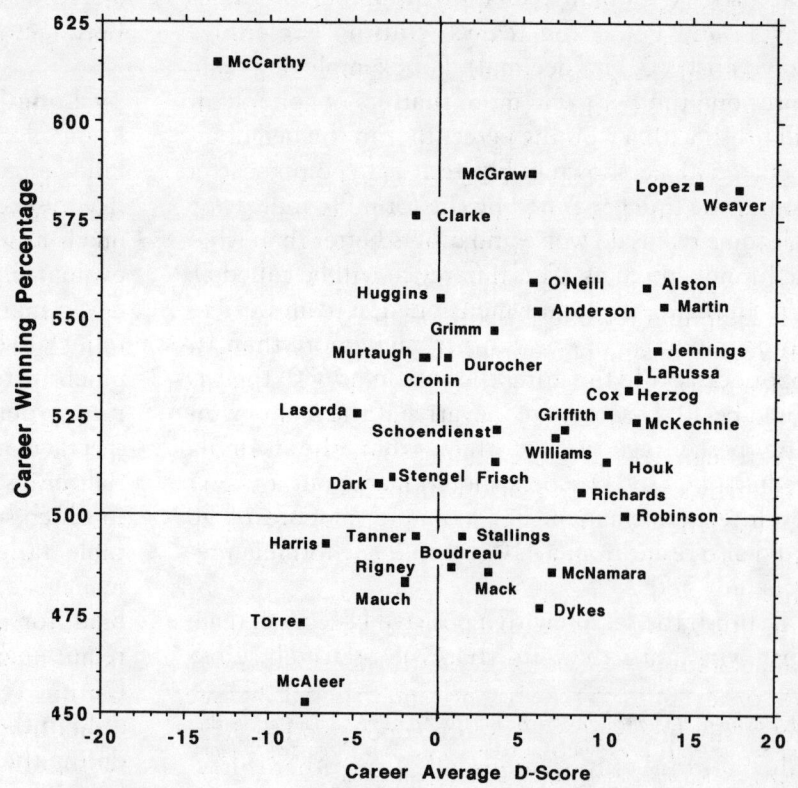

tant win department. Nevertheless, the evidence seems clear that the teams he managed consistently lost more relatively close games than they won. A likely explanation for this is that, with a rich and continuously re-plenished pool of top-notch Yankee talent at his disposal, winning required little managerial maneuvering of the sort employed by most managers in an attempt to eke out victories. Jimmy Dykes apparently sensed this when he needled McCarthy by calling him a "push-button manager."

The Mighty 1939 Yankees—Consider the 1939 Yankees as an example of a team calculated to arouse envy in Dykes or any other manager. This is the outfit that won the *Baseball Weekly* computerized greatest-team tourna-ment in 1994 by beating the legendary 1927 Yankees in the finals. In real life the 1939 team—despite the tragic loss of Lou Gehrig early in the season—scored 967 runs (most in the league) while giving up 556 runs (fewest in the league) for a 411-run difference. When divided by the 151 games they played, this yields an average run differential of 2.72 per game, the greatest such margin in history. The formula predicts an enormous winning percentage of 772 (500 + 272) instead of the 702 that this team actually achieved. To reach 772 would have required 118 in-stead of 108 wins, and no American League team has ever won more than 111. Despite a terrible D-score of mi-nus 70, a winning percentage of 702 was more than sufficient as the Yankees breezed to a pennant seven-teen games ahead of the second-place Red Sox.

Although the 1939 season is an extreme case, McCarthy's peculiar location in Figure 2 indicates that the tendency for his teams to lose relatively close games was a consistent one throughout his career. This is also illustrated in Figure 3, which plots D-scores for the twenty-one full seasons that McCarthy managed (upper left) together with those of a few of the other managers who are mentioned below. McCarthy had a positive score (open symbols) for only one-third of his seasons; all of the other thirty-

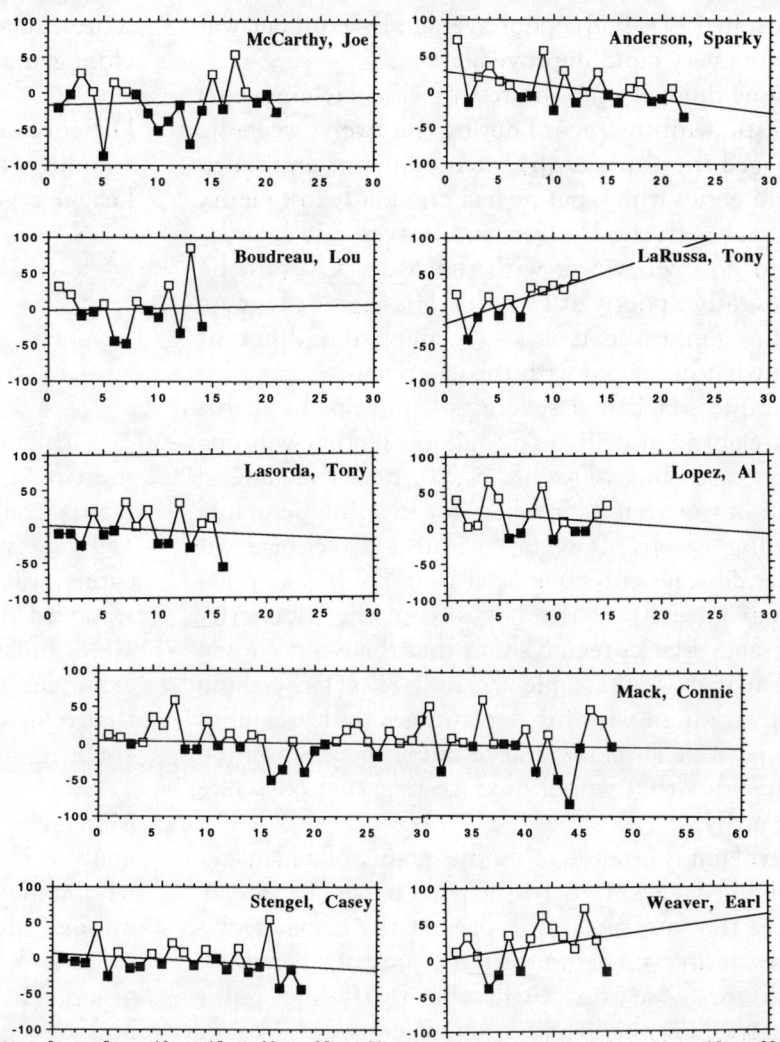

Figure 3. The course of D-scores over the careers of nine managers. In each panel, the x-axis represents full seasons, numbered in chronological order. The white squares represent positive D-scores, the black squares, negative ones. The lines fitted to the data are least-squares linear best fits. The slopes of these lines, for ten-year periods, are given in the column labeled "Career Slope" in the table in the appendix.

nine did better in this respect.

D-Scores of Some Other Managers—If McCarthy was the worst at winning close games, the best were Earl Weaver with an average D of 17.8 and Al Lopez at 15.4. These men are also third and fourth in life-time winning percentage. Of the five managers in 1993 who had completed ten or more full seasons, Tony LaRussa is clearly the best at 11.9, followed by Bobby Cox at 10.1. Tommy Lasorda, at -4.8, comes in last, while Sparky Anderson scores a respectable 5.9. Other than McCarthy, the all-time lowest average D-score of -7.8 was obtained by old-timer Jimmy

McAleer, who also suffered the lowest lifetime winning percentage. Joe Torre, who finished his tenth full season in 1993, had a poor average D-score but was showing very rapid improvement.

Casey Stengel is an interesting case. He enjoyed a fantastic winning record during the twelve years he managed the Yankees (623, ten pennants and seven World Series wins), but he had previously lost plenty of games with the Dodgers and Braves, and later he would do even worse with the Mets. Overall, he scores rather poorly at D = -3.5. His average D-score for the Yankee years was -3.3, negligibly different from what he scored with the bad teams.

Connie Mack had severe ups and downs in his forty-eight years, with an overall low lifetime winning percentage, and a D-score of 3.0, near the general mean of the group. However, for his nine pennant-winning seasons his average winning percentage was 657 and his D-scores averaged 18.6. For Mack's powerful teams, this is the opposite of the McCarthy syndrome. Mack's record shows that there is no statistical artifact (for example, a ceiling effect) associated with very high winning percentages that precludes high positive D-scores, and certainly there is nothing of that sort that would produce negative ones like McCarthy's.

No claim is intended that the quality of a manager should be gauged only by the percentage of strategic moves that are successful, or that the decisions he makes during games are the only cause of a team's D-score for a season. Still, the thirty-one point difference between the lifetime averages of Weaver and McCarthy suggests a meaningful influence. This difference implies that, for an average season with the same players, Weaver would win four or five more games than McCarthy.

Managerial Changes and Negative D-Scores—Because for every win there must be a loss, the average value of D for all teams and all seasons is zero. As it turns out, the full-season scores for those managers not in the select group of 39 (through 1992) average almost exactly zero. The positive average score of the select group is compensated by the average D of -9.5 for 280 instances in which two or more managers were employed during a season. This breaks down as follows:

2 managers (216 instances)	D= -9.0
3 managers (55 instances)	D= -9.5
4 managers (7 instances)	D= -19.6
5 managers (1 instance),	D= -46.

During these troubled seasons, the more often managers were dismissed, the lower were the D-scores, suggesting that managers who lose too many close games tend to get fired.

D-Scores Affect Season Standings—Consider the standings at the conclusion of the 1948 American League regular season:

Team	Games	Won	Lost	Pct	GBL	D
Indians	154	96	58	623	–	-49
Red Sox	154	96	58	623	–	-2
Yankees	154	96	60	610	2	-35

With zero D-scores, either the Indians, managed by shortstop Lou Boudreau, or the Yankees, led by Bucky Harris, could have won the pennant in the regulation 154 games. McCarthy, who was near the end of his career, was now the Red Sox manager. By his Yankee standards he achieved a relatively good D-score in 1948, but it wasn't good enough. This is only one example: many pennant races are sufficiently close that relative D-scores make a difference in the outcome.

Managers for five to nine seasons—A separate analysis has been undertaken for the sixty-five men who managed teams in the majors from five to nine seasons inclusive through 1992. Their average D-score is 3.3, little different from that of the other group. The correlation between winning percentage and average D-scores is .47, identical to that of the group of thirty-nine without McCarthy. Frank Chance has both the highest D-score (based on eight full seasons) of 31.4 and the highest winning percentage of 593. Dick Howser (eight years) has the second highest D-score. Jimmie Wilson has both the lowest D-score and winning percentage (-23.7, 401), with Hugh Duffy and Jeff Torborg also low scorers in both dimensions. The data through 1993 for sixty-seven managers (Art Howe finished his fifth complete season in 1993) are shown in Table 2.

An Index of Managerial Genius?—To finish the season with a positive D-score, a team must win more than its share of close games. Close games in turn are the ones most affected by managerial decisions that are made during the progress of those games. These contests are won or lost mostly by chance on any given occasion. Nevertheless, over long careers, good and bad luck will cancel, leaving the cleverest managers with the highest positive D-scores.

Decline of D-Scores Over a Career—After Bucky Harris was fired by the Yankees following the 1948 season, he returned to manage the Washington Senators for a third time. He concluded his career with the Tigers, who kept the original "boy wonder" occupied until he was almost sixty. But Harris never again finished in the first division, and he registered terrible Ds of -48, -40, -63, and -26 during his last four seasons. The decline of Harris was extreme but otherwise not unusual: twenty-six of the forty managers have shown declining D-scores during their careers. Included in Table 1 is a column headed "career slope," which is the per-decade linear tendency for the D-scores to rise or decline over the career of the manager. These are also represented by the fitted lines in Figure 3.

Validity of D-Scores—The negative D-scores associated with managerial changes during the season suggest that losing close games is a common and visible problem that is blamed on the manager. Further evidence, albeit more subjective, is provided by comparing D-scores with expert opinion about managerial quality. Such quality judgments have been made in Leonard Koppett's *The Man in the Dugout*. In his Introduction (page viii) he divides managers "…into three categories: (1) run-of-the mill, (2) successful, (3) successful and influential." He then states that he will focus on the third group. Each of these nineteen is treated in an individual chapter; together these make up the bulk of the book's contents. The seventeen members of this group who have managed for at least ten full seasons have an average lifetime D-score of 4.9. (If the anomalous McCarthy is removed, it jumps to 6.0.)

In his final chapter Koppett discusses twelve additional managers, each of whom is treated in a detailed, separately headed section. These presumably belong in his "successful" category. For those in this group who managed for ten or more seasons, the average of their D-scores is 4.3.

This leaves a group of managers from the group of thirty-nine who, by process of elimination, fall into Koppett's "run-of-the-mill" category, in the sense that they managed for at least ten seasons but are mentioned only in passing. (One of them, George Stallings, is not mentioned at all.) The average D-score of the run-of-the-millers is only 2.7. To summarize:

Category	Number	Ave D-score
Successful and influential:	18	4.9
Successful:	9	4.3
Run-of-the-mill	12	2.7
Total: 39		Average: 4.1

A preliminary game-by-game study within seasons helps to support the contention that D-scores relate to winning close games. During the 1939 season, according to an analysis kindly supplied by Bob Hoie, the Yankees were 22-16 in one-run games and 27-0 in games decided by six or more runs. For the 1931 season, these figures were 17-19 and 22-3 respectively.

Final Conclusions—The D-score is a valid index of a significant aspect of managerial performance, namely the ability to make tactical decisions that help a team win more than its share of close games. Considered over many seasons, the D-score provides evidence of this component of managerial skill. Joe McCarthy's record anomalously combines the highest lifetime winning percentage with the lowest average D-score of the forty managers who completed at least ten full seasons through 1993. Most other managers with high winning percentages also show relatively high D-scores. It appears that McCarthy was dealing with players of such exceptional ability that the aspect of "managerial genius" tapped by D-scores was simply not required. McCarthy's very low lifetime D-Score therefore provides objective evidence to support the claim of Jimmy Dykes that Joe McCarthy was indeed a "push-button manager."

The *Total Baseball* Formula—After this paper was completed and accepted for publication, the third edition of *Total Baseball* (1993) appeared, and for the first time it included a Manager Roster. (I thank Jim Vail of SABR for pointing this out at a meeting in Tempe.) Listed in that roster, for each manager's season, is a statistic called W-EXP (expected wins). It is based on a formula which turns out to be structurally identical to the one given on the first page of this paper, which was

$$Pct = 500 + \frac{100(R\text{-}OR)}{G}$$

The *Total Baseball* (TB) formula, when converted from wins to a baseball-style "percentage" basis becomes:

$$\text{Pct}_{TB} = 500 + \frac{100(R\text{-}OR)}{(G/3)\ \sqrt{(R+OR)/G}}$$

The *TB* formula differs from mine in that the fixed value of G in the denominator of my equation is replaced in the *TB* formula by $(G/3)\ \sqrt{(R+OR)/G}$. When $(R+OR)/G = 9$, which is approximately the average number of runs scored per game by both teams in a major-league contest, the *TB* denominator reduces to G, and the two equations become identical. Relative to my equation, the *TB* formulation causes the expected percentage of wins to decrease as the total number of runs scored per game increases beyond nine, and to increase as this value decreases from nine. (I thank Pete Palmer for his help with these equations.)

In its final column, the *TB* Manager Roster specifies, for each manager and season, a statistic called A-E, which is the actual minus expected number of wins. When converted to a percentage basis, this is almost equivalent to the D-score, differing only because of the adjustments of the denominator value of G caused by the *Total Baseball* formula.

By the *TB* formula, Bucky Harris and Tom Lasorda emerge with very slightly worse average lifetime A-E scores than McCarthy, but their winning percentages are relatively poor and they do not encroach upon the anomalous location of McCarthy.

I recommend that future calculations of D-scores make use of the *Total Baseball* A-E statistic.

Blowouts—Bob Tiemann, who did a superb job of reviewing my manuscript, has noted that there is a logical flaw in equating the D-score only with the selective loss of close games, since lopsided victories push a manager's score down, and blowout defeats push it up. Quite right. He supports this observation with data not available to me. Taking the 1939 Yankees as an example, he notes that they won fifteen games by ten or more runs, out-scoring their opponents by 198 runs in those games. Had they won those games by an average of five runs, the 411-run difference for the season would be reduced to 288, yielding a D-score for a .702 team of +13.

But blowouts do not explain McCarthy's overall record by any means. Tiemann reports that McCarthy's lifetime winning percentage in one-run games was .537. This sounds good until you compare it with his overall lifetime winning percentage of .615. Overall, then, he did relatively poorly in one-run games while managing his powerful teams.

Tiemann also notes that in his nine pennant-winning seasons, McCarthy's teams won 61 percent of their one-run games. This is essentially the same as his lifetime winning percentage. Bob also notes that Connie mack, in his nine pennant-winning seasons, won 57 percent of his one-run games. This should be compared with Mack's .486 overall record. I conclude that McCarthy's success during pennant-winning seasons was not related to winning close games, whereas Mack's definitely was.

For the first time, the fourth and latest edition of *Total Baseball* contains scores for individual games, limited so far to recent years. In a preface to this section, Tiemann and Braunstein state, and I strongly agree, that, "this new feature should prove invaluable to researchers and fans alike." They also note that, "In future editions we will provide game scores for earlier periods." Meanwhile, Palmer's statistic, which as noted above is very similar to mine, does discount blowouts to some extent by taking into account the total number of runs scored, which alters McCarthy's anomalous position a little but nevertheless leaves him in upper-left field in a class by himself. A challenge for the future will be to develop a better statistic for rating teams and managers by analyzing the full distribution of their game scores.

Table 1

This table lists data for the 40 men who have managed major league teams for at least ten full seasons from 1901 through 1993. Career span in parentheses includes partial seasons. D-scores are for full seasons only; winning percentage includes partial seasons. Career slope is based on the best fitting line relating D-scores over a manager's career, expressed as the change in D per ten years. Asterisks indicate those managers whose scores for individual seasons are plotted in Figure 3.

Manager	No. Full Seasons	Average D-Score	Winning Pct	Career Slope	Manager	No. Full Seasons	Average D-Score	Winning Pct	Career Slope
Alston, Walter (54-76)	23	12.4	.558	- 15.9	Houk, Ralph (61-84)	19	10.1	.514	- 10.6
* Anderson, Sparky (70-93)	23	5.9	.552	- 18.8	Huggins, Miller (13-29)	16	0.1	.555	1.5
* Boudreau, Lou (42-60)	14	0.9	.487	2.6	Jennings, Hughie (07-24)	14	13.0	.542	- 3.6
Clarke, Fred (97-15)	15	-1.4	.576	- 37.1	* LaRussa, Tony (79-93)	13	11.9	.535	47.8
Cox, Bobby (78-93)	11	10.1	.526	27.0	* Lasorda, Tommy (76-93)	17	-4.8	.526	- 7.1
Cronin, Joe (33-47)	15	-0.7	.540	0.2	* Lopez, Al (51-69)	15	15.4	.584	- 11.9
Dark, Alvin (61-77)	10	-2.7	.510	- 5.2	* Mack, Connie (94-50)	48	3.0	.486	- 2.5
Durocher, Leo (39-73)	22	0.5	.540	- 12.2	Martin, Billy (69-88)	10	13.4	.553	- 0.9
Dykes, Jimmy (34-61)	16	6.1	.477	- 8.2	Mauch, Gene (60-87)	22	-1.9	.483	- 4.9
Frisch, Frankie (33-51)	11	3.5	.514	- 24.7	McAleer, Jimmy (01-11)	11	-7.8	.453	- 36.3
Griffith, Clark (01-20)	19	7.6	.522	- 14.6	* McCarthy, Joe (26-50)	21	-13.2	.615	3.6
Grimm, Charlie (32-60)	12	3.3	.547	9.2	McGraw, John (99-32)	28	6.9	.587	- 17.7
Harris, Bucky (24-56)	27	-6.6	.493	- 15.8	McKechnie, Bill (15-46)	21	11.8	.524	10.8
Herzog Whitey (73-90)	13	11.4	.532	3.0	McNamara, John (69-91)	13	6.9	.486	-38.3

Manager	No. Full Seasons	Average D-Score	Winning Pct	Career Slope	Manager	No. Full Seasons	Average D-Score	Winning Pct	Career Slope
Murtaugh, Danny (57-76)	12	-0.9	.540	- 20.8	Stallings, George (97-20)	10	1.5	.495	- 27.3
O'Neill, Steve (35-54)	10	5.6	.559	32.2	* Stengel, Casey (34-65)	23	-3.5	.508	- 8.0
Richards, Paul (51-76)	10	8.6	.506	29.6	Tanner, Chuck (70-88)	17	-1.3	.495	- 27.9
Rigney, Bill (56-76)	15	-1.9	.484	11.9	Torre, Joe (78-93)	10	-8.0	.473	.69.9
Robinson, Wilbert (02-31)	18	11.2	.500	- 6.6	* Weaver, Earl (68-86)	15	17.8	.583	20.0
Schoendienst, Red (65-90)	12	3.5	.522	- 14.9	Williams, Dick (67-88)	15	7.0	.520	-7.9

Table 2

This table lists data for the 65 men who have managed major league teams for not less than five or more than nine seasons from 1901 through 1993. Career span in parentheses includes partial seasons. D-scores are for full seasons only; winning percentage includes partial seasons. Careers are too short to allow a meaningful calculation of career slopes.

Manager	No. Full Seasons	Average D-Score	Winning Pct	Manager	No. Full Seasons	Average D-Score	Winning Pct
Armour, Bill (02-06)	5	13.6	.524	Johnson, Davey (84-90)	6	21.7	.588
Bauer, Hank (61-69)	5	3.0	.522	Johnson, Walter (29-35)	5	3.0	.550
Berra, Yogi (64-85)	5	10.0	.522	Jones, Fielder (04-18)	6	9.5	.540
Bluege, Ossie (43-47)	5	16.4	.488	Kelly, Tom (86-93)	6	4.9	.517
Bresnahan, Roger (09-15)	5	-0.4	.432	Killefer, Bill (21-33)	6	16.8	.457
Bristol, Dave (66-80)	7	-1.3	.462	Leyland, Jim (86-92)	8	+1.5	.515
Bush, Donie (23-33)	6	-1.5	.480	Mele, Sam (61-67)	5	-10.9	.546
Callahan, Nixey (03-17)	5	-2.2	.462	Meyer, Billy (48-52)	5	1.0	.412
Carrigan, Bill (13-29)	6	24.7	.494	Mitchell, Fred (17-23)	7	-3.7	.476
Chance, Frank (05-23)	8	31.4	.593	Moran, Pat (15-23)	9	16.1	.561
Cobb, Ty (21-26)	6	-7.7	.519	Ott, Mel (42-48)	6	-13.0	.467
Collins, Jimmy (01-06)	5	10.4	.548	Ozark, Danny (73-84)	6	-2.5	.533
Corrales, Pat (78-87)	6	-10.8	.474	Piniella, Lou (86-93)	6	2.8	.527
Craig, Roger (78-92)	9	-6.4	.500	Rickey, Branch (13-25)	8	-15.9	.473
Donovan, Patsy (97-11)	8	-6.6	.438	Robinson, Frank (75-91)	7	8.7	.475
Dressen, Chuck (34-66)	9	13.9	.509	Rodgers, Buck (80-92)	7	10.0	.506
Duffy, Hugh (01-22)	8	-19.1	.444	Sewell, Luke (41-52)	6	-4.3	.485
Dyer, Eddie (46-50)	5	3.0	.578	Shotton, Burt (28-50)	8	1.0	.477
Fohl, Lee (15-26)	8	0.1	.474	Smith, Mayo (55-70)	7	10.3	.520
Franks, Herman (65-79)	6	22.2	.537	Southworth, Billy (29-51)	9	12.9	.597
Fregosi, Jim (78-92)	5	-21.0	.472	Speaker, Tris (19-26)	7	-15.3	.543
Gleason, Kid (19-23)	5	13.8	.519	Stanky, Eddie (52-77)	5	1.2	.518
Haney, Fred (39-59)	8	6.6	.454	Tebbetts, Birdie (54-66)	7	3.1	.515
Harris, Lum (61-72)	5	20.4	.488	Terry, Bill (32-41)	9	9.7	.555
Hendricks, Jack (18-29)	7	-6.4	.496	Torborg, Jeff (77-92)	5	-10.2	..427
Higgins, Pinky (55-62)	6	4.2	.502	Torre, Joe (77-92)	9	-12.1	.466
Hodges, Gil (63-71)	8	2.1	.467	Traynor, Pie (34-39)	5	2.0	.530
Hornsby, Rogers (25-53)	5	18.8	.463	Trebelhorn, Tom (86-91)	5	-2.2	.515
Howe, Art (89-93)	5	23.0	.484	Valentine, Bobby (85-92)	5	7.0	.490
Howley, Dan (27-32)	6	.-2.5	.431	Virdon, Bill (72-84)	9	6.9	.519
Howser, Dick (78-86)	5	28.8	.544	Walker, Harry (55-72)	5	-7.2	.511
Hutchinson, Fred (52-64)	8	15.6	.501	Wilson, Jimmie (34-44)	6	-23.7	.401
Johnson, Darrell(74-82)	5	8.8	.444	Zimmer, Don (72-91)	7	7.4	.508

Sources:

Herman, Bruce, "All-Time Greatest Team Playoff," *USA Today Baseball Weekly*, v. 3 No. 37 (on sale through January 25, 1994), p. 47.

Koppett, Leonard, *The Man in the Dugout: Baseball's Top Managers and How They Got That Way*, Crown Publishers, New York, 1993.

Thorn, John and Palmer, Pete (editors), *Total Baseball*, Warner Books, New York, 1989.

Will, George F., *Men at Work: The Craft of Baseball*, MacMillan, New York, 1990.

Wolff, Rick (Editorial Director), *Encyclopedia of Baseball* (Ninth Edition),Macmillan, New York, 1993.

Tommy McCarthy

How heavenly was this "Heavenly Twin"?

Eddie Gold

Tommy McCarthy

Who is Thomas Michael Francis McCarthy? And why is he in the Baseball Hall of Fame?

We've heard of Joe McCarthy, the fine manager, and Joe McCarthy, the not-so-fine Senator. Even Charlie McCarthy, the wooden dummy. But how about Tommy McCarthy?

The McCarthy era began in 1884 with the Boston Union League team and concluded in 1896 with Brooklyn.

He never led his league in batting, runs batted in, or homers, hitting only 44. And he finished with a .292 average, which was modest for that period.

Yet McCarthy was enshrined in Cooperstown by the Committee on Veterans in 1946. Superior hitting outfielders from McCarthy's era had to wait much longer. Sliding Billy Hamilton was finally elected to the Hall in 1961. Hamilton batted .344, topped by a .404 with the Phillies in 1894. He won two batting titles, stole 912 bases, and his 192 runs scored in 1894 is still the big league record. McCarthy never approached such offensive brilliance.

Sam Thompson had to wait until 1974. Thompson was Hamilton's teammate on the '94 Phillies and batted .407. His .331 career average tops McCarthy by 39 points. Thompson won one batting title, but was more dangerous as a run producer. His 166 RBIs with Detroit in 1887 were untabulated for 80 years, but were a big league record until the coming of Babe Ruth.

And why is McCarthy a so-called immortal when outfield outsiders Jimmy Ryan and George Van Haltren have far superior statistics?

Van Haltren, a pitcher-outfielder from 1887 to 1903, collected 2,532 hits, batted .316, and won 40 games. Ryan hit 118 homers, 22 as a leadoff batter, and had 2,502 hits and a .306 average.

Perhaps the reason McCarthy was enshrined is that he and fellow Boston outfielder Hugh Duffy (a legitimate Hall of Famer) were paired as the "Heavenly Twins." But if nicknames earn a Hall niche, why isn't Bob "Death to Flying Things" Ferguson enshrined ?

Baseball historians claim McCarthy was clever and scientific. So was Moe Berg.

McCarthy's manager at Boston was Frank Selee, who won pennants in 1891, 1892, 1893, 1897, and 1898. Selee later managed the Chicago Cubs and put together the Joe Tinker-Johnny Evers-Frank Chance double play trio.

Selee won 1,284 games and lost only 862 for a phenomenal .598 percentage. Sadly, Selee has never been a serious Cooperstown candidate. Only his record was heavenly, not his nickname.

Eddie Gold is a sportswriter for the Chicago Sun-Times and has been a SABR member since 1972.

Jimmie Reese

In his own words

James D. Smith III

At the time of his death, on July 13, 1994, at age 92, Jimmie Reese had been involved in professional baseball for 78 years. A major leaguer with the Yankees (1930-31, rooming with Babe Ruth) and Cardinals (1932), he earned distinction as the second baseman on the all-time Pacific Coast League team. In that league, he served the San Diego Padres as a player (1937-38), coach (1948-61) and short-term manager (1948, 1960-61). The California Angels' conditioning coach for the past two decades, renowned for his fungo hitting and host of friends, he was honorary American League captain at the 1992 All-Star Game. Above a doorway in his living room, on a wall adorned with pictures of friends (ballplayers and entertainers), there was a hand-lettered sign: "How rapidly doth fame fleeeth." Though grammatically an "error," the humble spirit expressed made a lasting "home run" with the legion of fans touched by the life of this playful, picture-framing, dedicated baseball man. Our conversation took place on September 18, 1989.

I was a batboy with the Angels in 1917. A fellow named Frank Chance was the manager—of the Cubs prior to that, but he came out here for his health and started to manage the Angels in the Coast League. And I was lucky enought to be his batboy. The Angels were at a place called Washington Park in Los Ange-

James D. Smith III *is pastor of Claremont Emmanuel Baptist Church in San Diego. With a Th.D. from Harvard, he has recently served as adjunct professor at Bethel Theological Seminary—West and the University of San Diego. He's been a SABR member since 1982.*

les. That was before they came to Wrigley Field.

I broke in with Oakland in 1924 [and stayed] until 1930. Lyn Lary and I were sold to the Yankees in 1927, and we were to report in 1929, but I had a bad year so I stayed and he went on ahead. I had my best year in 1929 and hit .337. That was with Oakland, and then I went out to the Yankees.

Buzz Arlett? He was one of the great hitters of any time that I have ever seen. Anybody. And Tony Freitas...well, I played against him when he was with Sacramento in the Coast League. He was quite a pitcher, a little bitty guy, had the heart of a lion, quite a boy.

I came to the Padres from Los Angeles in 1937. Coming to San Diego was fine. There was a lot of...not animosity but a lot of rivalry. The '37 team...Ted Williams, Tommy Thompson, Tiny Chaplin. Listen, you're bringing back names I'd almost completely forgotten about. Frank Shellenback was the manager. Tiny Chaplin to me was one of the finest young pitchers I've ever seen. And no doubt was going to eventually go to the big leagues. He had an accident, though. Coming from Tijuana, somebody hit him from the rear, killed him right there; he died right there. A very fine, a really good friend of mine. It really broke me up.

There was George McDonald, a fellow named Hal Patchett (an exceedingly good outfielder), George Detore, George Myatt. Bobby Doerr already went to Boston. I played second and Myatt was the shortstop. I was Bobby's replacement.

The only thing I know about Ted Williams...I recall very vividly that he used to stand in front of a mirror in our clubhouse and take different poses with the bat. Like [the old story about] the fellow who sat down to play the piano and everybody started laughing? Well, that's what happened to him. He went to take those poses and everybody said, "Look at what that busher's doing." But it turned out he wasn't that crazy. Probably one of the premier hitters of all of baseball, in any time. He had a great year...and then was sold to Boston for the big sum of $35,000. I think they got a bargain. Williams believed in himself, didn't think anybody could get him out, and Babe felt exactly the same way. Confidence.

Babe, of course. There's nobody in my book...he's the ultimate in baseball, from every angle. He could run, he could throw, he could field, of course his hitting was great, he had a great deal of charisma. He did more for baseball, I think, particularly after the Black Sox scandal, than any individual in baseball.

I remember the scandal because I was a batboy with some of the boys—some of those fellows were playing in the Coast League. Swede Risberg was playing with Vernon, Lefty Williams—I saw them in the Coast League—and Fred MacMullen was with the Angels. Oh, my God, what a blow! It took a lot out of me and millions of other baseball fans. We were disillusioned, we couldn't believe it happened. That's why I say Babe—during that heyday, that period, came back and started hitting home runs and drew a lot of praise, a lot of interest—and all the fans said, "Let's go out and see this big lug." Babe did more to bring 'em back than anybody in baseball.

There was a lot of excitement in San Diego when I played there [in 1937-38]. I played with a fellow named Bill Starr. He was a good friend of mine, a catcher at the time. We were going to San Francisco, somewhere, to play in the Coast League, sat down on the train, and he said, "Jimmie, I've got to give up this game. I don't make enough money. I make $400 a month, I want to get married, I want to raise a family." He went into the real-estate business and did an unbelievable job. To make a long story short, he became the owner of the ball club [in 1944] and one of the finest men I ever met in the game. And he knew more about the game than anybody. Many people

Jimmie Reese in the Pacific Coast League

James D. Smith III

from the Coast League wanted him to become president, but he turned it down.

I came back to the Padres in 1948, when Bill Starr was the owner. When I first came back, a fellow named Bucky Harris managed the ball club. I consider Bucky Harris one of the fine managers of all time. I coached third base for a year, and he wanted me to go back with him to Washington the following year. I asked Bill about that and he said, "Jimmie, why don't you stay here. You might be here a lot longer than Bucky will be there"—which no doubt became true, as I was with him for [a total of] fourteen years.

That 1949 team: Max West and, ah, Luke Easter! He drew more people to the Coast League than any individual in the entire [history of] baseball in the Coast League. He was the greatest drawing card you ever saw. He hit home runs wherever he went. He was a lefthand hitter and hit balls as hard to left field as he did to right. People from all over the League used to call Bill Starr and want to know if Luke Easter was going to play and, if he was, they'd want to make reservations.

Jack Graham was great there. In one period he had forty-eight home runs [actually forty-six] by July of 1948 and he got hit in the head. In [L.A.'s] Wrigley Field one time, an afternoon game, there's the sun and the shadows and he lost sight of the ball and it hit him right in the head.

Bill Starr brought in John Ritchey [who broke the PCL color barrier] and some of the other early black players. It was hard to adjust to it right away. The same situation occurred when Rickey brought Robinson in. People like Minoso, Simpson, and Easter helped speed the acceptance of black players—no doubt about it. You know, in one period you had to be twice as good; they were handicapped to start with...and now it's accepted without any problem. They're part of baseball and have played a big part, I'll tell you that.

The [PCL champion] 1954 Padres? You know, I don't get asked these questions very often. See, I've been in the game, altogether, about seventy years. We go back so many times, and there's a million people who ask me...and the most they ask me about is the Babe, of course. Any time I have an interview they say, "I want to ask you about the Babe," and I say, "Here we go again." But it's all right, it was fun. I'm happy that they're satisfied to ask. Now in '54, I was a coach and Lefty O'Doul was the manager. He had been in San Francisco and was a great hitter, you know. Right up until his late years, he used to hit in batting practice to kind of show the boys how it should be done.

You know, I miss the Coast League. I started here, I was a coach and player for years. The Coast League, in the period when I played there, when they had DiMaggio, Williams, and Oscar Eckhardt and those fellows, it was the finest minor league in the country. Very close to the major leagues. The only thing missing was the major leagues had a good pitcher out there every day when we had two and possibly three pitchers. By 1950 the ballparks were different. Portland, Seattle, most of the clubs had changed their ballparks, improved their parks. It was a good league, an eight-club league, you know. And now, of course, it's a different sort of league. It's hard for me to say whether the class of baseball is better. The major leagues are taking all the top players in the Coast League. When I played, the major leagues had sixteen ball clubs—I think we have twenty-six or twenty-seven now. So they're taking the cream of the crop from whatever other leagues. There were a lot of ballplayers—Smead Jolley, Buzz Arlett—who made a career in the PCL. By 1950, it was more of a farm system.

I was sorry to see Lane Field go. It was like old home week all the time. Of course, we later went to the one in Mission Valley [Westgate], and that was one of the finest little ballparks I ever played in. Lane Field was right near the railroad tracks, near the ocean. There were a lot of Navy ships and many sailors used to attend the games. It was only a stone's throw from the ocean. The fans were real close. When we won the pennant, I never saw such enthusiasm and excitement in my whole life. That was in 1937. Bill Lane owned the ballclub, an old miner, a gruff sort of fellow but very kindhearted…Bill Starr bought it from him.

Westgate was a pretty little park. The surroundings were nice, lots of flowers and a nice green hill there back of the yard. You'd see people driving in on the freeway, and everybody seemed to know one another. Of course, it was a lot smaller then than it is now. San Diego was a little country town, you might say, with the Navy. We drew [almost] 500,000 in the late '40s.

I really love the game—this is my life. I've got a couple of friends now that I wouldn't know what to do without. A fellow by the name of Nolan Ryan, with whom I've become very close, and who named one of his children after me…A fellow named Herb Plews, who lives in Colorado. I look forward to staying in the game until they back the wagon up. That's my life, I've enjoyed it. It's been good to me and I've made, I hope to say, a million friends. Without friends, I think you're lost, I don't think you have anything. To me that's more important than material things. I hear from them quite regularly. Just the other day I got a ball from Nolan, his 5,000th strikeout. He gave me his fifth no-hitter. The good Lord's had his arms around me for many years.

It's a pleasure talking with you. If you're this way, come and see me. I have a den and it brings back memories: from the Babe and from Gehrig, from Nolan Ryan and Reggie Jackson. And of course my great friend Jigger Statz. All the fellows I became very closely attached to. The season will be over in a couple of weeks. Any time you're here during the winter, come on over. So give me a call. The season's over the first of October, unless we get into the World Series. Then you'll have to wait a while.

Rube Parnham

He may have been the game's best pitcher in 1923

Mike Ross

It is strange how these research quests originate. If I had not spotted Bobo Newsom's statistics in *The Baseball Encyclopedia*, followed by an irresistible urge to set out across the U.S. in search of his mystique, I would not have learned why Newsom changed teams sixteen times in twenty years; nor would I have had the opportunity to "discover" Jim "Rube" Parnham. And that would have been a shame.

In 1942 Ruth "Kay" Griffiths, while enjoying a professional singing career in McKeesport/Pittsburgh, was spotted by a fellow musician looking for a singer for his band, which was contracted to play for Franklin Roosevelt at the "President's Ball" in Washington D.C.

After the ball, the band was held over, playing the main ballroom of the lavish Wardman Park Hotel. The 22-year-old Kay was living exotically with her own suite and a commensurate wage. On May 6, 1942, following a one-hit win over the Detroit Tigers, Bobo Newsom, pitching for Clark Griffith in Washington for the second of five occasions, strode into the dining room, sat at ringside, saw Kay Griffiths singing and fell for her. She forgot about her high school sweetheart back in McKeesport, and after a several months' courtship she and Bo married. Newsom died in 1962. Kay later remarried and divorced.

Mike Ross *has been a baseball publisher, editor, columnist, and pioneering TV broadcaster and analyst in the United Kingdom since 1987. He is the chairman of SABR's Bobby Thomson chapter for the United Kingdom and Europe.*

Recently, while visiting her home town of McKeesport for a high school reunion, she made contact with and subsequently married that same lost high-school sweetheart—Rube Parnham's son, Jim Parnham, Jr., himself a pitcher with splendid amateur achievements.

Fifty-two years from the time Kay and Jim had parted, I visited with the reunited pair in Orlando. Jim fetched two scrapbooks. One contained clippings on his own high-school baseball and basketball exploits. The second was full of photos and stories of Jim "Rube" Parnham's career.

Newsom and Parnham had much in common. Both characters at one time or another were talked of as the best pitcher in organized baseball. And both had been thirty-game winners in the minors. But one main difference became evident: Parnham eventually dissipated and wrecked a fabulous career through drink. Newsom, twenty-six years a pro, was a guy who liked to sip the wine, but he never missed a starting assignment.

Parnham took coffee with the Philadelphia Athletics in 1916-17, then became the ace of the Baltimore Orioles, playing on six of owner-manager Jack Dunn's seven consecutive championship teams. He became the International League's paragon in 1923 with a 33-7 record and twenty straight wins. He was the team's best pitcher on a staff that included Lefty Grove.

The facts and statistical details behind the career and greatness of Rube Parnham came to me as a near sensation. That these facts are not common knowledge among baseball-smart fans makes me wonder how such a discourtesy was maintained. Jim proudly points out that his father's winning streak is baseball's longest over a single season. On the final day of the season, with eighteen straight wins, Rube set out to break Rube Marquard's season record of nineteen. He started and won both ends of a doubleheader.

That was effectively his last hurrah. He was suspended for much of the next couple of seasons and eventually retired in 1929. For at least that one year, given the Orioles' near-major league status, he was arguably the best pitcher in baseball.

He hadn't been so bad in previous seasons either. Overall he combined for a 120-48 record despite being suspended for most of 1920 and 1921. Baltimore won five pennants with Rube as their ace. No surprise that Jack Dunn, notoriously tough to separate from his best players (Grove is only the best-known example), refused the $75,000 John McGraw tossed on the table for Parnham's contract. Said Dunn at the time, "I wouldn't sell him for one million dollars."

Rube was not exceptionally fast. He used control, guile, and savvy to fool the batters. "Rube didn't have anything really spectacular," teammate Fritz Maisel recalled. "One of his standby pitches was a low fast one between the belt and the knees. Most batters dribbled that one on the ground. Another was a fast, inside pitch which seemed—so help me—to shoot up as it crossed the plate. Batters popped that one up. His change of pace was what he called his 'nickel curve,' now known as a slider. It started out to cut the plate and slid off by six inches. Usually the batters didn't hit this one at all."

Rube was a drawing card and Dunn was determined to cash in on it. During his twenty-game win streak from July 12 to September 23, Rube often pitched with one, two or three days rest. His official record shows what appears as periods of four or five days' rest, but during those interims Rube pitched exhibitions against the Yankees, Braves, Pirates and Senators. In a twelve-inning contest at Oriole Park in 1923, Rube beat Walter Johnson, 2-1. He would claim that his arm was abused from overwork. The workload may have worn on his arm, but it was the liquor that finally got to him.

To Maisel the 6'4" Rube was a nice guy. "He was big and affable and easy going. In a way he was a boy who just never grew up, but he was a red-hot pitcher when he was with it. Off the diamond Rube was the dumbest. He didn't know the meaning of training rules. Many of us were afraid that Rube would send Dunn to an early grave. There'd come a day for him to pitch and he wouldn't be there. He'd go AWOL and stay away for a few days or a week. Then he'd show up in the dressing room and say he would like very much to pitch some baseball if Dunn could use him."

Fritz Maisel recalled, "Rube was always drawn ahead on his salary. Every season he would end up owing Dunn close to $1,000. When Dunn would send him a contract for another season, he would send it back unsigned with a note pinned to it, 'If we start even, I'll sign.' Dunn would send back the contract with a note, 'O.K. we're even.' Then Rube would sign and send back the contract with another note, 'Please advance me $200.'"

The situation deteriorated rapidly. Rube pitched in only 18 games in 1924 while incurring a total of $1,800 in fines, and was banned from organized ball for the 1925 season.

Following Rube's retirement Jim Jr. found success as a pitcher with the McKeesport High School team. But his father's actions mortified him. "He would come to the games and yell at me, abuse me, telling me what to do. He thought he was doing good but he embarrassed me. The cops had to ban him from coming to my games." Jim gazed sadly at an Orioles team photo from the scrap book and said, "I can tell he's drunk in this picture."

Rube's wife finally left him in 1936. "After that" recalled Jim, "he just bummed around the streets, didn't do any work." The local hero to the end, Rube was taken care of by the community. "The people loved him. He could do anything he wanted."

On July 30, 1959 Rube was elected to the International League Hall of Fame, notified by a letter sent to Wilson, Pennsylvania, enclosing his Lifetime Pass and a photo of his Hall of Fame plaque.

Rube hung on until November, 1963. When he died, such was the love and respect accorded by the community that the undertaker laid him out gratis in a new suit. And the respect from baseball was evident from the attendance of such notables as Stan Musial to witness Rube's final inning.

Batting Champs in the World Series

How have season leaders done in the Fall Classic?

Stan Grosshandler

Phil Cavaretta

John Olerud, Toronto Blue Jay first baseman, had two noteworthy accomplishments in 1993. He became the twenty-sixth player to win a batting championship and play in the World Series the same year, and along with teammates Paul Molitor and Roberto Alomar he became part of the first trio from the same team to finish win, place, and show in a batting race.

After hovering around .400 for most of the season Olerud finished with a .363 mark, followed by Molitor at .332, and Alomar with .326. Unfortunately, John averaged only .235 in the Series. Molitor won the Series MVP award with his sensational hitting.

The twenty-six players who have won the batting crown and participated in the Fall Classic have done it a total of 32 times.

In 1903 Honus Wagner, Pirate shortstop, beat out his manager Fred Clarke by .004 points to win the NL crown. In the first modern World Series Honus flopped to .222 as his team fell to AL champion Boston.

Ty Cobb repeated the Wagner feat in 1907 by beating out fellow outfielder Sam Crawford by .027 points—and then he had a miserable Series as the Tigers lost to the Cubs. The following year ('08) Ty again edged out Sam for the crown. He hit a lusty .368 in the Series, but the Tigers lost again to the great Chicago team.

The 1909 Fall Classic was the first in which both teams had the batting kings. Wagner and Cobb squared off, with the Pirate hitting .333 to the Peach's .231. The Tigers lost their third straight Series.

Two other Pirate bat kings led the Buccaneers into a Series. In 1927 "Big Poison" Paul Waner hit .333 in the Series only to have his team swept by the mighty Yankees, while shortstop Dick Groat in 1960 had an incredible year and then saw his team squeak past the Yanks in one of the most exciting World Series of all time.

Edd Roush, Hall of Fame Cincinnati outfielder, took his batting crown into the ill-famed 1919 Series where he hit .214 as the Reds defeated the crooked Black Sox.

Al Simmons of the mighty Philadelphia Athletics won the AL title in both 1930 and '31. Bucketfoot Al had two great Series, with the A's winning in '30, but losing in '31.

Stan Grosshandler is SABR member No. 50. He lives in Raleigh, North Carolina, where he is on the faculties of the University of North Carolina and North Carolina State.

The 1931 Series was the second time two bat leaders met. Simmons opposed Chick Hafey of the winning Cards. Chick had won one of the tightest batting races ever, with a .3489 to Bill Terry's .3486 and teammate Jim Bottomley's .3482. He hit so poorly (.167) in the Series, though, that Gabby Street benched him for the seventh game. Chick had had contract problems with Branch Rickey in the spring, and the Series was the straw that broke the camel's back. Hafey was soon on the train to Cincinnati.

Two other Cardinals, Stan Musial and Willie McGee, have appeared in two Series after winning the batting title. Musial achieved this feat in both '43 and '46, while McGee did it in '85 and '90, but that 1990 occasion deserves an asterisk. McGee was traded from the NL Cardinals to the AL A's on August 30. At the time he was second in NL hitting to Lenny Dykstra; Lenny's average eventually dropped below Willie's, and McGee was declared the NL bat champ. He is the only player to win a title in one league and play in the World Series for the other.

The lone Chicago Cub to win a batting title and appear in a Series was Phil Cavarretta in 1945, the last time the Cubbies appeared in the fall event. Phil's .423 is the highest average a batting champ has ever posted in the Series.

In 1941 the sensational young Pete Reiser became the first of three Brooklyn Dodgers to come to a Series as batting champ. Reiser, the classic "What Could Have Been But for Injuries" player, hit .200 in the Brooklyn loss to the Yankees. The second Dodger ('49) was Jackie Robinson, one of the most significant historical figures in the history of the game. Carl Furillo (1953) was the third.

Furillo was leading the league in hitting when, on September 6, he charged Giants manager Leo Durocher after he had been hit by a pitch. In the resulting scuffle someone stepped on Carl's hand and broke a finger, benching him for the rest of the season. His average was good enough to keep him ahead of Red Schoendienst by two points.

Though the Yankees have appeared in the World Series many times, on only two occasions have they brought a batting champ with them. In 1939 Joe DiMaggio came to the Series as champ, while in 1956 Mickey Mantle brought a triple crown to the fall event.

The 1954 season saw Giant centerfielder Willie Mays finish .003 points over right fielder Don Mueller. In the Series they faced AL champ Bobby Avila, the Cleveland second baseman. Willie is more remembered for his sensational catch on a Vic Wertz

drive than for anything he did with his bat in this Series, which the Giants swept in one of baseball's biggest upsets. Avila's .133 average is the lowest ever for a batting champ in the World Series.

During the 1960s five batting champs appeared in a World Series. Besides Groat, Tommy Davis of the Dodgers, Twin Tony Oliva, and triple crown winners Frank Robinson of the Orioles and Carl Yastrzemski of the Red Sox performed the feat.

More recent members of the club are George Brett—the only man to lead his league in hitting in three separate decades—Tony Gwynn, Wade Boggs, and Terry Pendleton. In the following chart, I have included an "H" for subsequent induction into the Hall of Fame, and an "MVP" if the player won that award in the season noted.

Year	National League		Season Ave.	WS Ave.
1903	Honus Wagner, Pitt (L)	H	.355	.222
1909	Honus Wagner, Pitt (W)	H	.339	.333
1919	Edd Roush, Cin (W)	H	.321	.214
1927	Paul Waner, Pitt (L)	H	.380	.333
1931	Chick Hafey, St.L (W)	H	.349	.167
1941	Pete Reiser, Brk (L)		.343	.200
1943	Stan Musial, St.L. (L)	H, MVP	.357	.278
1945	Phil Cavarretta, Chi (L)	MVP	.355	.423
1946	Stan Musial, St.L. (W)	H, MVP	.365	.222
1949	Jackie Robinson, Brk (L)	H, MVP	.342	.188
1953	Carl Furillo, Brk (L)		.344	.333
1954	Willie Mays, NY (W)	H, MVP	.345	.286
1960	Dick Groat, Pitt (W)	MVP	.325	.214
1963	Tommy Davis, L.A. (W)		.326	.400
1984	Tony Gwynn, S.D. (L)		.351	.263
1985	Willie McGee, St.L. (L)	MVP	.353	.259
1990	Willie McGee, St.L. (L-Oak)		.335	.200
1991	Terry Pendleton, Atl. (L)	MVP	.319	.367
	American League			
1907	Ty Cobb, Det (L)	H	.350	.200
1908	Ty Cobb, Det (L)	H	.324	.368
1909	Ty Cobb, Det (L)	H	.377	.231
1930	Al Simmons, Phil (W)	H	.381	.364
1931	Al Simmons, Phil (L)	H	.390	.333
1939	Joe DiMaggio, NY (W)	H, MVP	.381	.313
1954	Bobby Avila, Clev (L)		.341	.133
1956	Mickey Mantle, NY (W)	H, MVP	.353	.250
1965	Tony Oliva, Minn. (L)		.321	.192
1966	Frank Robinson, Bal (W)	H, MVP	.316	.286
1967	Carl Yastrzemski, Bos (L)	H, MVP	.326	.400
1980	George Brett, K.C. (L)	MVP	.390	.375
1986	Wade Boggs, Bos. (L)		.357	.290
1993	John Olerud, Tor (W)		.363	.235

The Six Greatest Throwing Outfielders in History!

(Or, who were King, Dode, Ross, Roy, Roberto, and Jesse?)

Cappy Gagnon

Ever since I saw my first baseball game, in the Cathedral on Lansdowne Street, I have admired outfielders with strong throwing arms. Traditionally, the strongest throwers have patrolled right field. The favorites of my youth were Clemente, Jensen, Colavito, Kaline, and Furillo.

Each was a little different. Clemente was the flashiest. Jensen and Kaline had classic form. Furillo had a very strong arm and developed the science of playing the unique caroms off the right field wall in Ebbets Field. But, for my money, Rocky Colavito possessed the most powerful throwing arm. In 5-2/3 major league innings pitched, Herb Score's roommate gave up only one big league hit.

I wanted to quantify the debate about outfield throwing by developing a rating system. The first person I found who produced such a rating was J. C. Kofoed, writing for the April, 1924 issue of *Baseball Magazine*. Kofoed's rating system was based on "assists per hundred games." This is a SABRmetric system, long before Alan Roth, Pete Palmer, and Bill James. I am indebted to Kofoed. I converted it to a percentage of "assists per games played." Thus we have OF A/G.

Project Scoresheet may have some special insight into this question by subjectively rating throws from certain locations to certain bases in an attempt to catch certain runners. A perfect measure would also rate the number of assists as a percentage of "opportunities for assists." Unfortunately, most of us do not have access to this data. I wanted something simpler, using readily available stats.

There has been a lot of debate about whether assists truly measure an outfielder's throwing arm. Some say that the great throwers don't get as many assists as they should because coaches and runners respect them. There is some data to support this. Al Kaline broke into the majors gunning down opposing runners, with totals of 16, 14, 18, 13, and 23. Thereafter, he hit double figures only one other time in his career, compiling such puny totals as 1, 4, 5, and 6. Conversely, some maintain that a lot of poor throwers get assists because of the frequency that their flippers are tested. There is some data to support this. Mickey Rivers had double digits in assists on six occasions, including a league leading 19, in 1980, yet had a very weak arm.

Bill James has written persuasively that both these arguments are fallacious. I strongly agree. The good throwers get their men. The poor ones do not. (There is a famous expression about "the exception that proves the rule." While I have no idea what this means, I will submit Rivers as Exhibit No. 1.) In this research I set out to objectify throwing and put it on a comparative basis. There could be some criticism about extreme ballpark shapes contributing to assist totals, but the fact remains that most of these men subjectively considered to have the best arms generally have high assist totals and the guys with the lame

Cappy Gagnon is a law enforcement and security consultant. In his first game as a Babe Ruth League right fielder in 1958 he threw out a runner at the plate.

arms do not.

Total Baseball is such an awesome lode (and load) of material that it has taken me a year to get to the third edition's page 2324—"Fielding Stats."

Range factor for outfielders is a misleading stat. Putouts plus errors, per game, defines range, or the ability to get to balls. Assists more appropriately rate throwing ability and not range. Mick the Quick had great range, but couldn't throw. Furillo and Colavito (maybe it's an Italian thing) had limited range but great arms.

Two observations leap out of the data. The first is that outfield assist totals form a continuum which starts in the prehistoric era, in right field, and moves through center to left and then down through the modern day in a similar pattern. The best thrower was a right fielder in the 1880's and the worst was a left fielder in the current game.

The second is that left fielders get fewer assists. They have one less throwing option than right fielders—the left fielder does not routinely make the cross-field throw to first. Left fielders are also stationed closer to third base, the key destination for many right field tosses. For these reasons, absent other considerations, managers usually place their stronger armed thrower in right. Maybe it's also because Ruth, Cobb, Williams, and I are all lefthanded hitters.

Changes over time—Assists have declined over time because outfielders have played progressively deeper as every Herbie Plews that comes along is hitting the ball to the warning track. Also in olden times, runners took more chances on the bases because one-run strategies are more important when the long ball is absent.

Because of the dramatic way that this data separates into eras, and with the help of Pete Palmer (not only a superb researcher, he is one of the most genuine and generous members of SABR), I have divided all outfielders into six eras: pre-1900; 1900-1920; 1921-1940; 1941-1960; 1961-1980, and 1981 to the present. Players are assigned to the era where they played the most games and placed in the position where they appeared the most. This provides some distortion, but, if life were fair, Ernie Banks would have played in the World Series in 1969. A minimum of 700 outfield games was required, thus eliminating a few guys with great arms, but limited appearances (e.g. Lou Sockalexis, Bullet Jack Thoney, George Washington...).

The same data that identifies the best also singles

out the worst. Some fans and researchers may be upset with the ranking of their favorite guy, but most choices of the experts have been borne out by the stats. In his *Historical Baseball Abstract*, James has selected the "best outfield arm" and "worst outfield arm" for each decade. Most of his selections are confirmed by this data.

Kicking the can—James is a very disciplined researcher who dislikes what he calls "kick the can" research. This is my favorite kind, since serendipity brings a special pleasure to me. While doing this study, I felt the need to locate a stat that would transcend outfield position and era. Voila! Along came OF A-E. This is sort of like the assists to turnover statistic for basketball. Most outfield errors occur on throws. Most of these throws are the high-risk situations where an outfielder is being challenged and has to cut loose. This is a high-risk, high-gain play. Those Yaz-like outfielders who can charge a ball like an infielder and get off a hard throw are going to pile up assists. They may also hit the runner, have the ball skip into the dugout or over the fielder, see the ball get lost in the tag play, and otherwise acquire in an error. Therefore, if you can peg out a lot of runners while keeping the errors down, you make it in my special mention list.

Only 17 men in baseball history have accumulated 100 assists beyond their total of "turnovers." This is a pretty good list. Most of them did very well on OF A/G, but a few were merely average. Among the "discoveries" were Hall of Famers Crawford, Cobb, and Keeler, plus Cy Williams, a personal favorite of mine. Cy may have preserved his arm strength with a unique versatility. A lefthander all the way in baseball, he became a prominent architect and accomplished artist as a righthander.

Another thing I like about this list is that it identifies players from every era of the game. There are very few statistics that don't merely reflect the type of baseball played during a certain period.

I have added one final bonus list—the fifteen men in baseball history who have played at least 300 games in each patch in the outfield. It seems that these flexible flychasers were average or worse in arm strength, although one of them does hold a career assist record. Stan the Man is the all-time leader in All Star Game assists, with his total of three being equally spaced around the outfield. This list also contains players from every epoch.

The best of all time—Using the OF A/G method, the

top nineteen outfield throwers of all time all played in the nineteenth century. The King was Kelly, with a 38 percent. In more than one out of every three games he played in the garden, King Kelly nailed someone on the bases. Jimmy Ryan, James' choice for the strongest arm of the 1880's, ranked thirteeth, with a 19 percent. Ryan is a defensible choice because of his position in center field and because he maintained his OF A/G for more than twice as many games played than any of the top five finishers on the list.

Other strong throwers were Big Sam Thompson, Big Ed Delahanty, and Little Dummy Hoy. Emmett Seery, ranking fifteenth, was the first left fielder on the list.

The weak arms included the usual suspects: James' choices of Billy Hamilton and Duff Cooley (he even sounds like a poor tosser). As for the Tipster, well, the late Speaker of the House could probably out-throw this guy. Ironically, it was another Speaker who played in Massachusetts who is one of the all-time best.

Nineteenth Century

	Strong Arms					Weak Arms			
King Kelly	Rf	750	285	.380	Tip O'Neill	Lf	1024	81	.079
Orator Shaffer	Rf	837	289	.347	Duff Cooley	Lf	1094	96	.088
Hugh Nicol	Rf	823	226	.274	Tommy Dowd	Rf	960	100	.104
Paul Radford	Rf	902	217	.240	Mike Tiernan	Rf	1474	159	.108
Dick Johnson	Cf	743	172	.231	Billy Hamilton	Cf	1584	182	.115

The Dead Ball Era broke with the pattern. For some reason, most of the big guns were in center field. James chose Gavvy Cravath, Harry Hooper, and Max Carey as the top throwers. The data liked the first two for ninth and fifteenth place. Carey was only twenty-seventh, but should get a bonus for huge game totals and playing a lot in the next era. The data would seem to suggest that James should have given Tris Speaker a mention, particularly since the Grey Eagle soared for nearly 2,700 games, more than the three men ahead of him combined! Here is where there may be a problem with my premise, because Spoke played very shallow and it is hard to determine whether his success was due to his strong arm or his quick feet. James was right on the money with his pick of Oldring as the worst thrower. Do people nick-named "Rube" excel at finesse tasks?

The surprise winner was Dode Birmingham, although his league-leading 33 assists in 1907 showed his arm strength, and Kofoed rated him number one. Birmingham is better known as the boy manager who benched Lajoie and as the man whose basehit and run

beat Walsh in the Addie Joss perfecto. He was serving as an umpire in Jorge Pasqual's Mexican League when he died in 1946. An oddity here is that Dode and Red Murray grew up together in Elmira, New York and both enrolled in the University of Notre Dame in 1905. Murray also finished well, sixteenth overall and the fourth best right fielder, behind James' two top choices and Mike Mitchell, Kofoed's top National Leaguer.

Dead Ball

	Strong Arms					Weak Arms			
D. B'mingh'm	Cf	709	130	.187	Topsy Hartsell	Lf	1312	108	.082
E. Heidrick	Cf	748	133	.177	Rube Oldring	Cf	1130	95	.084
Jimmy Barrett	Cf	855	143	.167	George Stone	Lf	837	76	.091
Tris Speaker	Cf	2698	448	.166	Buck Freeman	Rf	837	76	.091
Tilly Walker	Lf	1348	221	.163	Sherry Magee	Lf	1861	176	.095

The lively ball era continued the pattern of declining assist totals for outfielders. Bob Meusel is James' choice as the best arm, "by a wide margin." The data are not quite so definitive, placing him in twelfth spot, probably because of the uniqueness of Yankee Stadium. Meusel and Ruth swapped outfield positions, with the Babe playing right in the cozy confines of the house he built. Meusel patrolled the spacious left field garden at home and then took his more logical position on the road. Although George Herman must have had a strong arm, he had the tenth lowest OF A/G for right fielders in the lively ball era.

Ross Youngs led the heavers in this era. James' pick, Mel Ott, finished twenty-third overall, as the ninth best right fielder. Bill's choices for weak arms were Glass Arm Eddie Brown and Riggs Stephenson. The data is kinder to Stephenson, but Brown could not hide from the OF A/G. Lefty O'Doul does not fare well for a converted pitcher. As for Fats Fothergill, well, like Oldring and Brown, he was nicknamed out of any chance to be a success in the skillful arts. The poor throwers in this era would still be weak sisters six decades later. This is the first time that really poor fielders got the opportunity to last in the bigs.

Lively Ball

	Strong Arms					Weak Arms			
Ross Youngs	Rf	1199	192	.160	Bob Fothergill	Lf	832	37	.044
Ira Flagstead	Cf	1036	159	.153	Lefty O'Doul	Lf	804	35	.044
Carson Bigbee	Lf	1031	142	.137	Earle Combs	Cf	1387	69	.050
C. Heathcote	Rf	1157	157	.135	Rip Radcliff	Lf	887	45	.051
Jack Tobin	Rf	1491	202	.135	Eddie Brown	Cf	731	38	.052

The next era features Roy Cullenbine as the top

man, with DiMaggio as the second best arm. No, not him. And, not Dom either. It's the Vincemeister who leads the brothers. Dom ranks second, with Joe in fifth. James chose Willard Marshall and Carl Furillo as the best, and both scored well (Furillo was the eleventh best right fielder). My man Jensen came out okay, two spots above Furillo.

Fans of Mickey Mantle will not be happy with his fourth lowest ranking among middle fielders, but perhaps he was saving his arm for his post playing careers as casino handshaker and professional autograph signer. James' choice of Kiner as the worst arm is not contradicted by his .058 score (the same as Mantle's). King Kong Keller apparently threw more like Fay Wray than the Big Ape.

Frank Thomas finished with the best mark by a left fielder (.092).

Wartime

Strong Arms					Weak Arms				
R. Cullenbine	Rf	843	100	.119	Johnny Hopp	Cf	717	24	.033
V. DiMaggio	Cf	1081	125	.116	Rip Repulski	Lf	802	28	.035
W. Marshall	Cf	1145	125	.109	Dale Mitchell	Lf	832	37	.044
D. DiMaggio	Cf	1373	147	.107	Charlie Keller	Lf	1019	46	.045
Ron Northey	Rf	820	81	.099	B. McCosky	Cf	1036	48	.046

The Expansion Era was led by Clemente. Slam dunk. This paper would not be published if it weren't so. Roberto also finished thirteen points ahead of runner-up Ellis Valentine, the second largest margin of any leader, behind King Kelly. Yaz finished a bad call on a tag play behind Valentine's running mate, Warren Cromartie. I was surprised to find the third member of that great outfield, Andre Dawson, ranking far down the list at .068. Callison is no surprise to anyone who ever saw him play, but I must confess astonishment at Le Grand Orange.

Expansion Era

Strong Arms					Weak Arms				
R. Clemente	Rf	2370	266	.112	Mack Jones	Cf	871	27	.031
Ellis Valentine	Rf	856	85	.099	Don Baylor	Lf	822	27	.033
Rusty Staub	Rf	1675	165	.099	Lenny Green	Cf	883	29	.033
J. Callison	Rf	1777	175	.098	R. Office	Cf	771	27	.035
W. Cromartie	Lf	780	74	.095	Tito Francona	Lf	911	34	.037

The worst arms were no surprise. James pegged Baylor and Francona. They did not disappoint. Don may have suffered from having too many muscles;

Francona was doomed by his middle name (Patsy Dougherty fared poorly in his era, too.)

Moving into today's "what's a cutoff man?" era, there are several strong throwers. Barfield had a rifle. He is the only era leader who would have won a previous era, as he scored five points higher than Clemente. Cory Snyder and Glenn Wilson were also obvious choices. Youngblood, who was so versatile that he could play almost any position—even for both teams on the same day—also was a skilled player, but I (and a lot of Red Sox fans) am not able to explain Jim Rice being the fifth best. I could understand Sam Rice (.122), Harry Rice (.125) or Donna Rice, but Jimbo is a puzzler. He must have caught a lot of hard caroms off the wall.

The career totals for the modern alligator arms look like single season marks for most of the stars on these lists. All of the losers played center for significant periods of time. Wilson and Gibson were superb football players and were probably the two fastest men in the game. They may have been better off running in their throws. The other three were considered pretty good glove men, but all once played for the Cubs, so there may be a clue there.

Samuel Gompers Era

Strong Arms					Weak Arms				
Jesse Barfield	Rf	1387	162	.117	Bob Dernier	Cf	794	25	.031
Cory Snyder	Rf	827	88	.106	Kirk Gibson	Lf	1200	38	.032
Glenn Wilson	Rf	1131	109	.096	Mitch Webster	Cf	931	33	.035
J. Youngblood	Rf	745	71	.095	Willie Wilson	Cf	2021	76	.038
Jim Rice	Lf	1543	137	.089	Henry Cotto	Cf	760	32	.042

So, there you have it. Who's missing? Dwight Evans (.073) should have been higher. Willie Mays was a pedestrian .069, same as Musial. Kaline was a point lower. Paul Blair was a .059, so I guessed wrong on him by 40 points. Maris hit the speed limit (.055) which seems low. Overall, though, I still like the results. Oh, Rocco Domenico Colavito finished at .069—in his case, the runners probably held their bases!(Exception that proves the rule Exhibit No. 2.)

I have some friends on the Statistical Analysis Committee who will probably critique my work. A challenge I offer them is to find the best and worst throwing outfields of all time. Speaker, Hooper, and Lewis is not a bad place to start for the best.

Outfielders Who Assisted 100 Times More Than They Erred

(Even though this is a list of fielders, there are a lot of lumbermen listed here.)

1.	Tris Speaker	227	He stands alone. Cobb talent with grace.
2.	Harry Hooper	193	He stood next to Speaker for several years.
3.	Mel Ott	158	Also used his gun at third base.
4.	R. Clemente	126	*Sui generis.*
5.	Sam Crawford	125	Like Speaker, he was overshadowed by Cobb.
6.	Ty Cobb	121	Willie Mays with an attitude.
7.	Willie Keeler	120	Fielding percentage .140 higher than Kelly's.
8.	Johnny Callison	118	Wal-Mart Kaline.
9.	C. Yastrzemski	113	Played shortstop as college frosh.
10.	Sam Thompson	112	Very big man playing the o.f. 100 years ago.
11.	Max Flack	110	Does the name conjure up an athlete?
12.	J. Sheckard	110	Unsung. He and Yaz only left fielders on list.
13.	Paul Waner	109	Didn't play better because he was drunk.
14.	Max Carey	104	Started out as an infielder.
15.	Cy Williams	103	Played end at N. D. the year before Rockne.
16.	Jesse Barfield	100	A bazooka.
17.	John Titus	100	Silent John.

Men Who Played More Than 300 Games in Each Outfield Spot

(ranked according to highest level achieved)

		LF	CF	RF	
1.	Hugh Duffy	574	676	437	Could also hit a little
2.	Felipe Alou	434	484	736	Has the necessities as a manager
3.	Jose Cardenal	427	847	549	Took un-Latin 77 walks in 1975
4.	Gee Walker	742	463	420	Rube, Tilly, Chico, Dixie, Hub, Speed, Fleet
5.	Joe Carter	496	412	443	Dramatic
6.	Ben Chapman	404	583	541	Every position except 1B and C
7.	Russ Snyder	442	424	390	Big guy, no power; opposite of Cardenal
8.	Andy Pafko	362	803	443	Handy guy—played 3B too
9.	Ken Henderson	434	544	360	Good walker
10.	Dusty Baker	1117	490	348	Picked up necessities on Campanis-led Dodgers
11.	Kiki Cuyler	331	700	796	Played semipro baseball with George Gipp
12.	Stan Musial	943	325	750	Donora's second best to Griffey? NOT!
13.	C. Washington	324	320	1101	Free agent joke
14.	Jim Northrup	310	466	708	Moved around to fit Horton, Stanley and Kaline

Ted Williams, Premier Batting Coach

Big improvements for the '68 Senators

Jerry Hannan

During Carl Yastrzemski's early years with the Red Sox, Ted Williams was his special tutor and was credited with much of his improvement (although in later years Yaz would claim he never understood what Ted was talking about). But Williams' greatest coaching achievement was the renovation of the Washington Senators when he took over as manager and hitting instructor.

In 1968 the Senators ended 31 games below .500 during Jim Lemon's term as manager. Lemon, a free-swinging power hitter who led the league in strikeouts three times, was not one to stress pitch selection as a primary goal. In 1969 Williams became manager and placed great emphasis on waiting for the right pitch. In fact, he was obsessed with the thought that hitters should *never* swing at bad pitches.

During spring training Williams emphasized the need for swinging only at pitches in the strike zone and made life miserable for those who violated his precepts. Frank

Ted Williams in the dugout for the Senators.

Howard, one of his reclamation projects, probably had more power than any man in either league, but was always high in strikeouts and low in walks received. Williams vowed to correct this imbalance in Howard and others on the team who had not performed to their potential.

The personnel of the 1969 team was almost the same as in 1968, so we can accurately gauge Williams' effectiveness as a batting instructor. The main difference between the two years was at shortstop where Eddie Brinkman succeeded Ron Hansen, who was traded to the White Sox. Brinkman had been with the Senators for eight years and was known as a fine fielder with a magnificent throwing arm. But his highest average had been .229. In 1968 he had hit only .187 during limited service, being called to active duty with the National Guard during the Washington race riots.

At the other positions the personnel had not changed. With freshman manager Williams the 1969 team played exciting baseball, ending in fourth place after a ten-game winning streak that put them ten games

Patrick Hannan *is a chemist who retired from the Naval Research Laboratory in 1987.*

over .500, a net gain of forty games over the previous year. At the last night game in 1969 there was a standing ovation for Williams from the 17,000 attendees. Attendance overall jumped 68 percent, from 546,661 to 918,106. Washington's run production rose from seventh in a ten-team league to sixth in a twelve-team league. The team batting average improved from a pathetic .224 to a respectable .251. Runs scored increased from a pathetic 524 to 694. Even more noteworthy was the improvement in walks and strikeouts. Williams' insistence on swinging only at good pitches made a difference across the board.

I compared each player's performance for the three years prior to 1969 and the three years following. Del Unser had played only the previous year, and Brant Alyea had only 1-1/2 years of major league experience, but the other players were in the majors for the full six years under study (not necessarily with the Senators). Under Williams' platooning, the right field chores were split between Alyea and Ed Stroud, and the figures shown for them are a composite of their performances. In the accompanying table all performances are related to plate appearances—the sum of at bats and bases on balls.

In almost every case there was a notable improvement, with Bernie Allen, Eddie Brinkman, and Frank Howard the principal beneficiaries. Allen was not one to intimidate opposing pitchers, but his bases on balls average increased by 80 percent and his strikeouts declined by almost 27 percent. The change between 1968 and 1969 was particularly dramatic for Brinkman and Howard. Brinkman's 1968 season, with its .187 batting average and six runs batted in, hardly resembled his .266 average and 43 RBIs in '69. Howard increased his average from .274 to .296, increased his homer output from 44 to 48, walked 48 more times, and struck out 45 fewer times, while driving in 111 runs. In the following year he drove in 126 runs while leading the league in walks with 132.

To be accurate it must be said that two factors were significant in comparisons of '68 and '69. Most important was the lowering of the pitcher's mound to reduce the pitching dominance so apparent in '68 (the year of Denny McLain's 31 wins in the American League and Bob Gibson's 1.12 ERA in the National League). Another item was the addition of two expansion teams to the league. To quantify those effects would be difficult but, regardless, while the league

batting average rose from .230 to .246 the Senators' increase was much greater, from .224 to .251.

Another factor that must be mentioned was the influence of Williams on the whole league. Here was a deity from the past, away from the game since the beginning of the decade, whose effect on his own team was so apparent that he undoubtedly awakened in others an appreciation of waiting for the right pitch.

On the subject of pitch selection it is interesting that Eddie Yost, a member of the Senators for many years previous and referred to as "the walking man", averaged 18.0 bases on balls per 100 at bats. How about Ted Williams, the perfectionist? Over his full career he averaged 20.8 walks per 100 at-bats (Ty Cobb averaged 9.9). Undoubtedly, intentional walks contributed greatly to Williams' impressive average even though Ted was often followed in the order by some real bombers. Regarding strikeouts, he had only 7.3 per 100 at-bats—a 74 percent improvement over Babe Ruth's mark. Ted knew the strike zone!

Players' averages for three years before and after Williams' stint as Manager

Pos/Player		BB/100 PA	SO/100 PA	Avg.
1B Epstein	Before	11.5	20.3	.229
	After	15.7	21.5	.257
	Change	+36.5%	-5.9%	+12.2%
2B Allen	Before	7.1	11.6	.227
	After	12.8	8.5	.248
	Change	+80.3%	+26.7%	+9.3%
SS Brinkman	Before	6.2	16.6	.209
	After	8.2	7.3	.253
	Change	+32.3%	+56.0%	+21.1%
3B McMullen	Before	8.5	13.3	.242
	After	10.3	14.7	.251
	Change	+21.2%	-10.5%	+3.7%
LF Howard	Before	9.4	22.5	.270
	After	15.4	16.9	.286
	Change	+63.8%	+24.9%	+5.9%
CF Unser	Before	6.8	9.7	.230
	After	9.0	9.3	.268
	Change	+32.3%	+4.1%	+16.5%
RF Alyea & Stroud	Before	7.4	17.0	.232
	After	10.4	18.0	.247
	Change	+40.5%	-5.9%	+6.5%
C Casanova	Before	2.9	14.8	.237
	After	4.0	14.2	.216
	Change	+37.9%	+4.0%	-8.9%

The Mysterious Case of Rodney Pedraza

An up-and-down minor league season

Jim Storer

"**B**aseball people," and you know who you are, often warn the rest of us casual fans against the dangers of rushing young pitching prospects to the major leagues. In the context of a barroom baseball argument the mere mention of the name "David Clyde" by the person advancing this argument means that he wins the debate on this issue. Occasionally, the more sophisticated advocate will also remind us that Mike Morgan was brought up to the major leagues at the age of eighteen, and infer that were it not for his debut at such a precocious age, Morgan would have been another Tom Seaver.

This article is not about the merits or demerits of rushing young pitchers to the major leagues, but about the promotion of pitchers within the minor league system. It focuses on one very interesting example: Rodney Pedraza of the Eastern League New Haven Ravens, the Colorado Rockies' AA affiliate.

In 1994, Rod Pedraza was a 24-year old right-handed starting-pitching prospect for the Rockies. In three years of single-A ball, he had achieved a career won-lost record of 27-18. Although yielding well over a hit per inning, his phenomenal strikeout-to-walk numbers (career 253-79) were evidence of a successful control pitcher in the making.

As the Ravens' 1994 inaugural season got underway, so did Pedraza's coming-out party, or so it seemed. Though the Ravens struggled early on,

Pedraza certainly was the early favorite to become the ace of the Ravens' staff, spawning such headlines as "IN ROD WE TRUST." Starting the season 9-0 with a 1.86 ERA, he allowed only seventy-five baserunners in 77-1/3 innings, earning himself a promotion to the Rockies' AAA affiliate in Colorado Springs (Pacific Coast League).

The PCL's reputation for being a hitters' league is well established, and unlike many baseball reputations, is well deserved. This is the league that keeps producing all those Dodger prospects who hit .410 with eighty-seven home runs and never seem to make it in the major leagues. Well, that may be a slight exaggeration, but in 1994, three *teams* in the PCL had batting averages over .300, and five teams had ERA's over 5.00. Only six pitchers who qualified for the ERA title had ERAs under 4.00. Add to this equation the elevation at Colorado Springs, and you can imagine that young Mr. Pedraza's "promotion" to AAA was, for a pitcher, like being sent to Siberia.

Taking nothing away from Pedraza, the results were predictable. The wunderkind who soared through the Eastern League was sacrificed at the altar of the PCL hitters. Contrast the two statistical lines on the next page:

Jim Storer is a graduate of Harvard College and the University of Connecticut School of Law. He is a Sabermetrician and a practicing arttorney in Newtown, Connecticut.

	IP	H	ER	BB	SO	W	L	Pct.	ERA	MBA	K/W	K/9
New Haven	77.33	65	16	10	38	9	0	1.000	1.86	8.73	3.80	4.42
Colorado Springs	33.00	60	34	13	20	1	3	.250	9.27	19.91	1.54	5.45

Ouch! But, considering that the entire Colorado Springs' pitching staff posted an ERA of 5.73 for the season and that Pedraza's performance at Colorado Springs consisted of only seven starts, we should not infer a lack of ability on Pedraza's part. Quite the contrary, this difference probably is due to several factors: First, Colorado Springs and the PCL offer a superior hitting environment. Second, Pedraza was probably pitching a little over his head at New Haven. Third, the Ravens' offense was supporting Pedraza with almost eight runs per game during his first stint at New Haven.

But regardless of the *reasons* for the apparent shellacking that Pedraza absorbed at Colorado Springs, what happened to his performance at New Haven after he was demoted back to AA in July is truly remarkable. The following statistical lines include Pedraza's pitching performance after he returned to AA:

It is particularly instructive to examine the "Game Scores" of Pedraza's starts during these various times of the season. The Game Score is a statistic that I have shamelessly plagiarized from Bill James, which effectively measures the performance of a starting pitcher and ranks it on scale of one to 100, with one being the worst and 100 being the best. An average performance by a starting pitcher will rank somewhere around fifty. A pitcher who consistently posts Game Scores of sixty or better is an effective, "innings eating" starter, who, if not a Cy Young candidate, is a valuable asset to his team. A pitcher who regularly scores forty or lower had better start to seek an alternative career path. In fact, if your game scores consistently score under forty, then you simply won't be given an *opportunity* to pitch regularly.

Pedraza's Game Scores at New Haven averaged 59.3 before he was promoted to Colorado Springs, which is an outstanding average start. (An outing in

	IP	H	ER	BB	SO	W	L	Pct.	ERA	MBA	K/W	K/9
New Haven I	77.33	65	16	10	38	9	0	1.000	1.86	8.73	3.80	4.42
Colorado Springs	33.00	60	34	13	20	1	3	.250	9.27	19.91	1.54	5.45
New Haven II	50.33	64	30	13	20	4	3	.571	5.36	13.77	1.54	3.58
NH TOTAL	127.66	129	46	23	58	13	3	.813	3.24	10.72	2.52	4.09

The pitcher who deceived Eastern League hitters to the tune of that gaudy 9-0 record to start the season was not the same man who ended the season in New Haven. Something happened to Pedraza while he was getting beaten up at Colorado Springs. Maybe his confidence was shattered when, after emerging as the staff ace in New Haven, he got his big break in AAA, only to suffer a very understandable, if not inevitable, decline in his pitching statistics. Additionally, when Pedraza returned to New Haven, he found that his role as staff ace had clearly been usurped by right-hander Juan Acevedo, who was ultimately named Eastern League Pitcher of the Year.

which a starter pitches seven innings, allowing two earned runs on six hits and two walks, while striking out five would result in a Game Score of sixty). To put this in context, in 1987, when Roger Clemens won the Cy Young Award, his average Game Score was 61.3. After getting roughed up in the Mile High ERA state, however, Pedraza's average Game Score upon returning to New Haven was 40.3. (An outing in which a starter pitches 5-2/3 innings, allowing four earned runs on seven hits and one walk, while striking out two would produce a Game Score of forty). In fact, after returning to New Haven, Pedraza pitched three of the worst outings the Ravens had all season long, with Game Scores of sixteen, sixteen, and twenty-one. So it is no exaggeration to say that the type of performance turned in by Pedraza during his first stint at New Haven was Cy Young-caliber, while his return visit to Yale Field was more in the Walt Terrell category.

Potential explanations for Pedraza's relatively poor performance upon his return trip to New Haven abound. In the Connecticut *Post* of July 21, 1994, Pedraza himself stated that, "I think I put a lot more pressure on myself than I should have. I think I pressed a little and got out of what I was trying to do." He obviously was somewhat shaken up after his stint in Colorado Springs and may simply never have gotten back on track mentally at New Haven. Thus the pitcher's own statement and select statistical evidence appear to support those who warn against rushing young pitchers.

So what do we conclude from all this? Not much. This is only one season in the career of one young pitcher. Obviously a much more comprehensive study would need to be undertaken before we could justify *any* generalizations about the care and handling of young pitching talent. The Pedraza example is particularly interesting however, in its demonstration of the extremes of pitching in two radically different environments. Although I am skeptical of Pedraza's potential as a major leaguer because of his high hits allowed numbers and low strikeout totals, he probably would perform reasonably well at a higher level if he were backed up by an above-average defensive team.

To the extent that we can draw any legitimate conclusions from the Pedraza study, the following come to mind:

1. Don't judge the kid too harshly or apply any unjustified labels based on his limited exposure to the nightmarish pitching conditions of the PCL.

2. Maybe there is some validity to the notion that young pitchers should not be rushed from one level to another, at least when it involves thrusting a young pitcher into hostile pitching surroundings. (Remember 1984, when Mets' Manager Davey Johnson made sure to give a kid named Gooden his first major-league start at the pitcher-friendly Astrodome?).

3. The Rockies are blessed with terrific pitching prospects at the AA level. In addition to Pedraza and Pitcher-of-the-Year Acevedo, they had four other legitimate starting pitching prospects at New Haven in 1994: Lloyd Peever, Ivan Arteaga, Roger Bailey, and Phil Schneider. People and institutions often take for granted those resources that they already possess in abundance. Something tells me that the Rockies, on the other hand, are well aware of the gems that sparkle in their minor league system. Their difficult but enjoyable task will be in evaluating this talent as it develops throughout their minor league system and ultimately blossoms at the major league level.

(This article was written at the end of the 1994 season. Since then, Juan Acevedo and Roger Bailey have been promoted to the Rockies. Jorge Brito, one of the Ravens's two regular catchers in 1994, was also promoted to the majors. Rodney Pedraza was injured in spring training, had elbow surgery, and was out of action for the entire 1995 season.—J.S.)

Leading off and playing shortstop…Lou Gehrig?!

In the aftermath of Cal Ripken, Jr.'s breaking of Lou Gehrig's once inviolate record of consecutive games played, it's interesting to recall Gehrig's one career shortstop "appearance" at game number 1,427 of his streak.

On July 14, 1934 at Navin Field in Detroit, Gehrig was listed as the leadoff hitter in the Yankee lineup at the short-stop position rather than his usual fourth spot in the batting order at first base. The Iron Horse, suffering from back problems, stroked a single to right field off Tiger pitcher Vic Sorrell to open the game, but was promptly replaced by pinch runner Red Rolfe, who then took over the shortstop duties in the bottom of the first inning for the Yankees.

The day before, in racking up game number 1,426, Gehrig singled in the top of the first inning, played in the field at first base in the bottom of the inning, but then departed the game in the second inning.

Gehrig was back to full strength on July 15 when he went 4-for-4 and played the full game against the Tigers.

—Charlie Bevis

The California Winter League

A "sure-fire" idea that wasn't

R. Scott Mackey

The idea of a winter baseball league in sunny California seemed an exceptionally good one, a certain winner. This was especially true in 1921, when the Pacific Coast League rode a rising tide of popularity that had not been diminished either by its own 1919 betting scandal or the Black Sox scandal. Regular season ballpark attendance had hit all-time highs and PCL owners were making noises about becoming the nation's third major league. Why not keep baseball enthusiasm going through the winter, making money for the league's sponsors, and building momentum for starting a third major league?

Thus the California Winter League was born.

The league was sponsored by three Pacific Coast League franchise owners—the Vernon Tigers' Ed Maier, the Los Angeles Angels' William Wrigley, and the San Francisco Seals' Alfie Putnam. Their number one priority was to hire marquee names to give the league credibility and to draw fans. Ty Cobb was hired to manage the Seals, Harry Heilmann the San Francisco Missions, George Sisler the Tigers, and Rogers Hornsby the Angels. Reports as early as 1920 that Babe Ruth would manage one of the teams proved inaccurate.

Winter League President Frank Chance wrote the managers letters telling them the league's success depended on them: "The California Winter League is the start of something that may grow into one of the big things in baseball. It is up to the players to make the league go. If the men hustle on the field, there is no doubt the league will be a big success."

Finding the talent to play for future Hall of Famers Cobb, Heilman, Sisler and Hornsby was thought to be no problem. California was home to hundreds of professional baseball players in the off-season. Los Angeles alone had more than a hundred major league players wintering there. Between October and February dozens of semipro teams competed throughout the state, many in leagues sponsored by the Seals, the Angels, and the Oakland Oaks. And barnstorming sideshows with major league stars were huge successes.

The Winter League was to go beyond this by creating a top-flight circuit that featured major leaguers playing in highly competitive games. The concept seemed sound and the sponsors' pockets relatively deep, but from the outset the California Winter League faced an uphill battle for success.

Among the other PCL owners, support was lacking; Oakland Oaks owner Cal Ewing, a nationally known baseball figure, vehemently opposed the new league. Many major league owners shared Ewing's misgivings, fearing that one of their players might be injured. Or worse still in the owners' view, players might earn enough financial freedom from the off-season work to gain leverage in contract negotiations. Many forbade their players from participating in the league, promising to add such stipulations in the 1922 player contracts.

R. Scott Mackey is the author of Barbary Baseball: The Pacific Coast League of the 1920s, *published in 1995 by McFarland.*

The season opens—Nevertheless, the California Winter League launched its maiden season on Saturday, October 8, 1921, one week after the Pacific Coast League's season-ending game. Four teams competed over the next ten weeks: the San Francisco Seals, the San Francisco Missions, the Vernon Tigers, and the Los Angeles Angels. Though they took the names of PCL teams, rosters were mixed and bore little resemblance to their Coast League namesakes. Each team played a sixty-game schedule, using San Francisco's Recreation Park and Washington Park in Los Angeles.

An opening day crowd of approximately 7,000 at Recreation Park witnessed the Seals and Missions tangle. Down in Los Angeles the Tigers and Angels played before a crowd described as even larger. The California Winter League was off and running.

But the excitement didn't last. Fans grew disenchanted because teams featured only a few "name" major leaguers. Rumor had it that each of the four managers was paid more than he earned during the regular major league season. That meant little money left over for additional major league ballplayers. Furthermore, many major league owners held by their vows to bar their players from the league. As a result rosters were filled by Coast Leaguers—the same players fans had watched day-in and day-out for the past six months. Eventual champion Vernon, for example, featured only Sisler and two other major leaguers—Jimmy Austin and Dutch Ruether. Though most of the other Vernon players had once played or would go on to play in the majors, none could be considered a major star: Claude Cooper, Ike Wolfer, Carlisle "Red" Smith, Truck Hannah, Carl Sawyer, Honus Mitze, Walter Christensen, Wheezer Dell, Tom Hughes, Sam Lewis, Pete Schneider, and Jack Knight. To make matters worse, many of these players and those on the Angels came from the Oaks or the Seals, making it difficult for Southern California fans to root for their home teams.

Enthusiasm wanes—"After the first two weeks the curiosity of the fans with regard to Cobb, Sisler, Hornsby and Heilmann as managers and stars seems to have been satisfied," wrote Mert Smith in *The Sporting News*. "The promoters are realizing they must add some further attractions to draw interest."

Pacific Coast League fans already enjoyed the longest season in organized baseball. By November they had seen enough, especially when college football fever raged in both the San Francisco Bay area and the greater Los Angeles area.

Vernon's Ed Maier tried to drum up interest: "Why, the Los Angeles Chamber of Commerce ought to circularize the entire country informing the people that, in addition to shafts of sunlight this winter, it is possible for them to see George Sisler, Rogers Hornsby, Tyrus Cobb and Harry Heilmann and other big league players." Maier's vision was to attract vacationing Midwesterners eager to escape the winter cold back home, but his marketing plan never took off.

Following the first couple of weeks, attendance at ballgames settled in at about 200 to 300 fans for weekday games, and 1,000 to 3,000 for weekend games. The players' apathy grew as well, and a week before the season's end the Missions and Angels dispensed with normal protocol and played a whimsical yet legal game in just twenty-six minutes. The Angels won 6-1.

When the season ended, Vernon took first-place honors with little fanfare. They were followed by the Missions, the Angels, and the Seals. Vernon and the Missions played a best-of-three series for a $3,000 purse, with the Tigers winning.

Maier, Wrigley, and Putnam admitted that they had lost money on the league, but not the $50,000 that had been reported in *The Sporting News*. The financial shortfall and tougher restrictions placed on players by the major league owners doomed the California Winter League to its single season. What had seemed a sure-fire idea ended in failure.

Baseball's Longest Home Run (Nearly Five Minutes)

While much has been written about "tape measure" home runs, the longest home run in major league history was hit by Zack Wheat and had to be measured on a clock. On August 5, 1927, it took him nearly five minutes to round the bases after hitting a ball over the right field fence at Ebbets Field. Charley horses in both legs forced him to take a seat on second base. Finally, as Rabbit Maranville started out of the dugout to pinch run, old Zack struggled to his feet and limped the rest of the way home. It was his final round-tripper in Brooklyn.

—David McDonald

The Walk-A-Game Club

An exclusive group

Lary Bump

For the two-thirds of a season the major leagues played in 1994, Frank Thomas had a phenomenal number of walks. In 113 games played, he drew 109 bases on balls. Thomas was on a pace for more than 150 walks—a figure achieved by only Babe Ruth, Ted Williams and Eddie Yost in major league history.

However, even in a shortened season, Thomas fell short of becoming the ninth player in history and sixth in this century to walk more than 100 times and average more than one walk per game. He did exceed that rate as a Southern Leaguer at Birmingham (1990, 112 bases on balls in 109 games), and is likely to do it some day as a major leaguer.

The list of twentieth-century walk-a-game players has only one name that might not be familiar to today's casual fan: former Philadelphia A's player and manager Eddie Joost. It does not include well-known watchful waiters such as Max "Camera Eye" Bishop and Eddie "The Walking Man" Yost, who came within one low and outside pitch each of earning admission. Bishop walked 128 times in 129 games in 1929, and another 128 in 130 games the next season. Yost walked 151 times in 1956, but in 152 games.

Neither National League season record holder averaged one walk per game. Eddie Stanky played in 153 games when he walked 148 times in 1945, and Jim Wynn barely missed with 148 bases on balls in 149 games in 1969. Thus Jack Clark is the only twen-tieth-century National Leaguer with more than one walk per game.

The ability to draw walks is sometimes considered an "old player's" skill, but only three of the eight players listed were 30 or older when they had their first walk-a-game season. Williams, the all-time champ in this category, was a mere 22 the first time he achieved the feat. The complete list:

	G	BB	Yr	Team	Age
Yank Robinson	98	101	1890	Pittsburgh PL	30
Jack Crooks	128	136	1892	St. Louis NL	25
John McGraw	117	124	1899	Baltimore NL	26
Babe Ruth	142	148	1920	New York AL	25
Babe Ruth	152	170	1923	New York AL	28
Ted Williams	143	145	1941	Boston AL	22
Ted Williams	150	156	1946	Boston AL	27
Ted Williams	156	162	1947	Boston AL	28
Ted Williams	155	162	1949	Boston AL	30
Eddie Joost	144	149	1949	Philadelphia AL	33
Ted Williams	117	136	1954	Boston AL	35
Mickey Mantle	144	146	1957	New York AL	25
Jack Clark	131	136	1987	St. Louis NL	31

(ages as of July 1 for each season)

Here's a brief rundown on the one-per players:

William "Yank" Robinson was a walking man at a time when the season record for bases on balls was falling nearly every year. George Gore of the 1886 Chicago White Stockings was the first player to draw

---

Lary Bump is a freelance writer and editor from Rochester, New York. On his first trip to Fenway Park, he saw Ted Williams and Eddie Joost play as teammates.

Yank Robinson

the first player to hit four homers in a minor league game, with Omaha in 1889. That feat helped him earn a promotion to Columbus that September. Even so, he usually led off for the Browns. He hit 21 homers in his major league career. His high-water mark of seven in 1892 was second-best on his team behind Perry Werden's eight.

In Crooks' record-setting 1892 season he was one of the Browns' five captains, acting as the on-field leader of the club and compiling a 27-33 record with a team that finished 56-94. Crooks never again held such a position, and he played his last game in 1898. Like Robinson, Crooks met a tragic end, dying in an insane asylum in 1918.

John McGraw's inclusion on this list should come as no surprise. For one thing, The Little Napoleon stood just 5' 7". And even as a player, he was known as one who would scrap and push any advantage he could get. With Ned Hanlon's boisterous Baltimore Orioles, McGraw first walked 100 times (actually 101) as the regular shortstop in 1893. After moving to third base,

100 free passes in a season (102). The next year Paul Radford of New York's American Association club broke that record with 106. It was Robinson's turn the next two years, when he walked 116 and 118 times for St. Louis of the Association. Despite his walk-per-game pace in 1890, he lost his record that year to Bill Joyce of the Brooklyn Players' League club, who drew 123 bases on balls. That record lasted two years, until Crooks broke it.

The 5' 6-1/2" Robinson played every position except center field during his career, but mostly second base. He led the Union Association in walks with the modest total of 37 in 1884. He exceeded 100 only in that three-year stretch from 1888 to 1890. He played for teams in six cities and four leagues in ten seasons, with his career ending in 1892. By the next spring, a report in the *Sporting Life* said the heavy drinker was dying of "quick consumption," and he passed away in August 1894, a month short of age 35.

Jack Crooks, also primarily a second baseman, played only eight years. His first of three consecutive 100-walk seasons was in 1891, when he took his base 103 times for Columbus of the American Association. With St. Louis the next two years, he led the National League with 136 and 121 (in 128 games). He was known as "Home Run" Crooks because he was

Jack Crooks

he led the National League with 112 free passes in 1898. The next season Hanlon left for Brooklyn and McGraw became the player-manager. He joined the walk-a-game club in his final season as a regular player.

McGraw is among the four walk-a-game players who also managed. However, the list of the majors' year-by-year walks leaders is littered with players who became managers, with varying degrees of success. In addition to McGraw, Joost, Williams, and possibly Crooks, other future managers with high walks totals included Stanky, Cap Anson, Johnny Evers, Donie Bush, Miller Huggins, Eddie Collins, Burt Shotton, Gavvy Cravath, Ty Cobb, Mel Ott, Johnny Pesky, Gil Hodges, Eddie Mathews, Frank Howard, Toby Harrah, Gene Tenace and, currently, Mike Hargrove.

Only a few of those players drew walks because they were major threats at the plate. Thus, if we're looking for tomorrow's managers, we might want to focus on those who have developed the skill of working pitchers for walks as a way to remain regulars. Tony Phillips and Brett Butler leap immediately to mind.

Babe Ruth is the walkingest player in history. Crooks' season record lasted nineteen years, until Jimmy Sheckard drew 147 walks in 156 games for Chicago in the National League in 1911. Nine seasons after that, Ruth broke the season walks record, as well as his own year-old home run mark. Three years later, he achieved a walks total that only Williams has remotely approached.

Ruth had gigantic walks totals in the early '20s because he wasn't protected in the lineup the way he would be after Lou Gehrig arrived in 1925. No other Yankee had more than 11 home runs in either 1920 or 1923. With Gehrig following Ruth in the lineup, pitchers couldn't be quite so fine with the Babe. Still, Ruth had 100 or more walks a record thirteen times, and led the AL in eleven seasons.

Ted Williams—listed at 6' 3", an inch taller than the Bambino—ranks second to Ruth in career walks, in 100-walk seasons (eleven) and in years leading the league (eight). Williams also has five of the thirteen walk-per-game seasons of all time. He twice more

Eddie Joost

Transcendental Graphics

came within five walks of reaching one per game. His batting eye is legendary. Even as a 20-year-old rookie, he exceeded 100 walks (107), and he never again struck out as many times as the 64 Ks he chalked up in 1939.

Eddie Joost's lifetime batting average (.239) was more than 100 points lower than Williams'. But the Splendid Splinter's 1955 Red Sox teammate survived seventeen seasons, mostly at shortstop, largely because he could draw a walk. At 6' 0", Joost was the tallest of the walk-a-game players who had to work for their walks. He reached triple figures six consecutive years, 1947 to 1952. His high-water mark came in 1949, the only season in history with two walk-a-game players. It was the golden age of the base on balls. Ferris Fain finished third to Williams and Joost, with 136 walks in 150 games. Overall, walks increased 395 over the 1948 American League. The eight AL clubs averaged 703 walks each in a 154-game season.

Mickey Mantle and the Yankees were in their prime in 1957. The 25-year-old, 5' 11-1/2" Mantle was coming off a Triple Crown season, the first of two years in which he exceeded 50 home runs. He also walked more than 100 times each year from 1954 to 1958. It wasn't surprising that American League pitchers would walk the Mick more than once per game during a season in which he batted .365.

Mantle came close again in 1962, when he walked 122 times in 123 games. He exceeded 100 walks ten times in his eighteen major league seasons. In each of his last two years, 1967 and 1968, when he batted .245 and .237, he still walked more than 100 times.

Jack Clark was the Cardinals' offense in 1987, the first of the first baseman's four consecutive 100-walk seasons. That year the 6' 2" Clark hit 35 of the team's major league-low 94 home runs. Regardless, the team of speedy singles hitters won the National League pennant. But when Clark went down with a sprained ankle and was able to bat only once in the post-season, St. Louis lost a seven-game World Series to the Twins, possibly the least likely world champions in history. And a team led in walks by Kent Hrbek's 84.

Major League Umpires

What makes a rookie a rookie?

Ted Di Tullio

I have been a baseball fan since the mid '30s and became a complete fanatic in 1941 when Joe DiMaggio had his 56-game hitting streak and Ted Williams hit .406, the last player to do so until now. (Notice I have the first name of one and the near same spelling of the other).

Some 40 years ago, I started compiling baseball stats for batters, pitchers, teams, managers, coaches, and umpires. My primary umpire stat was and still is fifteen years as an umpire. As I went along, I noticed that most if not all umpires had come up in the September before their first full season. These appearances, unlike those of players who come up for a late-season cup of coffee, were omitted from their records.

Jocko Conlan is an extreme example of this. He umpired one game in 1935 during an emergency in the American League. His National League career began in 1941 and lasted until 1965 He is credited with a 25-year career, but he actually appeared in a 26th season. (Charlie Berry went the other way. He umped in the American League from 1942 through 1962, then appeared on opening day, 1970, to fill in during the umpire's strike. His record should show 22 yeas, not 21.)

I believe that umpires, like players, should be given credit for a season even when they appear in only a single game. I seem, however, to be in the minority. At the 1994 SABR convention, the Umpires and Rules Committee decided that these late-season umpires should *not* be considered major leaguers. Both leagues also refuse to acknowledge these umpires as official major league umpires, because they had not signed major league contracts. Since 1980, virtually all umpires have come up for a September trial in the year before they signed contracts.

Continuing to swim upstream, I provide on the next page a list active or recently retired umpires and what I believe was their "rookie" year (there are a few I can't yet pin down).

Ted Di Tullio *is the only fur designer in SABR.*

Umpires' Rookie Seasons

1.	Williams, Billy (retired)	1961, '62, or '63 (missing data)		46.	Bonin	1986
2.	Wendelstedt	1966		47.	McClelland	1986
3.	Barnett	1967		48.	Scott	1986
4.	Denkinger	1968		49.	Tschida	1986
5.	McCoy	1970		50.	Welke	1986
6.	Phillips	1970		51.	Poncino	1985
7.	Evans	1971		52.	Hirschbeck, M.	1989
8.	Froemming	1971		53.	Hohn	1989 (missing data)
9.	McSherry	1971				
10.	Pulli	1972		54.	Joyce	1989 (missing data)
11.	Brinkman	1973				
12.	Runge, Paul	1973		55.	Layne	1989 (missing data)
13.	Tata	1972 (missing data)		56.	Darling	1989
				57.	Reliford	1989
14.	McKean	1974		58.	Barnes	1990
15.	Ford	1975		59.	Cederstrom	1990
16.	Garcia	1975		60.	Craft	1990
17.	Quick	1974		61.	Hickox	1990
18.	Clark	1976		62.	Meriwether	1990
19.	Crawford, Garry	1976		63.	Rapuano	1990
20.	Kosc	1976		64.	Wickham	1990
21.	Merrill	1976		65.	Winters	1990
22.	Montague	1976		66.	Cuzzi	1991
23.	West	1976		67.	Evans, Jeff	1991 (only year)
24.	Gregg	1976		68.	Gisondi	1991 (only year)
25.	Hendry	1977		69.	Gorman, Brian	1991
26.	Kaiser	1977		70.	Harvey, Randy	1991 (only year)
27.	Reilly	1977		71.	Hernandez, A.	1991
28.	Voltaggio	1977		72.	Grinder	1983 (only year)
29.	Williams, Charlie	1977		73.	Kellogg	1991
30.	Cousins	1979		74.	Harris	1979
31.	Johnson, Mark	1979		75.	Potter	1991
32.	Morrison	1979		76.	Vanover	1991
33.	Reed	1979		77.	O'Nora	1992
34.	Roe	1979		78.	Bell	1992
35.	Palermo	1976		79.	Barron	1992
36.	Shulock	1979		80.	Long	1992
37.	Coble	1980		81.	Culbreth	1992
38.	Davidson	1980		82.	Henrichs	1993
39.	Marsh	1980		83.	Danley	1992
40.	Rippley	1980		84.	Meals	1992
41.	Davis, Gerry	1980 or '81 (missing data)		85.	Rieker	1992
				86.	Winans	1994
42.	Demuth	1983		87.	Barrett	1994
43.	Hallion	1981-'86 (missing data)		88.	Bean	1994
				89.	Larson	1994
44.	Hirschbeck, J.	1983		90.	Gibbons	1994
45.	Young, Larry	1984-'86 (missing data)				

Standardized Range Factor

A new method for measuring defense

Scott McClellan and Mark Schreiber

Paul Dickson's *Baseball Dictionary* refers to range factor as "a defensive statistic combining an individual's putouts and assists. It has been advanced by baseball statistician Bill James as a more accurate method of rating defensive ability than the standard fielding average. Many consider this to be James's most important contribution to baseball research."

Range factor ranks as a great contribution to baseball research because it measures fielders' ability to perform the function of defense, registering outs. Where fielding percentage basically considers only a player's competence at making the play when he has a chance, range factor measures the number of successful chances that fielders create with their effort and ability. But, while range factor is certainly a superior measure to fielding percentage, it fails to consider factors outside of a fielder's effort and ability which affect his chances.

The characteristics and tendencies of pitchers, and pitching staffs, have important effects upon fielders' chances which must be considered if fielding statistics are to be understood accurately. If a pitcher allows more ground balls than most, this will result in more chances for infielders, and fewer for outfielders. For a "fly ball pitcher," the opposite would be true. Pitchers with relatively high strikeout totals will reduce the number of chances for all the fielders on their team compared to teams with lower strikeout totals. The standardized range factor formula adjusts for these effects by compensating for the characteristics of the pitching staff of the team for which the fielder plays in relation to the league. The resulting "standardized" range factors measure fielding statistics by a neutral standard, factoring out the influence of the pitchers, as shown in the formula:

$$\text{Range factor} \cdot \frac{\text{Strikeouts (league)}}{\text{Total Batting Outs* (league)}} \times \frac{\text{Average K of league staff}^\dagger}{\text{K (fielder's team's staff)}} + y$$

For infielders, y=

$$1 - \frac{\text{Strikeouts (league)}}{\text{Total Batting Outs* (league)}} \times \frac{\text{Groundout/Flyout**ratio (team)}}{\text{Groundout/Flyout**ratio (league)}}$$

For outfielders, y=

$$1 - \frac{\text{Strikeouts (league)}}{\text{Total Batting Outs*(league)}} \times \frac{\text{Flyout/Groundout**ratio (team)}}{\text{Flyout/Groundout**ratio (league)}}$$

†Strikeouts for the league in question divided by the number of teams in that league.

* AB-H for the league in question.

** Ground ball/Fly ball and Fly ball/Ground ball ratios for team and league pitchers may be used in place of these, and were in fact used for this article.

The first part of the formula measures the relative impact of strikeouts in a league on defensive chances, and whether a team's pitching staff increases or decreases the number of chances for its fielders relative to the league in this regard. The respective "y" factors

---

Scott McClellan is a recent college graduate who would like to work in baseball in some capacity. Mark Schreiber is a college student majoring in electrical engineering.

measure the impact of a pitching staff's Ground ball or Fly ball tendencies, again relative to the league, on the number of chances for infielders and outfielders. The impact of pitching staffs on fielders can be seen by a demonstration of the formula using the range factors of Ryne Sandberg of the Cubs and Paul O'Neill of the Yankees. Both teams had high Ground ball/Fly ball ratios.

Sandberg's range factor for 1993 was 5.06, according to STATS 1994 *Major League Handbook*, so

$$\frac{5.06}{\left(0.234 \times \dfrac{954.1}{905}\right) + \left(0.776 \times \dfrac{1.53}{1.35}\right)} = 4.54$$

The data in the denominator of the formula comes from STATS 1994 *Player Profiles*. As the formula shows, the Cubs struck out 905 batters, fewer than the league average, which was 954.14. Cubs pitchers compiled a Ground ball/Fly ball ratio of 1.53, second in the National League only to the Dodgers 1.54, and greater than the league ratio of 1.35. These two factors combined to inflate Sandberg's chances. The formula estimates that Sandberg's range factor would have been 4.54 in a neutral setting. (0.234 is 13,358, the NL strikeout total, divided by AB-H for the league, 77489-20427. 0.776, of course, is 1-0.234.)

The formula would work similarly for O'Neill, only using the data for his respective team and league, and employing the "y" factor for outfielders:

$$\frac{2.00}{\left(0.228 \times \dfrac{925.14}{899}\right) + \left(0.772 \times \dfrac{0.641}{0.8}\right)} = 2.34$$

0.8 is the Fly ball/Ground ball ratio for the American League, the reciprocal of the league's Ground ball/Fly ball ratio. 0.641 is the Fly ball/Ground ball ratio for the Yankees. 925.14 is the average strikeout total for an American League team in 1993, 899 is the Yankees' staff's total for that year, 0.228 is 12, 952 strikeouts divided by AB-H for the 1993 AL, which is 77506-20661, and 0.772 is 1-0.228. Thus O'Neill's range factor of 2.00, one of the lowest in the league due to a pitching staff which allowed many ground balls, is "standardized" at 2.34, second best among the regular American League right fielders listed in the tables accompanying this article, which list the 1993 leaders by position in terms of standardized range factor.

Standardized range factor cannot address all of the external factors that influence a fielder's defensive statistics, but the formula can measure the most obvious of these factors, and can further understanding of fielders' defensive ability.

Second Basemen

AL	Team	Range	Standardized	NL	Team	Range	Standardized
Carlos Baerga	Cle	5.46	5.69	Robby Thompson	SF	5.41	5.92
Brent Gates	Oak	5.29	5.62	Bret Barberie	Fla	5.34	5.52
Lou Whitaker	Det	5.79	5.51	Mark Lemke	Atl	5.34	5.32
Chuck Knoblauch	Min	5.12	5.35	Mickey Morandini	Phi	4.80	5.28
Torey Lovullo	Cal	5.04	5.28	Luis Alicea	StL	5.56	5.22
Harold Reynolds	Bal	5.15	5.21	Carlos Garcia	Pit	4.84	5.16
Joey Cora	Chi	4.87	5.15	Eric Young	Col	5.27	5.16
Scott Fletcher	Bos	5.38	5.09	Craig Biggio	Hou	5.02	5.14
Doug Strange	Tex	5.17	5.08	Jeff Gardner	SD	5.03	5.12
Bill Spiers	Mil	4.88	5.03	Jody Reed	LA	5.47	5.03
Roberto Alomar	Tor	4.77	4.97	Delino DeShields	Mon	5.24	4.86
Rich Amaral	Sea	5.20	4.97	Ryne Sandberg	ChN	5.06	4.54
Jose Lind	KC	4.92	4.93	Jeff Kent	NYN	4.72	4.42
Pat Kelly	NY	5.26	4.39				
Bret Boone	Sea	4.57	4.36				

Third Basemen

AL	Team	Range	Standardized	NL	Team	Range	Standardized
Rene Gonzales	Cal	3.03	3.18	Jeff King	Pit	3.02	3.22
B. J. Surhoff	Mil	2.82	2.91	Matt D. Williams	SF	2.69	2.94
Robin Ventura	ChA	2.56	2.71	Terry Pendleton	Atl	2.89	2.88
Mike Blowers	Sea	2.80	2.67	Ken Caminiti	Hou	2.80	2.86
Craig Paquette	Oak	2.49	2.64	Mike Lansing	Mon	3.09	2.86
Ed Sprague	Tor	2.50	2.61	Sean Berry	Mon	2.87	2.66
Wade Boggs	NYA	3.09	2.58	Charlie Hayes	Col	2.86	2.66
Dean Palmer	Tex	2.44	2.40	Tim Wallach	LA	2.81	2.58
Scott Cooper	Bos	2.46	2.33	Todd Zeile	StL	2.71	2.54
				Chris Sabo	Cin	2.28	2.50
				Dave Hollins	Phi	2.13	2.34
				Steve Buechele	ChN	2.59	2.32

Shortstops

AL	Team	Range	Standardized	NL	Team	Range	Standardized
Pat Meares	Min	4.77	4.99	Jay Bell	Pit	5.23	5.58
Gary DiSarcina	Cal	4.68	4.90	Ozzie Smith	StL	5.54	5.20
Greg Gagne	KC	4.84	4.85	Royce Clayton	SF	4.75	5.20
Mike Bordick	Oak	4.56	4.84	Barry Larkin	Cin	4.68	5.14
Omar Vizquel	Sea	4.89	4.67	Rey Sanchez	ChN	5.61	5.03
John Valentin	Bos	4.92	4.65	Kevin Stocker	Phi	4.49	4.94
Ozzie Guillen	ChA	4.38	4.63	Ricky Gutierrez	SD	4.56	4.64
Cal Ripken	Bal	4.55	4.61	Jose Vizcaino	ChN	5.16	4.63
Pat Listach	Mil	4.47	4.61	Vinny Castilla	Col	4.69	4.59
Travis Fryman	Det	4.84	4.60	Walt Weiss	Fla	4.34	4.48
Felix Fermin	Cle	4.21	4.38	Jeff Blauser	Atl	4.18	4.16
Spike Owen	NYA	4.81	4.01	Jose Offerman	LA	4.52	4.15
				Andujar Cedeno	Hou	3.87	3.96
				Wil Cordero	Mon	4.27	3.96

Left Fielders

AL	Team	Range	Standardized	NL	Team	Range	Standardized
Mike Greenwell	Bos	2.15	2.35	Eric Davis	LA	2.36	2.66
Juan Gonzalez	Tex	2.21	2.28	Luis Gonzalez	Hou	2.58	2.64
Albert Belle	Cle	2.41	2.27	Phil Plantier	SD	2.33	2.29
Kevin McReynolds	KC	2.16	2.22	Jerald Clark	Col	2.28	2.28
Dion James	NYA	1.89	2.22	Moises Alou	Mon	2.08	2.22
Mike Felder	Sea	1.95	2.18	Derrick May	ChN	2.04	2.21
Greg Vaughn	Mil	2.38	2.16	Vince Coleman	NYN	2.02	2.06
Luis Polonia	Cal	2.26	2.06	Pete Incaviglia	Phi	2.02	1.96
Brady Anderson	Bal	2.10	2.05	Milt Thompson	Phi	2.01	1.96
Tim Raines	ChA	2.03	1.96	Barry Bonds	SF	2.08	1.92
				Kevin Mitchell	Cin	2.07	1.92
				Jeff Conine	Fla	1.95	1.88
				Ron Gant	Atl	1.79	1.86
				Bernard Gilkey	StL	1.91	1.83

Center Fielders

AL	Team	Range	Standardized	NL	Team	Range	Standardized
Bernie Williams	NYA	2.73	3.21	Ryan Thompson	NYN	3.19	3.25
Milt Cuyler	Det	3.11	3.10	Marquis Grissom	Mon	2.81	2.99
Lance Johnson	ChA	3.14	3.04	Chuck Carr	Fla	3.05	2.94
Devon White	Tor	2.88	2.89	Otis Nixon	Atl	2.80	2.92
Kenny Lofton	Cle	2.99	2.81	Lenny Dykstra	Phi	2.98	2.90
Chad Curtis	Cal	3.01	2.74	Derek Bell	SD	2.87	2.82
Brian McRae	KC	2.66	2.73	Brett Butler	LA	2.44	2.75
Ken Griffey, Jr.	Sea	2.41	2.70	Ray Lankford	StL	2.83	2.71
David Hulse	Tex	2.61	2.69	Alex Cole	Col	2.68	2.68
Robin Yount	Mil	2.87	2.61	Darren Lewis	SF	2.90	2.68
Billy Hatcher	Bos	2.34	2.55	Steve Finley	Hou	2.61	2.67
Mike Devereaux	Bal	2.53	2.47	Bobby Kelly	Cin	2.71	2.51
Kirby Puckett	Min	2.50	2.36	Andy Van Slyke	Pit	2.75	2.40

Right Fielders

AL	Team	Range	Standardized	NL	Team	Range	Standardized
Mark McLemore	Bal	2.49	2.43	Sammy Sosa	ChN	2.28	2.47
Paul O'Neill	NYA	2.00	2.34	Jim Eisenreich	Phi	2.47	2.40
Wayne Kirby	Cle	2.49	2.34	Larry Walker	Mon	2.25	2.40
Tim Salmon	Cal	2.55	2.33	Dante Bichette	Col	2.39	2.39
Ellis Burks	ChA	2.31	2.23	Orlando Merced	Pit	2.60	2.27
Ruben Sierra	Oak	2.35	2.14	Dave Justice	Atl	2.15	2.24
Jay Buhner	Sea	1.90	2.13	Reggie Sanders	Cin	2.37	2.20
Joe Carter	Tor	2.07	2.08	Tony Gwynn	SD	2.22	2.18
Felix Jose	KC	1.95	2.00	Mark Whiten	StL	2.23	2.14
				Eric Anthony	Hou	1.96	2.00
				Bobby Bonilla	NYN	1.96	2.00
				Cory Snyder	LA	1.74	1.96
				Willie McGee	SF	2.02	1.87

GAME 5 Sunday, October 2, 1955

New York   000 100 110 - 3 6 0
Brooklyn   021 010 01x - 5 9 2

NEW YORK (2-2)

7 Howard	k	k	sx	wx	43
8 Noren	6^	7	463p	363p	
5 McDougald	e6	63	w	13	
2 Berra	3-	S	3-	H	
3/9 Collins	w	k	43	k	
3 ERobinson	w	w	k	sx	
r Carroll 8					
9 Bauer 8					
4 Martin	13	s'	e5	543p	
6 Rizzuto	3^				
o Skowron 4	2^f				
6 JColeman 4	9				
o Carey 9	53				
1 Grim	53	6\			
o Cerv 7	H				
1 Turley 7					
o Byrne 9	43				

BROOKLYN (2-2)

4 Gilliam	3-	s+	53	w
6 Reese	wx	53	8	k
8 Snider	f46	H	H	d
2 Campanella	k	8	wx	k
9 Furillo	5\	k	43p	S
3 Hodges	S	k	sx	14b
5 JRobinson	6\	w	643p	s'
7 Amoros	H'	k	k	k
1 Craig	w	14b		
1 Labine 7	k	k		

Pitchers: NEW YORK, Grim L (998x), Turley (xx19). BROOKLYN, Craig W (9991x), Labine S (xxx81).
Left on Base- NY 7, Bkl 7. T- 2:40. A- 36,796.
Ump-Summers, Ballanfant, Honochick, Dascoli, Donatelli, Flaherty.

The Busher from Dubuque

Pants Rowland wore many hats

Joseph P. Murphy, Jr.

The sixth and final game of the 1917 World Series had just ended and John McGraw was beside himself. His New York Giants had just lost their fourth World Series in the past seven years, the last game being highlighted by the memorable and ignominious dash of the Giants' Heinie Zimmerman, as he vainly pursued Eddie Collins across home plate with the game's first run. In his biography of McGraw, Frank Graham stated that as the Giants manager furiously headed for the clubhouse, he met the manager of the victorious Chicago White Sox, who extended his hand and said:

"'Mr. McGraw, I'm glad we won, but I'm sorry you had to be the one to lose.'

And McGraw had snarled:

'Get away from me, you _____ _____ Busher!'"[1]

The "_____ _____ Busher" was Clarence (Pants) Rowland, whose remarkable baseball career spanned seven decades of the twentieth century, but whose name is unknown to the average fan today. Although he never played a major league game, he managed the Chicago White Sox to a World Series championship in 1917. As president of the Pacific Coast League in the 1940s, he pioneered the concept of major league baseball on the West Coast. In the intervening years, he was an owner-manager in the high minors, a productive scout, and an American League umpire. At the age of seventy-five, he became executive vice-president of the Chicago Cubs, serving as owner

Philip K. Wrigley's chief assistant. The consummate achiever, he approached each task with enthusiasm and dedication.

Clarence Rowland was born on February 12, 1879 in the small town of Platteville, Wisconsin, about twenty-five miles northeast of Dubuque, Iowa. His father, who had been an engineer on the Burlington Railroad, moved the family to Dubuque, where he ran a grocery store and bar. Young Rowland's formal education ended after his second year in high school, but at an early age he displayed a sense of initiative which characterized his entire life. When barely in his teens, he was organizing and managing sandlot baseball teams and working as a bellhop at Dubuque's Julian Hotel. In the company of two young ballplaying associates, he journeyed to Chicago during the 1893 World's Fair, and, at the age of fourteen, earned $12.50 a month, plus board and room, as a bellhop in the Windsor-Clifton Hotel in downtown Chicago. He admitted that most of his wages were spent on riding the giant Ferris wheel.

Pants—During his early years as a sandlot ballplayer, Rowland acquired the nickname which, in his own words, "has followed me in the ten different leagues with which I have been associated as manager, scout, umpire, club president, league president and club owner." As the organizer of Dubuque's Ninth Street Blues, he was wearing his dad's blue trousers, folded under the knee and girded by stout twine. While trying to score from first on the team slugger's long

---

Joseph P. Murphy, *a retired judge, spent most of his adolescence (and all of his allowance) in Wrigley Field's bleachers, rooting for the Cubs.*

smash, Clarence stumbled at second base (a rock), tripped at third when the pants leg predictably lengthened, and successfully stumbled home to beat the replay. The umpire, Billy Baumann, said, "Pants, I didn't think you were going to make it!"—and thus was born the distinctive nickname by which Clarence Rowland was known thereafter.[2]

Dubuque had an established baseball history. Long before the National Association of Professional Baseball Leagues was formed in 1902, minor league teams had existed, and one such, the Dubuque Rabbits, featured Charles A. Comiskey and Old Hoss Radbourn, who were teammates in the Northwest League in 1879. Comiskey's ties to Dubuque, including his 1892 marriage to Nan Kelly, of that city, without question contributed to what developed into a close relationship with Pants Rowland, who was instrumental in introducing modern organized baseball to Dubuque.[3]

Beginning a minor league career—In 1903, at age twenty-four, Rowland headed to Chicago for a second time. The Three-I League was reorganizing and Rowland was the self-appointed spokesman for his adopted home town. He brought with him a petition signed by fifty-two of Dubuque's leading citizens. He returned with a franchise in the new league and was promptly appointed as manager. The club finished in seventh place and Pants, to use his own words, "was bounced."[4] There followed a three-year hiatus in his baseball career, but after the 1907 season, in which the Dubuque Dubs fell into the basement, with 22 wins and 109 losses, he was summoned back and led the club to a more respectable fifth-place finish in 1908.[5]

Attracted by a salary of $3,000, Pants went west in 1909 to manage Aberdeen to third place in the Northwestern League. 1910 found him back home in the Midwest. He piloted Jacksonville (IL) in the ill-fated Northern Association, which folded in July despite the talents of such future big leaguers as Casey Stengel, Bobby Veach, Fritz Maisel, and Bill Burwell. Rowland finished out the year as the manager of Winnipeg in the Western Canada League.

Dubuque beckoned him once again, and as owner-manager of the team between 1911 and 1913, he led the Dubs to sixth, fifth, and second-place finishes. He switched to Peoria in the Three-I League in 1914, and turned a last-place club into a contender, winding up in second place, only three games behind Davenport.[6]

Meanwhile, in Chicago, Charles Comiskey was frustrated. After the World Series season in 1906, the White Sox had never finished higher than third, and since Nixey Callahan had become manager in 1912, the club had declined to fourth, then fifth, then sixth place. In the late summer of 1914 the old Roman summoned Rowland to Chicago.

Probably because of his own ties to Dubuque, Comiskey was well aware of Pants Rowland's career in baseball. He knew also that Rowland had recommended both Larry Doyle and Bobby Veach to big league scouts, and when Commy was filling out his roster for an around-the-world tour in 1913 he asked Rowland to suggest a promising pitcher from the Three-I League. Pants gave him the name of a young man named Red Faber, who pitched so well on the tour that he began his Hall of Fame career with the White Sox the following season.

During their visit in Chicago, the two men discussed how to revitalize the Sox's sagging fortunes. Their talk resulted in Chicago's purchase of Eddie Collins from the Philadelphia Athletics on December 8, 1914. Nine days later, Commy startled the baseball world by naming Rowland, then 35 years old, the new manager of the Chicago White Sox.[7]

The busher takes over—He was a virtual unknown. He had never played an inning of major league or minor league baseball. A Class B league had been the highest rung on his managerial ladder. In eight minor league seasons, Rowland-managed teams had never won a pennant. He was perhaps the classic personification of a "busher," and that is how he was regarded by fans and skeptical baseball personnel.

Comiskey was determined to have a winner, and the notoriously tightfisted owner opened his checkbook. He had paid $50,000 to acquire Collins, and in 1915 he purchased Shoeless Joe Jackson for $31,500 and three players. Eddie Murphy came over from the Athletics; $12,000 purchased Oscar Felsch from Milwaukee of the American Association. Lefty Williams and Dave Danforth bolstered the 1916 pitching staff.

Rowland's club played hard-nosed baseball. Rowland's reputation in the minors was that of a scrappy, umpire-baiting leader. One sportswriter even dubbed him the "Muggsy McGraw of the Three-I League."[8] His 1915 White Sox won 93 games and finished in third place. Sportswriters around the league were impressed by the demeanor and the competence of the new manager, and the following year the club finished in second place, losing out in the final days to the Boston Red Sox.

The start of the 1917 season saw two new faces in Chicago's lineup. Chick Gandil was acquired from Cleveland in February to play first base, and young

Swede Risberg took over the shortstop position. Collins, Jackson, Weaver, Felsch, and Schalk rounded out an impressive starting lineup. Paced by Eddie Cicotte's 28 wins and a league-leading 1.53 ERA, the White Sox battled Boston through midseason, then spurted away in August to win the pennant by nine games. In the World Series against the Giants, Red Faber pitched in four of the six games, winning three of them. When the victorious White Sox returned to Chicago they were greeted at the LaSalle Street Station by 5,000 fans, who hoisted Rowland onto their shoulders and carried him into the street, blocking traffic for twenty minutes.[9]

Pants had attained celebrity status. He accompanied his boss to Comiskey's cabin in the Wisconsin woods, he headlined an eight-act vaudeville program at a downtown Chicago theater (delivering a monologue entitled "Right Off the Bat"), and he was even the subject of a ditty by George Moriarty, who had just switched from playing third base to umpiring:

> When Rowland, pert and frisky,
> signed up with Charles Comiskey,
> the wise guys laughed until they had to bawl.
> But he who laughs the greatest
> is he who laughs the latest;
> Now Comiskey laughs the merriest of all.[10]

It had been a great year. The team had won 100 games, a total which no White Sox club has ever equalled. Rowland became the first manager of a World Series winner in this century never to have played in the major leagues.[11]

The Sox slide—However, despite their startling success, the White Sox were not a happy club. Eddie Collins, well-educated and well-paid, was nicknamed "Cocky," and was so disliked by his fellow infielders that they wouldn't throw him the ball during pre-inning warmups. His $15,000 salary exceeded the combined incomes of Gandil, Risberg, and Weaver. Happy Felsch led the team in batting during 1917 and was rewarded with a $3,750 contract. As the 1918 season began, a spirit of dissension and revolt was starting to build.[12]

Moreover, the nation was at war. Baseball had been declared a "nonessential industry," and ballplayers, like everyone else, were subject to Secretary of War Newton Baker's ultimatum to "work or fight." Urban Faber joined the Navy. Joe Jackson, Lefty Williams, and reserve catcher Byrd Lynn went to work in shipyards, enraging Charles Comiskey, who accused them of evading the Army draft. Happy Felsch opted for employment at a Pittsburgh steel plant. In mid-August Risberg, McMullin, and Eddie Collins left to join the service. At one point, Rowland headed East for a road trip with sixteen players. A young man named Dan Cunningham left the team after sitting on the bench during several tough losses. He announced that he intended to become a minister of the gospel, and the language of the dugout was jeopardizing his vocation.[13]

The 1918 season was disastrous. Cicotte led the league with 19 losses. The White Sox finished in sixth place, seventeen games behind the pennant-winning Red Sox. Comiskey concluded that Rowland had lost control of his players, and on December 31 announced that Kid Gleason would replace Pants as manager.

During his four-year tenure with the White Sox, Rowland's teams won 339 games and lost 247, for a percentage of .578. Charles Comiskey was not an easy man to work for. Since the league's founding in 1901, he had employed six different managers. A former star player himself, he expected and demanded instant and continued success. His parsimonious salary schedule guaranteed the unrest and resentment that ultimately produced the Black Sox scandal several years later. Rowland's departure resulted from a combination of factors: the team's internal struggles, the "work or fight" edict which siphoned off so many of the team's mainstays, and the impatience of the club owner. Rowland had, however, come a long way from Peoria.

Back to the bushes—There was much speculation as to Rowland's future. Everyone seemed to concede that he had performed capably as a major league manager. In February, 1919, Rowland, in company with Hugh Brennan, a Chicago businessman and close friend, purchased the Milwaukee Brewers franchise in the American Association for a reported $80,000. The Milwaukee fans were ecstatic. Seven hundred people attended a civic banquet in Rowland's honor. The guest of honor shook hands with all who attended and announced that Big Ed Walsh would join the Brewers' pitching staff.

The Milwaukee club, with Pants at the helm, lost its first five games and never recovered. Walsh turned in his uniform in July, bemoaning the fact that the spitball was prohibited in the Association. The team never rose higher than seventh place in the standing, and finished the season dead last, with a winning percentage of .384. Rowland and Brennan chose to bail out, and sold the franchise (at a profit) to a group of Milwaukee businessmen.[14]

In the 1920s Rowland was on the move. He spent a year as a scout for the Detroit Tigers. When Hughie Jennings resigned as their manager after the 1920 season, Ty Cobb was mentioned as the leading candidate to fill the vacancy. Cobb, still riding high as a Detroit player, indicated no interest in the job. Rowland's name was then put forth, and it appeared that he would be selected. When Cobb, off on a December duck-hunting trip, was told about this proposal, he erupted. In his autobiography, he recalled the scene:

> That was a jolt. I couldn't play under Rowland, nor could anyone who knew the facts. Pants Rowland never had appeared in a game of big-league ball, in fact had been running a short-order grill in a small Illinois town until 1915. He was a typical fan, up until the day Charley Comiskey and Ban Johnson arrived in his town on a hunting trip. Rowland fell into the most fantastic lucky break in the history of managing. Comiskey took a fancy to him and shocked baseball by naming Rowland his new manager. To cap the cockeyed story, the White Sox won a pennant and World Series in Rowland's third year. Posies were tossed at Rowland for that, but everyone around the league knew that Kid Gleason had been the actual tactical genius behind the victory. Big-leaguers called Pants Rowland "The Bush-League Manager." When the White Sox fell to sixth place in 1918, he was released in favor of Gleason.[15]

As we know, Cobb, the passionate perfectionist, was a man of violent dislikes. He doubtless recoiled from the thought of playing every day under a manager who had never played in a major league uniform. However, his characterization of Rowland as just "a typical fan" at the time Comiskey chose him as manager conveniently overlooked a respectable eight-year career as a minor league manager. It is difficult to assess Cobb's comment that "everyone around the league know that Kid Gleason had been the actual tactical genius…." Gleason, whose twenty-year major league career included service as both a pitcher and an infielder, served as a White Sox coach between 1912 and 1917. In the first three years, under manager Jimmy Callahan, the White Sox fell from fourth to sixth place. When Rowland took over the tide was reversed, although the acquisition of quality ballplayers was obviously a major contributing factor. Although he certainly was regarded as a busher when the arrived in Chicago, he had proven himself to be a competent and successful leader. And when Ed

Walsh was asked, two thirds of the way into the 1915 season, "What do you think of Rowland as a big league manager?" he replied, "Clarence Rowland forgot more inside baseball ten years ago than some of the fellows who are calling him busher ever knew."[16]

In any event, Cobb reluctantly agreed to become the Tiger manager. Rowland moved on to manage the Columbus Red Birds of the American Association for two losing seasons. In 1923 he accepted president Ban Johnson's offer to become an American League umpire, and served as such through 1927. He came to his new position without previous umpiring experience, and his career as an arbiter appears to have been an undistinguished one. Billy Evans recalled a day when he and Pants were working a Yankee game and Babe Ruth was on first base. The next batter hit safely and the Babe headed for third.

> I ran down to third from the plate," said Evans, "to call the play. Babe beat the throw a good two feet and I was already to call him safe when I heard somebody yell: 'You're out.' It was Rowland, dashing over from second. Then, as Babe got up, Clarence began brushing him off…patting the dust from Ruth's uniform…and saying, 'that was a great slide, Babe…a helluva slide…and you almost made it.'
>
> Well, I went back to the plate and Ruth came down there. 'I was safe a mile,' he told me. So I said: 'Why tell me? You didn't say a thing to him out there…I didn't hear you beef at the decision then.' The Babe just looked at me and cracked: 'Hell, did you see him brushing me off…and telling me what a great slide it was! He had me so rattled I felt like giving him a tip….'[17]

Although a rookie umpire, he was not bashful about asserting his authority. He bounced Tris Speaker, Bucky Harris, and Cobb, among others. Cobb drew a five-day suspension when he renewed the quarrel with Rowland after the game. However, both the Cleveland and Washington clubs were said to have complained about the rookie ump's performance, and Clark Griffith at one point asked for his dismissal.[18] Pitchers felt that he had a "floating" strike zone. Walter Miller, who pitched for Cleveland, reminisced:

> He just missed too many. Honest to God, he was pitiful behind the plate. You never knew what he was going to do. He just missed them, that's all. He didn't miss them intentionally, he just wasn't qualified, I guess.[19]

George Pipgras, who later became an umpire himself, felt that Rowland was the worst umpire he saw in the American League. He recalled Bill Dineen telling him that once after a game he and Pants had worked together, Rowland said, "I had a good game today. I didn't miss one call," and Dineen replied, "Good day! You missed a hundred!"[20]

So it may have been time to move on, and when E.S. Barnard took over as American League president in 1928, he dropped Rowland from the umpire roster. After a year of scouting for the Cincinnati Reds in 1928, Rowland returned to the minors for the next four years. He managed Nashville in the Southern Association in 1929 and 1930, and then took advantage of an opportunity to buy the Reading (PA) franchise in the International League. He did business with an old friend. The Chicago Cubs owned the Reading club, and the Cub president at that time was William Veeck, Sr., better known nowadays as Bill Veeck's father. The senior Veeck had been a sportswriter, under the pseudonym of Bill Bailey, with the Chicago Evening American back in 1915, when Pants arrived as the new White Sox manager, and Veeck held him in high regard. After Rowland spent two years in Reading as owner-manager, Veeck introduced him to Philip K. Wrigley, the owner of the Cubs. It was a meeting which marked the beginning of a remarkable association which ended with Rowland's death thirty-six years later.[21]

Wrigley had inherited the club upon the death of his father some months earlier. He had no background in baseball, but had a genuine interest in carrying on the Cub tradition. In Veeck he had an experienced executive, and it was doubtless on Veeck's recommendation that Rowland signed on as chief scout in charge of the Cubs' farm system. He served in this capacity throughout the Thirties, and is credited with discovering Big Bill Lee, Phil Cavarretta, Dolph Camilli, Eddie Stanky, and Augie Galan, among others. One of his important assignments was to negotiate with Branch Rickey in the trade which brought Dizzy Dean to the Cubs in 1938. Dean's great years were behind him by then, but his seven victories in the Cubs' stretch drive that year helped the club to the pennant.[22]

In 1942 Wrigley dispatched Rowland to Los Angeles. The Cubs had acquired the Pacific Coast League Angels as a farm club, and Pants was placed in charge as general manager. The team climbed from deep in the second division to second place that year, and won the Pacific Coast League championship in 1943, 21 games ahead of the closest contender.[23] Night baseball was banned on the Pacific Coast in those wartime years, and there was talk of suspending play entirely. It was Rowland who rallied the league's executives to keep the game going. The Sporting News named Rowland the minor league executive of the year, and when W. C. Tuttle retired as the league's president, the owners elected Rowland in 1944 as his successor, giving him a ten-year contract.[24] Back in Chicago, Phil Wrigley praised his selection, but indicated there would always be a place for him in the Cubs organization.

The fact that Rowland was chosen by his peers to be president only two years after he had come to the West Coast says much about him—his personality and his character. Despite his scanty educational background, he was an urbane, articulate, self-confident salesman. He had the ability to attract the attention, and to win the confidence, of men in high places: Ban Johnson, Comiskey, Bill Veeck, Phil Wrigley. He was personable and diplomatic; he was aggressive without being confrontational; he was the eternal optimist. Ed Burns, a columnist for the Chicago Tribune, once wrote:

> Pants is one of my most beloved pals, but sometimes at the start of the year, when I am trying so sweetly to steam up hope for a glorious Chicago baseball season, the sight of his radiant face and his constant enthusiasm depresses me.[25]

Rowland assumed his new duties with typical ebullience. He immediately began a campaign to achieve major league status for the Pacific Coast League, and he worked tirelessly to convince the baseball establishment that the West Coast was ready to support such a move. His efforts met with predictable skepticism. Committees were formed and feasibility studies were conducted, but his proposal was ultimately rejected. Undaunted, he shifted gears and announced that the Pacific Coast League was prepared to withdraw from the National Association and go "outlaw" unless its players were exempted from being drafted by major league clubs. He won an unprecedented "open classification" for the Pacific Coast League—a notch above the AAA classification—with substantial concessions on drafting procedures.[26]

Rowland employed Emmett Ashford, the first black umpire to serve in the Pacific Coast League. Ashford advanced to the majors in 1966 and credited Rowland as the moving force behind his promotion.[27] Back in 1943, Rowland had suggested that the Angels sign two outstanding black players, Chet Brewer and Lou

Dials, but Phil Wrigley vetoed the idea, fearing too much criticism from his major league colleagues.[28]

Rowland was an activist and outspoken leader for his league. The PCL directors thought so highly of him that they recommended his appointment as Baseball Commissioner when Kenesaw Mountain Landis died in November, 1944.[29] Senator Happy Chandler was chosen to succeed Landis, but Pants continued to enjoy the confidence of the Coast League directors. In 1952, two years before the expiration of his ten-year term, they voted to extend the contract until 1957, and substantially increased his salary. Emil Sick, owner of the Seattle club, declared: "We feel we have the best president in baseball."[30]

Re-enter Phil Wrigley. Back in Chicago, things were not going well. Since the Cubs' pennant-winning year in 1945, the club had usually languished deep in the second division. Attendance had fallen sharply and managers had come and gone. Wrigley told Rowland he needed him, and Pants, now 75 years old, couldn't turn him down. Over the years he had served as Wrigley's troubleshooter, and a bond of mutual admiration and respect had developed between them. The Coast League accepted his resignation "with deep regret," and he headed back home to the Midwest in 1955 with a new title: executive vice-president of the Chicago Cubs.

However, more than a troubleshooter was needed. The Cubs were mired in a deep depression which extended throughout the next decade and which included the infamous innovation of "rotating managers." In November, 1956, Rowland reappeared in Los Angeles, where, as general manager, he presided over that city's last season in the Pacific Coast League.[31] In 1958, when major league baseball finally arrived in Los Angeles, fourteen years after Pants had started his drumbeating campaign, the franchise was shifted to Spokane.

Returning to Chicago, he went into gradual retirement. Still active at age 80, he was gifted with a gold-plated telephone on his birthday, in recognition of his frequent use of that instrument as a Cub official. In later years, an honorary vice president, he was a frequent visitor at Wrigley Field. He died in a Chicago rest home on May 17, 1969. He was 90 years old.

Footnotes:

1. Graham, Frank, *McGraw of the Giants*, New York, G. P. Putnam's Sons, 1944, p. 108.

2. *The Sporting News*, March 2, 1955, p. 18.

3. Appel, Martin and Burt Goldblatt, *Baseball's Best: The Hall of Fame Gallery*, New York, McGraw-Hill Book Company, 1977, p. 101.

4. *The Sporting News*, March 2, 1955, p. 18.

5. Dowling, John R., *The III League: 1901-1961*, Watseka, Illinois, 1992; The Encyclopedia of Minor League Baseball, pp. 114, 117.

6. *The Sporting News*, March 2, 1955, p. 18; Encyclopedia, pp. 120, 123, 125, 126, 130, 133, 138; *The Story of Minor League Baseball*, the National Association of Professional Baseball Clubs, 1952, p. 78.

7. *The Sporting News*, March 2, 1955, p. 17; December 24, 1914; *Chicago Daily Tribune*, December 18, 1914.

8. Chicago *Daily Tribune*, December 19, 1914.

9. New York *Times*, October 18, 1917.

10. New York *Times*, October 19, 1917; *Baseball Digest*, March, 1955, p. 95; *The Sporting News*, January 24, 1918.

11. *The Story of Minor League Baseball*, p. 631.

12. Voigt, David Q., *American Baseball*, vol. II, Norman, Oklahoma, University of Oklahoma Press, 1970, p. 23; Asinof, Eliot, *Eight Men Out*, New York, Henry Holt and Company, 1987, p. 18.

13. *The Sporting News*, June 13, 1918; June 20, 1918; July 4, 1918; July 11, 1918; July 18, 1918; August 1, 1918; August 15, 1918.

14. *The Sporting News*, January 16, 1919; February 20, 1919; April 3, 1919; July 11, 1919; September 25, 1919; January 15, 1920; March 2, 1955, p. 18.

15. Ty Cobb, with Al Stump, *My Life in Baseball: The True Record*, Garden City, New York, Doubleday & Company, Inc., 1961, pp. 195-196.

16. *The Sporting News*, August 5, 1915.

17. *The Sporting News*, March 2, 1955, p. 18; December 30, 1943.

18. *The Sporting News*, May 26, 1925; August 20, 1927; Charles C. Alexander, *Ty Cobb*, New York, NY, Osford University Press, 1984, p. 176; New York *Times*, February 19, 1928., p. 18; December 30, 1943.

19. Eugene Murdock, *Baseball Between the Wars: Memories of the Game by the Men Who Played It*, Westport, CT., 1992, p. 192.

20.. Pipgras interview by Norman L. Macht, circa 1984.

21. *Encyclopedia*, 173, 1976; *The Sporting News*, June 27, 1929, October 31, 1929; February 23, 1955, p. 13; March 2, 1955, p. 17.

22. *The Sporting News*, February 23, 1955, p. 14; Angle, Paul M., *Philip K. Wrigley*, Chicago, Rand McNally & Company, 1975, pp. 65-67.

23. New York *Times*, November 19, 1941; Angle, *Philip K. Wrigley*, p. 101.

24. San Francisco *Chronicle*, January 19, 1944.

25. *The Sporting News*, January 2, 1952.

26. New York *Times*, December 5, 1945; December 12, 1945, San Francisco *Chronicle*, August 2, 1946; New York *Times*, August 30, 1951; January 1, 1952.

27. Larry R. Gerlach, *The Men In Blue: Conversations with Umpires*, New York, Viking Press, 1980, p. 273.

28. Dick Dobbins and Jon Twichell, *Nuggets of the Diamond*, San Francisco, Woodford Press, 1994, p. 212.

29. New York *Times*, January 14, 1945; San Francisco *Chronicle*, October 25, 1952.

30. San Francisco *Chronicle*, November 1, 1956.

31. Los Angeles *Times*, November 1, 1956.

RBI Average

A new statistic for baseball

Daniel Lee Swetman

The batting title in major league baseball is not determined by the "hits" category, rather it is determined by the "batting average" (BA) category. The reason for this is that the player who is credited with the most hits may have had more opportunities to obtain hits than other players. The BA is the ratio between hits and at bats. The runs batted in (RBI) title, however, is awarded to the player who bats in the most runs, regardless of the number of opportunities he has had to do so. A player who consistently bats with runners on base has a distinct advantage over one who frequently bats with the bases empty. Thus, the batting title is purely an individual award, while the RBI title, although bestowed on an individual, is actually, at least partially, a team award.

Baseball needs an individual RBI Award for the player who is most productive at batting in runs, given the opportunities he has had. This award should be based on a statistic called Run Batted In Average (RBIA). The RBIA will also be a helpful statistic for scouting and evaluating players.

The RBIA should not be an attempt to determine the "best overall" offensive player. Other statistics, such as Steve Mann's Run Productivity Average (RPA) and the Linear Weights System introduced in *Total Baseball*, which include such actions as advancing runners and stolen bases, are more suited for that purpose.

It is also tempting to try to make the RBIA seem more meaningful than it is. It will *not* determine the best clutch hitter, the best two-out hitter, or the best hitter with runners in scoring position—only the best hitter at batting in runs. Therefore, the only action that will increase a player's RBIA is batting in a run; and the only action that will decrease a player's RBIA is failure to bat in a run when given the opportunity. Furthermore, the location of the potential run is considered. A player who bats with a runner on third base, for example, has a better opportunity to earn an RBI than a player who bats with a runner on second base. The final characteristic that the RBIA has is simplicity. Many aspects of a situation that contribute to whether a run scores, such as the speed of the base runners, field conditions, and ability of the defense, are not considered. The statistic is more complex than the BA, but it is not so complex as to be unwieldy.

Background—There are eight different situations in which a batter may come to the plate. They are as follows: bases empty, runner on first, runner on second, runner on third, runners on first and second, runners on first and third, runners on second and third, and bases loaded. Each is different in terms of the opportunity it presents the batter to ring up one or more RBI. Similarly there are twenty-eight different results that can occur in terms of run production, depending on how many runs score as a result of that batter's turn at bat. It is important to remember that,

Daniel Lee Swetman is a professor of math education at Auburn University and a lifetime diehard Chicago Cubs fan.

for the purpose of this statistic, the action of the batter that scores the run(s) is of no consequence—only the original situation and the number of RBIs recorded. For example, if a batter's turn at bat begins with a runner on third base, and the runner scores; whether the batter hit a single, double, triple, fielder's choice, or sacrifice fly does not matter—only that the run scored. Like the batting average, the RBIA is a ratio, expressed as a decimal for simplicity.

Procedure—We need to decide what weight to give the various situations and results. Here's how it works. (Because of unique aspects of the situations involving home runs, bases-loaded-walks, and squeeze bunts, they will be discussed separately.)

Numerator: one point for each base advanced to score, plus one point for each run scored.

Denominator: the reverse of the numerator points for location, plus one point for each potential run (i.e., third-base runner: 4+1=5; second-base runner: 3+1=4; first-base runner: 2+1=3; batter: 1+1=2).

Table 1: RBIA formula

	Numerator Points: (Score from...)	Denominator Points: (Runner on...)
3rd base	2	5
2nd base	3	4
1st base	4	3
Batter	5	2

A player's RBIA for a particular turn at bat is his numerator points divided by his denominator points. His RBIA for more than one turn at bat is the sum of his numerator points divided by the sum of his denominator points. Table 2 shows all possible situations and results that will affect the RBIA.

Table 2: RBIA—all possible at bats

Base Runners	RBI	Formula	RBIA	Runner on third, 2 outs Formula	RBIA
None	0	0/2	0.000		
	1	5/5	1.000	x	x
1st	0	0/5	0.000		
	1	4/5	0.800		
	2	8/8	1.000	x	x
2nd	0	0/6	0.000		
	1	3/6	0.500		
	2	8/8	1.000	x	x
3rd	0	0/7	0.000	0/6	0.000
	1	2/7	0.286	2/6	0.333
	2	8/8	1.000		
1st & 2nd	0	0/9	0.000		
	1	3/9	0.333		
	2	7/9	0.778		
	3	11/11	1.000	x	x
1st & 3rd	0	0/10	0.000	0/9	0.000
	1	2/10	0.200	2/9	0.222
	2	6/10	0.600	6/9	0.666
	3	11/11	1.000		
2nd & 3rd	0	0/11	0.000	0/10	0.000
	1	2/11	0.182	2/10	0.200
	2	5/10	0.455	5/10	0.500
Full	0	0/14	0.000	0/13	0.000
	1	2/14	0.143	2/13	0.154
	2	5/14	0.357	5/13	0.385
	3	9/14	0.643	9/13	0.692
	4	14/14	1.000		
Exceptions (bases-loaded walk, squeeze)	1	1/1	1.000		

For example, a batter who comes to bat with runners on first and second receives nine denominator points (two for the batter, three for the runner on first base, and four for the runner on second base). If he bats in two runs, he gets seven numerator points (three for the runner who scored from second base and four for the runner who scored from first base). This results in an RBIA of 0.778 for that turn at bat. Walks are not considered a turn at bat, with the exception of bases-loaded walks, which are discussed below. A sacrifice bunt is calculated as a turn at bat only if a run scores, and that situation is also explained later. (This is not an attempt to change the requirements for official at bats. The "turn at bat" referred to here will only be considered for tabulating the RBIA.)

Table 3 lists the occurrences from lowest to highest RBIA. All occurrences of no RBI receive an RBIA of 0.000, and all home runs receive an RBIA of 1.000.

Table 3: RBIA situations in ascending order

RBIA	RBI	Situation
0.000	0	All
0.143	1	Full
0.154	1	Full*
0.182	1	2nd & 3rd
0.200	1	2nd & 3rd*
0.200	1	1st & 3rd
0.222	1	1st & 3rd*
0.286	1	3rd
0.333	1	3rd*
0.333	1	1st & 2nd
0.357	2	Full

0.385	2	Full*
0.455	2	2nd & 3rd
0.500	2	2nd & 3rd*
0.500	1	2nd
0.600	2	1st & 3rd
0.643	3	Full
0.666	2	1st & 3rd*
0.692	3	Full*
0.778	2	1st & 2nd
0.800	1	1st
1.000	1	Empty
1.000	2	1st
1.000	2	2nd
1.000	2	3rd
1.000	3	1st & 2nd
1.000	3	1st & 3rd
1.000	3	2nd & 3rd
1.000	4	Full

*2 outs

It may at first seem inaccurate that, in some cases, a lower number of RBI is rewarded more than a higher number of RBI. For example, one RBI with a runner on second receives an RBIA of 0.500, while two RBI with runners on second and third receives only 0.455. This occurs because RBIA is a ratio of "production to opportunity." Even though the player with two RBI had greater productivity, he also had greater opportunity.

Since the only values that need to be determined for each at bat in order to figure the RBIA are the numerator points and the denominator points, only two questions need to be answered (with modifications for the exceptions listed in the following section). They are, "What was the situation when the batter came to the plate?" and "How many RBI resulted?" A simple computer program can calculate the RBIA instantly.

Exceptions—The situation involving home runs is more complex than the situations involving batting in other runners only. Statistics, baseball, and philosophy all enter into the formula. Figured strictly by the criteria presented previously, a solo home run would receive an RBIA of (5/2), or 2.500, while a grand slam home run would receive an RBIA of (14/14), or 1.000. Philosophically, the idea of an average that is based on a ratio of successes to attempts, and that exceeds 1.000 is difficult to justify. There is, however, a precedent in baseball: slugging average. A player's SA can exceed 1.000, if he or she gets an unusually large number of extra-base hits.

A bigger problem is that this approach to home-run-related RBIA rewards a solo home run more than a grand slam home run. This is not acceptable.

To solve the first problem, we could lower the numerator points to be equal to the denominator points for any home run. The 5/2 for a solo home run would become 2/2. This would result in an RBIA of 1.000 for that at bat, which would be accurate and acceptable.

It would create another problem, though. A player would receive only two numerator points for hitting a solo home run, the same amount awarded for batting in a runner from third base. Over the course of a season, this would result in an inaccuracy in the RBIA. There must be a continuous increase in numerator points for increased productivity, along with a continuous increase in denominator points for increased opportunity. To accomplish this, we assign an equal number of numerator and denominator points for any home run: five for a bases-empty homer, eight for a two-run shot, eleven for a three-run home run and fourteen for a grand slam. Using this procedure, a home run rewards the batter with more numerator points for a given number of RBI than any other event that scores the same number of RBIs, while the denominator points increase as the opportunity to score increases.

Similarly, a batter who is issued a bases-loaded walk has not had the opportunity to bat in four runs. Likewise, a batter who is asked to participate in a squeeze bunt is realistically only given the opportunity for one RBI. These two situations are rewarded with one numerator point and one denominator point, signifying that the batter did "all that he could do," hence RBIA=1.000.

The final exception concerns the number of outs in situations involving a runner on third base. A runner on third base with fewer than two outs presents a greater opportunity to score than a runner on third base with two outs, because there are more ways to score that run. This consideration is appropriate to all situations involving a runner on third base. We address this inequity by subtracting one denominator point (indicating a decrease in the opportunity) from a batter's RBIA for any at bat in which there are two outs *and* a runner on third base. (See far right column, Table 2)

Application—It sounds good, but does it really work? Only time will tell, but we can make an educated guess. If some actual RBIAs were to be calculated for an actual season, for some actual players, some questions might be answered. Will the RBIA differentiate players with seemingly similar statistics? Will it tell us anything we don't know? Will it be accurate? Will we have to be mathematicians to understand it? Will it be unwieldy to report? What is a "good" RBIA? To answer these and other questions, I calculated the RBIA for six players from the Atlanta Braves organization for the 1994 season. (Thanks to the Braves organization for making their score sheets available to me.) Although the results are unofficial, they can be used to answer some of the questions that might arise in relation to the RBIA. Tables 4 and 5 show the year-end statistics for the six players. Table 4 includes the RBIA, calculated to five decimal places, and the formula used to calculate the RBIA, listing the total numerator points and denominator points for the season.

Table 4: Year-end statistics (detailed)

Players	AB	BA	RBI	RBIA Formula	Avg.
Blauser	380	.258	45	147/1639	.08969
Justice	352	.313	59	205/1468	.13965
Klesko	245	.278	47	174/1126	.15453
Lemke	350	.294	31	84/1424	.05899
McGriff	424	.318	94	345/1866	.18489
Pendleton	309	.252	30	101/1283	.07872

Table 5 lists the year-end statistics as they might appear in a media guide or newspaper.

Table 5: Year-end statistics (for publication)

Players	AB	BA	RBI	RBIA
Blauser	380	.258	45	.090
Justice	352	.313	59	.140
Klesko	245	.278	47	.155
Lemke	350	.294	31	.059
McGriff	424	.318	94	.185
Pendleton	309	.252	30	.079

Modifications and detail will have to be determined by any League or Conference that chooses to use the RBIA as an official statistic. How many at bats or RBI will be necessary to qualify for the League Title? Is the official situation determined when the batter steps into the box, or when he/she executes? (e.g., If a runner on first base is caught stealing, does the batter's situation reflect "Runner on first," or "Bases empty"?) This procedure is also not intended to change the rules for determining official RBI. A batter, for example, who hits into a double play which results in a run scoring will receive a zero in the numerator for that turn at bat, because no RBI is recorded. The procedure presented here, can, however, be the basis of a useful tool for coaches, scouts, players, and fans in determining who are, in fact, the better players at batting in runs—which, after all, is what wins games.

GAME 6 Monday, October 3, 1955
Brooklyn   000 100 000 - 1 4 1
New York   500 000 00x - 5 8 0

BROOKLYN (3-2)

7/4 Gilliam	7	53	s	wx
6 Reese	k	S	53	f36
8 Snider	k			
4o Zimmer 4	k	w	k	
2 Campanella	8	w	k	63
9 Furillo	p	s'x	63	k
3 Hodges	wx	f64x	53	63
5 JRobinson	543p	f64	8	53
8/7 Amoros	13	3-	s	k
1 Spooner				
1 Meyer 1	k	43		
o Kellert 7	4^			
1 Roebuck 8				

NEW YORK (2-3)

6 Rizzuto	Ws	5^	63	63
4 Martin	k	k	s	e5x
5 McDougald	W	6^f	8	1^
2 Berra	S'+	wx	sx	f36
9 Bauer	S'	s	f54	s+
3 Skowron	H"	8		
3o Collins 6	w	43		
8 Cerv	s	53p	6^	1\
7 Howard	k	k	k	9
7 Noren 9				
1 Ford	7	53	13	3-

Pitchers: BROOKLYN, Spooner L (6xxx), Meyer (3991), Roebuck (xxx8). NEW YORK, Ford W (WP).
Left on Base- Bkl 7, NY 7. T- 2:34. A- 64,022.
Ump-Ballanfant, Honochick, Dascoli, Summers, Flaherty, Donatelli.

Total Production Average

The best overall batting performance measure—so far

Eugene E. Heaton, Jr. and Alan W. Heaton

From almost the dawn of the game's history, baseball officials, writers, and fans have sought a valid, easy-to-compute measure of players' batting performance as a yardstick by which their effectiveness could be judged, and by which players could be compared against each other.

Baseball is truly a game of numbers, which are gathered, analyzed, chronicled, and argued about incessantly. Batting average, home runs, runs batted in, and so on, are trotted out as needed to make the case that one player is or was superior to another.

For many years, the most widely used statistic to summarize a batter's overall performance has been the batting average (BA): simply the number of hits divided by the number of plate appearances minus bases on balls (and reached base by catcher's interference or hit by pitch). This statistic is easy to calculate but is also both misleading and incomplete.

The batting average ignores the "power" that is or could be involved in reaching base on a hit. A batter who is basically a singles hitter receives as much credit for his batting as does a batter who pounds out a high proportion of extra-base hits.

This problem was corrected to some extent by the creation a number of years ago of the slugging average (SA), in which the number of total bases represented by a batter's hits is divided by the number of at-bats. This is a very useful statistic, but at least in the pre-

computer era it was more difficult to compute than the batting average. For whatever reason, it does not get as much attention as the batting average, though it has been seen in the baseball media much more frequently in recent years.

Moving back to the batting average, another of its disadvantages is that it ignores the contribution that reaching base by drawing a walk has on a batter's overall performance. There has been great variation among players over the years in their ability—or willingness—to reach first by a base on balls rather than a hit. And while the old saying, "A walk's as good as a hit.," is both trite and not strictly true (in that a hit has greater potential to advance baserunners), it gets the batter to first base with the opportunity to score a run. Actually, if the saying were revised to: "A walk's as good as an infield single," it would be correct in most cases.

The absence of bases on balls in performance measurement was corrected somewhat by the calculation of the on-base average (OBA), which is simply the number of hits *and* bases on balls divided by total number of plate appearances (again excluding hit by pitch and catcher's interference). However, this measure seems to have had relatively limited or specialized use, primarily being called into play to show that, for example, a leadoff hitter is good at getting on base to "set the table" for the batters who follow him. It is rarely used to show that power hitters have brought something extra to the game beyond just hitting.

Eugene and Alan Heaton are both public opinion researchers, the former with Response Analysis Corporation in Princeton, N.J., and the latter with the Food and Drug Administration in Washington, D.C.

In recent years, there has been an attempt to pull all the relevant figures together, so to speak, by publishing combined on-base plus slugging average (OB+SA) figures for batters. While in one respect a step in the right direction because it considers both ability to reach base and ability to hit with power, OB+SA has a major weakness: it contains duplicate or overlapping statistics, in that a batter's hits are counted twice: in raw form as part of the on-base average, and in "weighted" form in terms of the number of bases a given hit represents.

Above and beyond the drawbacks of the various performance measures already cited is one more, very major one: they consider *only* a player's ability to reach one or more bases in a given at bat.

What determines the winner of a baseball game is not hits, but the number of times a team scores *runs*. Batting average, on-base average, slugging average, and on-base plus slugging average all completely ignore this crucial point.

For a number of years, a relatively obscure statistic has been available to provide an answer to the question of how much a player helps his team score runs. The run production average (RPA) is one of the most easily computed figures in baseball. It is based on runs scored, plus runs batted in, minus home runs (to avoid double-counting), divided by at bats.

The run production average truly separates the greats from the very goods from the average or mediocre batters of the past and of today. A case could be made for using RPA as a complete substitute for batting average, or the other statistics already discussed, as a measure of total batting performance. However, focusing on run production alone is perhaps too extreme or one-dimensional, and it ignores a player's ability to get on base and help "make things happen."

There is need for a statistic that includes the relevant data contained in all the various measures described above, which constitutes one all-encompassing measure of a batter's skills. That statistic now exists, and in the computerized world of today is easy to calculate. And it is remarkably simple in its concept.

The total production average (TPA) is computed by summing the total number of bases resulting from the batter's hits, adding bases on balls, runs scored, and runs batted in (minus home runs, to avoid double counting), and dividing this sum by number of plate appearances. (Ideally, hit-by-pitches and catcher's interference figures would be part of this statistic as well. They are not included in the figures presented in this paper because they are not readily available. For most players, however, inclusion of these additional data would make very little difference in their overall performance records.)

The TPA, in effect, combines the on-base average, the slugging average, and the run-production average, without the kind of duplication present in the OBA+SA. It takes into account a player's ability to hit (and builds in a measure of his power), his ability to reach base via a walk, to score runs, and to drive in runs.

One feature of baseball offense that is not included in the total production average is the stolen base. There are two reasons this statistic has been omitted. First, it is not a reflection of batting skill. Second, data on times caught stealing are not generally available, and it would be foolish to build successful base stealing attempts into the TPA without penalizing a player for the unsuccessful ones.

In addition to the fact that it includes so much more relevant information than, for example, the batting average, the TPA is easier to interpret in the sense that, as will be seen, the range of scores is much greater than for the batting average.

Over most of the "modern" baseball era, the practical range of most batting averages has been (for position players) from around .250 (for all but the weakest hitters) up to .350. In contrast, the range of the TPA begins below .500 and extends to about 1.000.

So much for the background and calculation of the TPA. Let us move to a review of actual TPA scores, to show the practical application of the statistic.

One approach might be to take examples of high- and low-scoring TPAs for randomly selected famous and not-so-famous players over their careers, or for particular good or poor seasons by an individual.

This paper focuses instead on each of the eight every-day positions, offering examples of five distinct categories or levels of batting accomplishment. These five categories are based on an analysis of the distribution of TPA scores among a large sample of players over the years, as will be discussed immediately following a brief description of each category.

Mediocre batters: This level represents about the minimum TPA that a player can achieve and have more than a very brief, unsuccessful major league career.

Good hitters: This level includes a large number of players who were reasonably successful over their careers. (This category might also be called "average," but the fact is that, to achieve this level, a player has to be quite a good batter. We have therefore omitted the somewhat disparaging category of average.)

Very Good batters are well above average, though not quite good enough to be called "great".

Great hitters are essentially the best batters at their position. However, we will see that not all Hall of Famers were great hitters.

Legends make up a very small pantheon that includes the greatest hitters of all time.

Shown below is a listing of selected players in each category, at each position. Four players are shown at each level, except in the Legend group, where there are fewer than four at each position. It is worth noting that Hall of Famers can be found in all categories except Mediocre.

Some notes on the figures below, to aid in their interpretation:

TPAs were computed from data in the eighth edition of *The Baseball Encyclopedia*.

All players shown had completed their careers. TPAs were not computed for active players.

Some players had considerably longer careers than others. Obviously, if two players with similar TPAs had markedly different career lengths, the one with the longer career was more valuable over time. However, in terms of the players' "average" year, the two can be considered as comparable in batting productivity.

The TPA calculations are not adjusted in any way to reflect different "periods" of baseball, between which overall batting performances have shown considerable variation. (See Harry Hollingsworth, "The Best & Worst Baseball Teams of All Time," p.18, for a decade-by-decade chart showing variation in batting average, slugging average, and team home runs.)

In general, we have shown players who had most or all of their career since 1900.

The data have not been adjusted to reflect the particular ballparks in which each player played.

Ranges for the five categories have been developed so that approximately two thirds of all the players in each position fall into the Good and Very Good categories, split about evenly between the two groups. The remaining third are classified as Mediocre (about one-sixth of all players at that position) at the low end of the scale, or Great/Legend (again, about one sixth in total) at the high end of the scale. Combining the Greats and Legends, and looking at the distribution across the resulting four groups produces a reasonable approximation of a normal bell-shaped curve.

While the ranges of TPA scores for the five performance levels are generally comparable across the eight positions, they are not identical. Historically, catchers and shortstops have been the least productive batters. Second and third basemen come next, with first basemen and outfielders being the most productive. (Of all eight postions, left field, with its less demanding requirements of the fielder's arm, seems to have attracted, on average, the most productive batters.)

Finally, it is important to note that the four players used to illustrate each level of Total Production are just *examples*. Let these players represent a starting point for further analysis and discussion.

First Base:

Mediocre (-.610)

  .541 Tony Muser
  .564 George Stovall
  .589 Walter Holke
  .601 Tommy McCraw

Good (.610-.699)

  .613 Eddie Waitkus
  .643 Stuffy McInnis
  .653 Babe Dahlgren
  .687 Mike Epstein

V. Good (.700-.799)

  .718 George McQuinn
  .733 Dale Long
  .766 George Sisler
  .795 Jim Gentile

Great (.800-.949)

  .820 Willie McCovey
  .830 Dolph Camilli
  .851 Hal Trosky
  .901 Johnny Mize

Legends (.950+)

  .991 Hank Greenberg
  .996 Jimmie Foxx
  1.047 Lou Gehrig

Second Base:

Mediocre (-.540)

  .494 Sandy Alomar
  .504 Al Weis
  .525 Billy Gardner
  .529 Emil Verban

Good (.540-.599)

  .542 Jerry Adair
  .563 Glenn Beckert
  .576 Sibby Sisti
  .583 Bill Mazeroski

V. Good (.600-.699)

  .613 Nellie Fox
  .639 Red Schoendienst
  .668 Roberto Avila
  .690 Billy Herman

Great (.700-.849)

  .739 Marty McManus
  .772 Eddie Collins
  .818 Jackie Robinson
  .842 Charlie Gehringer

Legend (.850+)

  .935 Rogers Hornsby

Third Base:

Mediocre (-.560)

  .468 Dave Hilton
  .483 Lee Tannehill
  .544 George Moriarty
  .547 Fred Marsh

Good (.560-.639)

  .565 Billy Hitchcock
  .601 Clete Boyer
  .614 Billy Cox

.637 Hans Lobert

V. Good (.640-.709)

.647 Brooks Robinson

.664 Grady Hatton

.681 Eddie Yost

.692 George Kell

Great (.710-.799)

.717 Ken Keltner

.749 Ken Boyer

.767 Pie Traynor

.782 Harland Clift

Legends (.800+)

.825 Al Rosen

.826 Eddie Mathews

Shortstop:

Mediocre (-.510)

.452 Ray Oyler

.482 Billy Hunter

.493 Bobby Bragan

.494 Ed Brinkman

Good (.510-.589)

.512 Mickey Doolan

.555 Wally Gerber

.573 Luis Aparicio

.586 Billy Jurges

V. Good (.590-.699)

.596 Marty Marion

.618 Mark Koenig

.666 Alvin Dark

.693 Johnny Pesky

Great (.700-.799)

.711 Luke Appling

.715 Lou Boudreau

.744 Joe Sewell

.780 Vern Stephens

Legends (.800+)

.806 Honus Wagner

.821 Joe Cronin

Catcher:

Mediocre (-.525)

.453 Bill Killefer

.475 Pat Corrales

.497 Bob Swift

.519 Bob Rodgers

Good (.525-.599)

.534 Jerry Grote

.569 Joe Ginsberg

.575 Andy Etchebarren

.585 Ray Schalk

V. Good (.600-.689)

.612 Birdie Tebbetts

.631 Tim McCarver

.675 Frankie Hayes

.681 Sherm Lollar

Great (.690-.799)

.708 Smoky Burgess

.720 Ernie Lombardi

.739 Walker Cooper

.798 Yogi Berra

Legends (.800+)

.814 Bill Dickey

.818 Roy Campanella

.843 Mickey Cochrane

Left Field:

Mediocre (-.625)

.547 Ivan Murrell

.584 Ted Uhlaender

.608 Gil Coan

.618 George Case

Good (.625-.709)

.627 Alex Johnson

.663 Lou Brock

.676 Curt Blefary

.703 Gates Brown

V. Good (.710-.799)

.728 Andy Pafko

.740 Beau Bell

.766 Carl Yastrzemski

.790 Vic Wertz

Great (.800-.899)

.810 Riggs Stephenson

.833 Willie Stargell

.870 Ken Williams

.888 Stan Musial

Legend (.900+)

1.030 Ted Williams

Center Field:

Mediocre (-.600)

.538 Jose Tartabull

.544 Ty Cline

.592 Johnny Rucker

.595 Charlie Hemphill

Good (.600-.664)

.600 Bill Virdon

.616 Cesar Tovar

.635 Curt Flood

.641 Lloyd Waner

V. Good (.665-.774)

.666 Max Carey

.673 Terry Moore

.736 Edd Roush

.773 Pete Reiser

Great (.775-.899)

.792 Earle Combs

.831 Larry Doby

.846 Tris Speaker

.883 Ty Cobb

Legends (.900+)

.904 Mickey Mantle

.914 Hack Wilson

.960 Joe DiMaggio

Right Field:

Mediocre (-.600)

.550 Jesus Alou

.555 Johnny Cooney

.577 Rich Coggins

.595 Al Pilarcik

Good (.600-.684)

.622 Gino Cimoli

.636 Gene Stephens

.652 Debs Garms

.659 Tommy Davis

V. Good (.685-.779)

.687 Casey Stengel

.724 Sam Rice

.754 Roberto Clemente

.769 Bing Miller

Great (.780-.899)

.784 Al Kaline

.795 Paul Waner

.862 Frank Robinson

.892 Mel Ott

Legend (.900+)

1.102 Babe Ruth

At last, it is possible to compare players by a single number, instead of having to deal with the convoluted thinking that has to be brought to bear when trying to assess player A (batting average of .312; slugging average of .401, and 168 career home runs over a ten-year career (not to mention such other relevant statistics as number of bases on balls, runs scored, runs batted in, and even doubles and triples)) against player B (batting average of .286; slugging average of .438, and 257 career home runs over a 14-year career). The TPA is a real "argument settler" when it comes to batting skills.

Also, although the TPA does not address a player's fielding skills, the TPA makes it possible to compare two players, one an average fielder and one with an above-average glove, to see whether the better-than-average fielder is preferable, even though his total batting productivity may be significantly lower.

Finally, and indeed serendipitously, there is something inherently satisfying about a statistic whose apparent practical maximum stands just beyond the realm of decimals, at the whole number of 1.000, a target that has been approached by some (including Jimmie Foxx's almost heartbreakingly close figure of .996), but achieved by only three of the game's greatest icons—Gehrig, Ruth, and Williams. And of these, the Sultan of Swat remains supreme.

Only time will tell whether any of the stars of today will ever join this legendary trio.

Baseball Put to the Test

And England beats the U.S.

Ian Smyth

The United States Olympic Baseball team, under the management of Leslie Mann, secretary of the International Baseball Federation, and a former National League player with Boston, Chicago, St. Louis and New York, arrived in Plymouth, England on August 11, 1938 to compete in a five-match "Test Series" against England.

The American team had been selected from among the country's best non-professional players at the National Amateur Baseball Trials held the previous month in Lincoln, Nebraska, under the auspices of the U.S. Baseball Congress. The team was a mixture of college and high school players, and included Mike Schemer, who went on to play with the New York Giants. The tour was in preparation for the 1940 Olympic Baseball Tournament in Tokyo, Japan.

Once in England the tourists' schedule was hectic, comprising the five-game series against England and another five games against provincial opponents including Yorkshire, Lancashire, London, Birmingham, and the Royal Air Force.

However, the main part of the tour was the "Test Series" against England. The bulk of the England team came from the Yorkshire-Lancashire League, a professional circuit in the north of England. For the series to be competitive the England team included

players from the British Empire, the result being a team consisting almost entirely of Canadians. England was skippered by George "Chummy" MacNeil. The Yorkshire *Evening News* described MacNeil as:

> ...one of the most versatile fellows in the game...who has taken the trouble to master so perfectly the various phases of the baseball game.

The rest of the England squad, many of whom had played semipro ball in Canadian leagues, are listed (along with their clubs and league batting averages) below:

England Test Team

Robinson (Oldham)	.477
Ritchie (Liverpool Giants)	.476
McNeill (Leeds Oaks)	.456
Marsh (York)	.456
Holden (Bradford City Sox)	.432
Cadorette (Halifax)	.422
Wright (Halifax)	.403
Hanna (Halifax)	.437
Kendrick (Oldham)	.370
Strong (Hull)	.346
Bissett (Birmingham)	—
Ruvinsky (London)	—

The test games were scheduled from August 13 to 19, at Liverpool, Hull, Rochdale, Halifax and Leeds. The press and baseball followers in England were

Ian Smyth *is an executive member of the British Baseball Federation. He is also a member of the Bobby Thomson Chapter of SABR, which is researching the history of baseball in Great Britain.*

excited about the prospect of seeing the "American Olympians" and played up local interest by advertising the games as the first-ever "International Series."

Game 1. Wavertree Stadium, Liverpool, August 13, 1938—In the buildup to the first Test, the Liverpool *Evening Express* predicted that pitching would be the deciding factor:

> ...if Kendrick, the Oldham pitcher, shows anything like his form, American batters will need to be at their very best.

However, it also noted that:

> ...the tourists will have three brilliant pichers available: Virgil Thompson, a curve ball man; Clyde Dean, who favours the fast ball; and Wendell Ringland, who specializes in a side-arm delivery.

Expectations for a pitchers' duel between Kendrick and Thompson were satisfied.

> The brilliant pitching of Ross Kendrick and great work of catcher Ivan Ruvinsky were the main features of the first baseball Test Match...England won 3-0. There was no score until England's seventh frame when Danny Wright hit the only home run of the match. Virgil Thompson, America's opening pitcher, never found his real form. He was benched in the eighth frame when Sam Hanna hit a double and brought in Sid Bissett for the second run. (Liverpool *Evening Express*.)

England's third run was scored by skipper MacNeil on a single by Marsh in the eighth inning. Despite the fact that the Americans were much quicker and surer "base throwers," Kendrick's pitching kept them off the bases. He pitched a two-hit (both singles) complete game and struck out sixteen. A crowd of 10,000 watched the game.

Game 1

	1	2	3	4	5	6	7	8	9	Total
England	0	0	0	0	0	0	1	2	0	3
U.S.	0	0	0	0	0	0	0	0	0	0

This victory was clearly enjoyed by the press, which ran a cartoon poking fun at the Americans.

Game 2. Craven Park, Hull, August 15, 1938—The visit of the "American Olympians" was undoubtedly a highlight for people of Hull. The Hull *Daily Mail* of August 13 noted that:

> There should be no qualms about the attendance at Craven Park on Monday night, because the finest baseball attraction ever staged in the city will be the fare then. It will certainly be a red letter day in as much as the city has never staged a Test Match between England and America.

Craven Park, host to the Test, was the home of Hull Kingston Rovers Rugby League Club, and had been opened in 1922.

Pitching again paved the way for an England victory. The Hull *Daily Mail*:

> After a shaky start England gained their second Test Match Victory over America when they met at Craven Park last night. There was only one change in the England team, this was the inclusion of Jerry Strong, the Hull captain and pitcher, who recorded twelve strikeouts. The 5,000 spectators were entertained to a game which could have been anybody's until the closing frame. America scored two runs in the opening frame, Buger and O'Rourke scoring. England were shut out in their first attempt, but in the second frame Cadorette lessened the margin by scoring on an error by Buger. There was no further scoring until the fifth innings, when England's batsmen had a hectic time and had scored five runs before they were dismissed. First Robinson and Ritchie came in on a hit by Bissett, who was brought round when MacNeil hit a great 'two bagger'. To crown all this, Sam Hanna hit a glorious homer, which also brought in MacNeil. This appeared to have put England in a sound position, but in America's seventh and eighth innings they ran in four runs through Dean, Benson, Buger and O'Rourke. England scored one run in each of the seventh and eighth innings, Bissett and Robinson reaching the plate amid great excitement. England received a shut out in the ninth, and with two men on base, O'Rourke was caught out to dismiss the Americans, and England had won by eight runs to six.

Strong, the England pitcher, recorded twelve strikeouts. Schemer, the American pitcher, had five.

Game 2

	1	2	3	4	5	6	7	8	9	Total
England	0	1	0	0	5	0	1	1	0	8
America	2	0	0	0	0	0	2	2	0	6

Game 3. Spotlands, Rochdale, August 16, 1938— As in Hull the local press was looking forward to the visit of the "American Olympians."

The game was played at Spotlands, home of Rochdale Football Club, and attracted only about 1,000 spectators. The uncertain weather and the lack of Rochdale's U.S.-born players in the England team were held responsible by the Rochdale *Observer* for the low turnout.

> ...It was a poor night for England, for not only did they fail to record a run, they did not even manage to occupy third base on a single occasion. Whereas the American players made only one fielding error, the England side were responsible for five. The Americans also enjoyed an advantage in the pitching department. Sid Bissett, a reserve pitcher utilized by England had only five strike outs, whilst Clyde Dean scored seven for America.
>
> The work of the American players was a joy to behold, and...provided the chief feature of the match. Time and again the ball was picked up with remarkable celerity and hurled to a base with unerring accuracy and enormous power. On two occasions there was a perfectly dizzy switching about of the ball from man to man with consequent paralysing results to the England innings.

America scored in each of the first two innings, then three runs in a two-out rally in the seventh, which included two England errors.

Game 3

	1	2	3	4	5	6	7	8	9	Total
England	0	0	0	0	0	0	0	0	0	0
America	1	1	0	0	0	0	3	0	0	5

The series now moved to Halifax. The American team had improved with every game. However, England now had their ace, Ross Kendrick pitching, where a win would clinch the series.

Game 4. The Shay, Halifax August 18, 1938— The Shay was home of Halifax Town Football Club. Despite hopes of the biggest crowd to date only 5,000 spectators turned up. England bombed America in this game, out-hitting them ten to three, behind the pitching of Kendrick. The next day's Halifax *Guardian* reported:

England took the lead in the second when their captain, McNeill, roused the crowd by hitting a magnificent home run. In the fourth, three more runs were scored. Hanna walked, Kendrick singled, Cadorette got on base through an error. Wright singled to bring home Hanna and Kendrick, then Benson singled to score Cadorette.

Controversially, the game was called during the ninth inning due to bad light, giving England the game and the series. Kendrick recorded his second shutout of the series, striking out twelve batters, while allowing only three singles.

Game 4

	1	2	3	4	5	6	7	8	9	Total
England	0	1	0	3	0	0	0	0	0	4
America	0	0	0	0	0	0	0	0	0	0

Game 5. Headingley, Leeds, August 19, 1938— The fifth test was staged at the home stadium of Leeds Rugby League Club. The game did not attract much interest, and the Leeds papers gave it little coverage.

In a rain-shortened game England won by five runs to three in six innings. This victory gave England a 4-1 winning margin in the series, which delighted all concerned with the game in England. The Liverpool *Evening Express* noted that,

> The National Baseball Association must be feeling well satisfied with the fillip the American game has received this last few weeks.

Subsequently, due to the success of the England team, the International Baseball Federation crowned them as the Inaugural World Amateur Champions.

After the test series the American Olympians played five exhibition games throughout the country, winning them all. They then headed off to the continent to play games in Belgium, France, Italy and Holland. Unfortunately, due to the Sino-Japenese conflict the Olympic Games were initially moved from Tokyo, then cancelled altogether with the outbreak of World War II. The outbreak of war also brought about the demise of the game in England. Baseball in Europe was brought to a standstill for over six years. Regrettably the game had not developed strong-enough roots in the English sporting psyche, and it never regained its pre-war popularity.

The Strange Case of Rapp's Missing Raps

Something was not right about Goldie Rapp's rookie hitting streaks

Jamie Selko

Several years ago, while perusing Joe Reichler's informative and entertaining *The Great All-Time Baseball Record Book*, I was struck by the performance of one Joseph "Goldie" Rapp. During Benito Santiago's last really good year (his rookie one), a hoopla was raised by his record-setting rookie 34-game hitting streak. Amidst this buzz, Goldie's name surfaced in the national media for the first time in some seventy years as the former panjandrum and poobah of National League Consecutive-Game-Hitting-Rookies. Goldie, who was thrown out only eighteen of the twenty-seven times he tried to steal during his rookie year of 1921 (not a misprint, and another fact of Goldie-teria which caught my eye), is listed as having two twenty-game-plus hitting streaks (twenty-three and twenty-six) that year for the Phillies. Now, considering the fact that he played in fifty-two games for the Phils that year, it struck me as odd that, having hit in forty-nine of them, his batting average for the Phillies was only .277. That, plus the fact that he got only fifty-six hits *total*, led me to investigate what I like to call…"The Strange Case of Rapp's Missing Raps."

To the Phillies—Goldie started the season with the Giants, but was traded (with others) to the Phillies for (among others) Casey Stengel on or about July 1. He had been hitting a puny .215 for the Giants and

had gotten but thirty-nine hits for them in the fifty-eight games in which he appeared, laying to rest any thought that perhaps he had one of those streaks with the McGrawmen. In his last game as a Giant, on June 29, he went 0-1, so there was no possibility of a carryover effect regarding the two alleged streaks.

For some reason, Rapp did not break into the Phillie lineup until July 7, against St. Louis. He had not played in the July 2 doubleheader against the Dodgers, the day England's A. G. Hill set a new mile record, blazing the four laps in 4:13.8. Nor did he appear against the Dodgers on the third.

On the fourth the Phils played a doubleheader against the Braves. Goldie appeared in neither game. In Toronto, Edward Marquis was killed by a pitched ball. Charlie Paddock also equaled his own world record of 9.6 in the hundred-yard dash that day.

Goldie did not play against the Bostons on July 5 or 6 either, and in not doing so he missed a doozy of an internecine baseball brawl. It seems that, in the fifth inning of the Boston-Philadelphia game, Braves player Tony Boeckel got into a slam-bang with third-base coach Dick Rudolph because Rudolph sent Ray Powell home on Boeckel's hit, and Powell was "meat" at the plate. Tony apparently didn't take kindly to the coach's gamble, so he popped him.

Beginning the streak—Finally, on the seventh, Goldie got his chance to play for the hapless Phillies and went one for three versus the Cards. Also on the seventh, Babe Ruth played in a game at St. Paul's

Jamie Selko lives in Eugene, Oregon

Orphan Asylum in Pittsburgh and fanned against the kid pitcher he faced. (Can you see Jose "All they care about is winning" Canseco or David "Where's the wimmins" Cone playing in an exhibition game against orphans—for free? I knew you couldn't.) On the eighth, Goldie went 3-for-5 and scored two runs vs. those same Cards. He followed that up with a 2-for-4 day on the ninth.

There was no game on the tenth, the day Joe Judge put on the greatest power display of his career, hitting two homers and a triple against the Browns. On July 11, Goldie went 1-for-4 against the Redbirds. On the twelfth, he mauled the Bucs for a hit in five at bats. Goldie's game was rained out on the thirteenth. On the fourteenth Goldie did the Bucs' pitchers again to the tune of 1 for 3.

The Phillies were rained out on July 15, but Goldie made the headlines anyway. Five Phils, Rapp included, were charged with disorderly conduct in an altercation involving two foot-bound citizens whom the ballplayers, ensconced in a fine automobile, apparently perceived to be wending their pedestrian way a bit too slowly for the players' liking at a crosswalk. The players were "alleged to have yelled at them to 'get a move on,' which is said to have started the argument."

On the sixteenth the Phils played a doubleheader versus the Reds. (Remember those? During the first month Goldie was on the team, the Phillies played six double-dips, including three in five days at one stretch). Goldie went 5-for-7 in the twin bill and scored three runs, his best day of the season. Although the Phillies were idle on July 17, there was some hot action up in Buffalo, where umpire O'Brien and pitcher Tomlin were arrested for assaulting each other. It seems Tomlin took umbrage at the umpire's ball-and-strike decisions and proceeded to deck him, whereupon, regaining his feet, umpire O'Brien pummeled pitcher Tomlin about the face with his mask.

The Reds and the Phillies played another doubleheader on the eighteenth. Goldie had cooled off during the off-day, and was only 2-for-8, getting one hit in each game. The nineteenth saw the same two teams play their fifth game against each other in four days. Robert Norton "Speed" Geary made his National League debut for the Reds and picked up what would ultimately prove to be his only win for them. He went 7-2/3 innings and struck out five to earn the victory (he would strike out only five more in his next—and last—30-1/3 innings). He was no mystery to Goldie that day, however, as the Rappster solved him for two hits in five at bats.

The next day it was on to Chicago for another doubleheader. Goldie went 2-9. On the twenty-first Goldie had a good day, going 3-for-4. Also of note that day, the Yankees got sixteen hits and lost, 17-8, as their pitchers gave up twenty-two hits in a contest that saw fourteen doubles hit.

Fifteen straight—On the twenty-second, the same day that saw the Yankees pummel the Akron Firestones, champs of the Akron Industrial League 23-3, Goldie had two hits against the Cubbies in a game that the New York papers noted (correctly) as the fifteenth consecutive in which the feisty lead-off man had gotten a hit. The next day, a record crowd of 39,000 in Boston watched the Beaneaters split a twin-bill with the Pirates. In Philadelphia, Goldie went 2-for-5 against the Cubs.

The next day is when things begin to go awry in Rappville. Playing the Giants in New York (where he received an ovation from the fans), Goldie went 2-for-4. It was Goldie's seventeenth consecutive game with a hit, yet the New York papers referred to it as his eighteenth, an amazing error, considering that a mere two days previously they had gotten his streak correct at fifteen games. He may well have cost the Phillies the game that day (they lost 4-3) by trying to score from third on a ball hit to first baseman Kelly. "Highpockets," who also drove in all four Giant runs, fielded a hot smash and tossed to pitcher Ryan who had rushed to cover the bag. Rosy took a tumble, and Goldie, sensing an opportunity, thought he could make it home. He was wrong.

The Phillies had the twenty-fifth off, but on the twenty-sixth, Goldie hit in his eighteenth straight—barely—against the Cards, going 1-for-6. The big story the next day was Babe Ruth. Playing an exhibition in Cincinnati, the Babe went 3-for-5 with six RBIs. No big deal, you say? Well, one of his hits was a homer over the center field fence. Not only was it the first home run ever to straightaway center in Crosley—no one had ever hit the fence on the fly before! The Bambino was not done yet, however. His next at bat yielded an even longer smash, this one reaching the bleachers in center.

On July 27 Rapp hit in his nineteenth consecutive game, 1-for-4 against the Redbirds, who turned a triple play that day.

The streak reached twenty on the twenty-ninth when he went 1-for-4 against St. Louis. In Cleveland Cy Young whiffed two in a two-inning stint in a Cleveland "Old Pros vs. Old Sandlotters" game, and our Goldie hit in consecutive game number twenty-one—but the New York papers called it game twenty-four! Somehow, Goldie had picked up two more games in the press. Goldie hit a leadoff home run in this contest, giving Bobby Bonds and Ricky Henderson a target to shoot for in later years.

On July 30 Goldie went 5-for-9 in a doubleheader versus the Cubs to make it twenty-three straight games in which he had connected safely. The New York papers called it twenty-six. The next day, he went 0-for-4 against the Cubs, and the streak was over. (In fact, the headline for the game read "RAPP HELD HITLESS.")

What happened?—Is the mystery of Goldie's two streaks solved? Well, just to make sure, I researched the rest of the season. Goldie would only play (play, not hit) in as many as ten consecutive games once the rest of the season. From September 14 until the season ended on October 1, he played in fourteen games (and corralled hits in ten). In fact, he would play in less than half his team's remaining games. There were two streaks of ten games played by the Phillies in which he did not appear at all. After hitting .392 during his streak (including a combined .436 (24-55) against the Reds and Cubs), he would hit under .200 for the rest of the season.

There are two possibilities which may serve to explain the error. One is that someone looked up the twenty-three-game streak and read about the twenty-six-gamer and accepted them both. The other is a simple misreading of the box score. Then, as now, runs followed at-bats in the boxes, so the box for what would have been game twenty-four reads: 4-1-0. That could have been misread as a hit instead of a run, and, as Goldie did get hits in the next two games, that would indeed have been twenty-six in a row.

Either way, sorry Goldie—no dual twenty-pluses. Still, Goldie fans, take heart. I do believe he holds the record for the longest hitting streak with a new team right after being traded. (If not, I'm sure I'll hear from Bob Davids!)

Young at Heart

Boston baseball teams during 1908 presented some tricky problems for the postman. Pitching for the Boston Red Sox was a big guy named Denton True Young, called "Cy" by everybody. On the crosstown Beaneaters, Irving Melrose Young was finishing his fourth season sharing Boston with the more famous Young, but he too was called "Cy"—either "Young Cy" or "Cy the Second." "Cy the Second" broke in with 20 wins in 1905, leading the National League in starts, complete games, and innings. He led the real Cy in those categories plus wins, games pitched, and shutouts (7).

Cy the Imposter declined during each year, until, on June 18, 1908, he was shipped over to Pittsburgh for Tommy McCarthy and Harlan Edward "Harley" Young—dubbed "Cy the Third."

Harley-Cy was not too successful in the win department, finishing 0-3 for his one and only big league season, but his ERA or 2.62 was one tick better than his namesake's career mark. He also eventually beat the big guy in the longevity department, 92-88. None of the three Cy Youngs had given names that suggested future greatness as hurlers: Denton, Irving, and Harley sound more like a congressman, a jeweler, and a tractor salesman.

Charles "Charley" Young of the Baltimore Feds of 1915 was also called "Cy," but by then all of his predecessors were gone and he was free to be mediocre all by himself, sans roman numerals.

The "W" Boys

In 1931, Earl Webb hit 67 doubles for the Red Sox, the all-time record. It was also more doubles than he hit in his next two best seasons combined. The Sox must have known something about Webb, because they swapped him during the middle of a .285 season the next year. The Tigers, not very shrewdly, sent over Dale Alexander, who proceeded to raise his average well over 100 points to win the batting title (.367). The Bengals also threw in Roy Johnson, who gave the Red Sox three consecutive .300 seasons and much more than they could have expected from the mystery doubler. Alexander and Webb were both out of the majors after '33. After the '35 season, the Sox shipped Johnson and the fading Carl Reynolds off to Washington for one season of the aging Heinie Manush.

Owen Wilson was the Earl Webb of triples. In 1912 he hit 36, for the all-time standard. He was always a pretty good tripler, but his six best years shows an aberration (12, 13, 12, 36, 14, 12).

The two "W" boys are probably the two least likely single-season record holders: Webb finished 638 behind Tris Speaker in his specialty; Wilson a hefty 198 behind Sam Crawford.

—Cappy Gagnon

Lost in the Ninth

Near no-hitters from a different perspective

Stew Thornley

Near no-hitters are often regarded as games in which a team gets only one hit; after all, one is close to zero. But if a fan leaves a game saying, "I almost saw a no-hitter," which is more likely: She witnessed a one-hitter in which the lone hit took place in the second inning, or a game in which a team was held hitless until the ninth, even if it then broke through for more than one hit?

This article will focus on the latter situation—no-hitters broken up in the ninth inning. There has been no definitive source of information, however, that has isolated games in which the first hit did not occur until the ninth inning.

Since *The Sporting News* annually lists all one- and two-hit games, along with when the hits took place, it's a straightforward process to identify most (80 to 90 percent) of the no-hitters lost in the ninth. Finding the rest—no-hitters that are broken up with three or more hits—requires digging into a variety of sources. Two invaluable sources for this article were Society for American Baseball Research members William Ruiz and the late Keith Sutton; Sutton compiled and maintained until his death a list of no-hitters broken up with two out in the ninth.

This article will expand on Sutton's work to include all no-hitters broken up in the ninth. From this, we can get an idea of a pitcher's chances of hanging onto a no-hitter that he carries into the

ninth.

Rather than try to identify all such games since Alexander Cartwright was a lad, this article will cover an arbitrary period, the expansion era (since 1961), that yields enough trials to render meaningful percentages of no-hitters either completed or broken up. (It should be noted, however, that the quirkiness of no-hitters makes any kind of probability analysis of the subject shaky. At the very least, it shows what happened in the past—that, since 1961, approximately half the no-hitters taken into the ninth have been broken up. Whether this is a valid percentage for predicting a pitcher's chances into the future is up to the reader to decide.)

A note on the definition of a no-hitter for this article: We're looking at no-hitters that survive the ninth. For most, that is the end of the no-hitter. But some are carried into, and broken up, in extra innings. Although these are no longer considered official no-hitters, they will be counted as no-hitters here for comparison purposes. Between 1961 and 1994, there have been two—one by Jim Maloney in 1965 and the other by Mark Gardner in 1991.) On the other hand, we are not counting no-hitters that don't get a chance to be extended into the ninth, either because the game is shortened by rain or because the hitless team doesn't bat in the last of the ninth because it has already won the game (Andy Hawkins and Matt Young have pitched these types of no-hitters since 1961).

From 1961 through 1994, 49.3 percent (ninety-

*A SABR member since 1979, **Stew Thornley** has seen all kinds of no-hitters and near no-hitters. This list of near no-hitters was compiled with the assistance of William Ruiz and Keith Sutton.*

nine of 201) of no-hitters have been completed. After one out has been recorded, the percentage increases to 63.1; it is 79.2 percent after two are out. (A summary, along with a decade-by-decade breakdown, follows the list of "Lost in the Ninth" no-hitters.)

Of the 102 no-hitters broken up in the ninth since 1961, fifty-three finished as one-hitters, thirty as two-hitters, eleven as three-hitters, five as four-hitters, one as a five-hitter, and two as six hitters. Eight of these games extended into extra innings, sometimes as a result of the game being tied (usually scoreless) even before the first hit, meaning that the game would not have been finished even with another hitless inning. In a few of the games, though, it was the late hit (or hits) that tied the game and resulted in extra innings.

Cesar Tovar, Billy Williams, and Eddie Milner have often been credited with breaking up the most no-hitters since each had his team's only hit (or hits) in a game five times. Although that doesn't fit the near no-hitter definition being used here, two of the three have broken up no-hitters in the ninth, Milner in 1983 and Tovar twice in 1969.

The most frequent spoiler of the expansion era is Horace Clarke of the Yankees, who broke up three, all within a month in 1970. Nelson Liriano spoiled a pair within a week in April, 1989.

Nolan Ryan is not only the all-time leader in no-hitters, he also holds the record for one-hitters and five times has had a no-hitter broken up in the ninth. But the National League record holder for one-hitters, Steve Carlton, never pitched a no-hitter nor did he ever carry one into the ninth inning.

Tom Seaver experienced ninth-inning disappointment three times, once having a perfect game broken up, before finally pitching a no-hitter in 1978. The real title of tough-luck pitcher, however, goes to Dave Stieb. He lost a no-hitter in the ninth in 1985, then two—both with two out in the ninth and one of them on a bad-hop single—in his final two starts of the 1988 season. The following August, he had a perfect game spoiled by Roberto Kelly with two out in the ninth (Stieb, like Seaver, did eventually complete a no-hitter).

Perhaps the closest play to break up a no-hitter with two out in the ninth was Carlos Garcia's infield hit off Jeff Fassero in July 1994. Garcia hit a liner back at Fassero, who thought he had caught it. The moment of hesitation, as Fassero looked vainly into his glove and finally discovered the ball near the edge of the mound, was fatal as he grabbed the ball and fired too late to get Garcia at first.

Tom Browning is the only pitcher to carry a perfect game into the ninth after having once before pitched a perfect game. His attempt at a second perfect game in 1989 was broken up by Dickie Thon.

Preston Gomez's legacy as a manager includes the fact that he twice pinch hit for pitchers who had a no-hitter through eight innings but still trailed in the game. One was Clay Kirby in July, 1970, the other Don Wilson (who had already pitched two no-hitters in his career) in September, 1974. In both cases, the relief pitcher was unable to complete the no-hitter in the ninth.

Except for Ken Landreaux's one-out double in the ninth, Bruce Kison would have been the holder of the most lopsided no-hitter ever, as his Angels beat the Twins, 17-0, in April, 1980.

How great a disappointment is it to lose a no-hitter in the ninth inning? Here are some reactions of those who've been there:

The Royals' Danny Jackson said the words he uttered after his no-hitter was spoiled in 1986 "can't be printed in a newspaper…It's disappointing. It's really disappointing."

Jim Slaton of the Brewers held the Twins hitless for eight innings in 1981 and admitted to these thoughts before Sal Butera spoiled it leading off the ninth: "I was thinking about how it would feel afterward. The happy part, about being elated…A no-hitter—you want it awful bad."

A year later the Twins broke up not just a no-hitter, but a perfect game that Toronto's Jim Clancy had been working on. Clancy said, "My legs were shaking on every pitch," adding that after Randy Bush singled to lead off the ninth, "I felt like crying."

Tom Seaver said he felt numb as he watched Jim Qualls' single ruin his perfect-game bid in 1969. "It was within my grasp. I could have had it," he said after the game. "You just don't get another chance. I can't measure the disappointment."

Ron Robinson of the Reds was still another who saw a perfect game disappear in the ninth, his with two out. Robinson responded simply, "That's baseball."

Here is a list of no-hitters broken up in the ninth since 1961, along with the name of the spoiler and the number of outs when the first hit occurred. (When more than one pitcher is listed, it means the last pitcher is the one who gave up the first hit. Relief pitchers who entered a game after it was broken up are not included in the list.)

Lost in the Ninth (Since 1961)

(# Perfect game broken up)

1961 1 no-hitter kept through 9 innings; 1 broken up in ninth

9/27, Al Schroll, Minnesota vs. Cleveland, Don Dillard (0)

1962 5 no-hitters; 2 broken up in ninth

5/1, Bill Stafford/Roland Sheldon, New York at White Sox, Nellie Fox (0)

5/22, Whitey Ford/Jim Coates, New York vs. LA Angels, Bob Rodgers (1)

1963 3 no-hitters; 4 broken up in ninth

5/11, Ted Bowsfield, Kansas City A's at Minnesota, Vic Power (0)

7/29, Joel Horlen, White Sox at Washington, Chuck Hinton (1)

8/27, Jim Bouton, New York vs. Boston, Russ Nixon, (0)

8/4, Johnny Podres, Los Angeles at Houston, Johnny Temple (1)

1964 3 no-hitters; 2 broken up in ninth

4/18, Jim Maloney/John Tsitouris, Cincinnati vs. Los Angeles, Frank Howard (2)

6/26, Gerry Arrigo, Minnesota vs Chicago, Mike Hershberger (0)

1965 4 no-hitters (including Maloney's); 0 broken up in ninth

1966 1 no-hitter; 2 broken up in ninth

9/25, Ken Holtzman, Cubs vs. Los Angeles, Dick Schofield (0)

#9/30, Larry Dierker, Houston at NY Mets, Ed Bressoud (0)

1967 4 no-hitters; 2 broken up in ninth

4/14, Billy Rohr, Boston at New York, Elston Howard (2)

4/16, Steve Barber, Baltimore at California, Jim Fregosi (1)

1968 5 no-hitters; 2 broken up in ninth

6/1, Dean Chance, Minnesota at Chicago, Bill Voss (1)

6/7, Blue Moon Odom, Oakland vs. Baltimore, Dave Johnson (2)

1969 6 no-hitters; 5 broken up in ninth

5/15, Dave McNally, Baltimore at Minnesota, Cesar Tovar (1)

5/31, Joe Sparma, Detroit at Pilots, Don Mincher (1)

#7/9, Tom Seaver, NY Mets vs Cubs, Jim Qualls (1)

8/10, Mike Cuellar, Baltimore vs. Minnesota, Cesar Tovar (0)

9/13, Larry Dierker, Houston at Atlanta, Felix Millan (2)

1970 4 no-hitters; 4 broken up in ninth

6/4, Jim Rooker, Kansas City at New York, Horace Clarke (0)

6/19, Sonny Siebert, Boston vs. New York, Horace Clarke (0)

7/2, Joe Niekro, Detroit at New York, Horace Clarke (1)

7/21, Clay Kirby/Jack Baldschun, San Diego vs. NY Mets, Bud Harrelson, (0)

1971 3 no-hitters, 2 broken up in ninth

4/16, Juan Marichal, San Francisco vs. Cubs, Ken Rudolph (0)

7/18, Luke Walker, Pittsburgh vs. Los Angeles, Joe Ferguson (0)

1972 3 no-hitters; 4 broken up in ninth

6/18, Jerry Reuss, Houston vs. Philadelphia, Larry Bowa (0)

7/4, Tom Seaver, NY Mets vs. San Diego, Leron Lee (1)

7/11, Marty Pattin, Boston at Oakland, Reggie Jackson (1)

7/18, Steve Arlin, San Diego vs. Philadelphia, Denny Doyle (2)

1973 5 no-hitters; 4 broken up in ninth

6/13, Rick Wise, St. Louis at Cincinnati, Joe Morgan (1)

#6/16, Jim Palmer, Baltimore vs. Texas, Ken Suarez (1)

7/6, Ron Schueler, Atlanta at NY Mets, Ron Hodges (0)

8/21, Stan Bahnsen, Chicago at Cleveland, Walt Williams (2)

1974 3 no-hitters, 5 broken up in ninth

#5/27, Ken Brett, Pittsburgh vs. San Diego, Fred Kendall (0)

7/15, Wayne Garland, Baltimore vs. Oakland, Dick Green (0)

7/20, Doc Medich, New York vs. Kansas City, Fran Healy (0)

8/7, Nolan Ryan, California at White Sox, Dick Allen (1)

9/4, Don Wilson/Mike Cosgrove, Houston vs. Cincinnati, Tony Perez (0)

1975 3 no-hitters; 3 broken up in ninth

6/8, Ken Holtzman, Oakland at Detroit, Tom Veryzer (2)

7/2, Rick Wise, Boston at Milwaukee, George Scott (2)

9/24, Tom Seaver, Mets at Chicago, Joe Wallis (2)

1976 4 no-hitters; 7 broken up in ninth

5/2, Rudy May, New York at Kansas City, Amos Otis (0)

6/4, Andy Messersmith, Atlanta at Montreal, Pepe Mangual (1)

5/26, Ken Brett, Chicago at California, Jerry Remy (2)

7/23, Doyle Alexander, New York vs. Boston, Rick Burleson (0)

8/7, Steve Luebber, Minnesota at Texas, Roy Howell (2)

8/28, Vida Blue, Oakland vs. Detroit, Mickey Stanley (1)

10/2, Phil Niekro, Atlanta at Cincinnati, Cesar Geronimo (1)

1977 3 no-hitters; 0 broken up in ninth

1978 2 no-hitters; 1 broken up in ninth

9/26, Mike Flanagan, Baltimore vs. Cleveland, Gary Alexander (2)

1979 1 no-hitter; 2 broken up in ninth

7/13, Nolan Ryan, California vs. New York, Reggie Jackson (1)

7/13, Steve Renko, Boston at Oakland, Rickey Henderson (1)

1980 1 no-hitter; 2 broken up in ninth

4/23, Bruce Kison, California at Minnesota, Ken Landreaux (1)

8/20, Dan Spillner, Cleveland vs. White Sox, Leo Sutherland (1)

1981 3 no-hitters; 4 broken up in ninth

5/6, Bert Blyleven, Cleveland at Toronto, Lloyd Moseby (0)

8/25, Dennis Lamp, White Sox at Milwaukee, Robin Yount (0)

9/5, Jim Slaton, Milwaukee at Minnesota, Sal Butera (0)

9/12, Bob Ojeda, Boston at New York, Rick Cerone (0)

1982 0 no-hitters; 1 broken up in ninth

#9/28, Jim Clancy, Toronto vs. Minnesota, Randy Bush (0)

1983 3 no-hitters; 4 broken up in ninth

#4/15, Milt Wilcox, Detroit at White Sox, Jerry Hairston (2)

6/26, Storm Davis, Baltimore vs. Detroit, Rick Leach (0)

7/31, Jose DeLeon, Pittsburgh at New York, Hubie Brooks (1)

9/23, Chuck Rainey, Cubs vs. Cincinnati, Eddie Milner (2)

1984 2 no-hitters; 1 broken up in ninth

5/12, Mario Soto, Cincinnati vs. St. Louis, George Hendrick (2)

1985 0 no-hitters; 3 broken up in ninth

5/8, Mike Moore, Seattle at Milwaukee, Robin Yount (0)

6/6, Jimmy Key, Detroit at Toronto, Tom Brookens (0)

8/24, Dave Stieb, Toronto at Chicago, Rudy Law (0)

1986 2 no-hitters; 4 broken up in ninth

6/16, Charlie Hough, Texas vs. California, Wally Joyner (1)

8/20, Walt Terrell, Detroit vs. California, Wally Joyner (2)

#8/20, Don Carman, Philadelphia at San Francisco, Bob Brenly (0)

10/1, Danny Jackson, Kansas City vs. California, Dick Schofield (0)

1987 1 no-hitter; 2 broken up in ninth

5/5, Eric Bell, Baltimore at Minnesota, Tom Nieto (0)

6/7, Mike Jackson, Philadelphia vs. Montreal, Tim Raines (0)

1988 1 no-hitter; 8 broken up in ninth

4/27, Nolan Ryan, Houston vs. Philadelphia, Mike Schmidt (1)

#5/2, Ron Robinson, Cincinnati vs. Montreal, Wallace Johnson (2)

5/8, Doug Drabek, Pittsburgh vs. San Diego, Randy Ready (0)

5/28, Odell Jones, Milwaukee at Cleveland, Ron Washington (1)

6/6, Tom Browning, Cincinnati at San Diego, Tony Gwynn (1)

6/12, Mike Scott, Houston vs. Atlanta, Ken Oberkfell (2)

9/24, Dave Stieb, Toronto at Cleveland, Julio Franco (2)

9/30, Dave Stieb, Toronto vs. Baltimore, Jim Traber (2)

1989 0 no-hitters; 6 broken up in ninth

4/23, Nolan Ryan, Texas at Toronto, Nelson Liriano (1)

4/28, Kirk McCaskill, California vs. Toronto, Nelson Liriano (0)

5/4, John Farrell, Cleveland vs. Kansas City, Kevin Seitzer (0)

#7/4, Tom Browning, Cincinnati at Philadelphia, Dickie Thon (0)

#8/4, Dave Stieb, Toronto vs. New York, Roberto Kelly (2)

8/10, Nolan Ryan, Texas vs. Detroit, Dave Bergman (1)

1990 7 no-hitters (not counting Hawkins'); 5 broken up in ninth

#4/20, Brian Holman, Seattle vs. Oakland, Ken Phelps (2)

5/27, John Smoltz, Atlanta at Philadelphia, Lenny Dykstra (1)

6/13, Trevor Wilson, San Francisco at San Diego, Mike Pagliarulo (0)

7/29, Scott Garrelts, San Francisco vs. Cincinnati, Paul O'Neill (2)

8/3, Doug Drabek, Pittsburgh at Philadelphia, Sil Campusano (2)

1991 8 no-hitters (includes Gardner's); 2 broken up in ninth

4/10, Scott Sanderson, New York at Detroit, Tony Phillips (0)

8/14, Randy Johnson, Seattle vs. Oakland, Mike Gallego (0)

1992 2 no-hitters (not counting Young's); 2 broken up in ninth

9/13, Bob Welch/Kelly Downs, Oakland vs. Seattle, Harold Reynolds (1)

9/30, Frank Viola, Boston at Toronto, Devon White (0)

1993 3 no-hitters; 3 broken up in ninth

4/6, Jose Guzman, Cubs vs Atlanta, Otis Nixon (2)

5/16, Randy Johnson, Seattle at Oakland, Lance Blankenship (1)

9/29, Tim Pugh, Cincinnati at San Diego, Billy Bean (1)

1994 3 no-hitters; 3 broken up in ninth

4/13, Pedro Martinez, Cincinnati at Montreal, Brian Dorsett (0)

5/29, David West/Heathcliff Slocumb, Phillies vs. Houston, Steve Finley (0)

6/13, Jeff Fassero, Montreal, vs. Pittsburgh, Carlos Garcia (2)

Summary

1961-70: 36 no-hitters; 24 broken up in ninth—60%

11 broken up with 0 out

9 broken up with 1 out (73.5% survived)

4 broken up with 2 out (90% survived)

1971-80: 28 no-hitters; 30 broken up in ninth—48.3%

10 broken up with 0 out

12 broken up with 1 out (58.3% survived)

8 broken up with 2 out (77.8% survived)

1981-90: 19 no-hitters; 38 broken up in ninth—33.3%

18 broken up with 0 out

8 broken up with 1 out (48.7% survived)

12 broken up with 2 out (61.3% survived)

1991-94: 16 no-hitters; 10 broken up in ninth—61.5%

5 broken up with 0 out

3 broken up with 1 out (76.2% survived)

2 broken up with 2 out (88.9% survived)

1961-94: 99 no-hitters; 102 broken up in ninth—49.3%

44 broken up with 0 out

32 broken up with 1 out (63.1% survived)

26 broken up with 2 out (79.2% survived)

#Perfect Game until ninth:

From 1961 through 1994, eleven pitchers who brought perfect games into the ninth finished with neither a perfect game nor a no-hitter. In addition, Jack Kralick and Milt Pappas lost perfect games but maintained no-hitters for a total of 13 perfect games broken up in the ninth since 1961. During that period, there had been eight perfect games (Bunning, Koufax, Hunter, Barker, Witt, Browning, D. Martinez, Rogers) pitched.

The Thief

Harry J. Rothgerber, Jr.

"Keen perception,
  Sound judgment,
    Young blood."
      (And a good jump.)
        Two steps and a slide away,
          Two and a half and a dive,
            Skip, don't cross
              Your feet.
                Pitcher rubbered,
                  Ball uncovered.
                    (Big righthander.)
                      Longer lead,
                        Hands off knees,
                          Weight balanced,
                            Eyes seeking
                              Pitcher's movements.
                                Make a break!
                                  No change of mind!
                                    Crossover pivot,
                                      Body low,
                                        Begins to raise,
                                          Pistons pumping,
                                            Short quick sprint.
                                              Hook slide,
                                                Pads scraping,
                                                  Spikes gleaming,
                                                    Dirt spraying.
                                                      Looks safe.
                                                        Wait!
                                                          Signals crossed!
                                                            (Line drive,
                                                              First Base,
                                                                Step on bag,
                                                                  Double play!)
                                                                    Quick starter,
                                                                      Speedy runner,
                                                                        Clever slider
                                                                          Sometimes equals . . .
                                                                            Inning Over!

Harry J. Rothgerber, Jr. is deputy chief of the juvenile and mental health division of the public defender's office in Louisville, Kentucky. He is also a legal writer and former chair of the Kentucky Parole Board.

"Mr. October"? Not!

Munson, Brett, others outperformed Jackson in the post-season

Alan Hirsch

Reggie Jackson was undeniably a tremendous World Series performer. In five Series, Jackson batted .357, with 10 home runs and 24 RBIs in 98 at bats. True, most of the damage was done in two series (1977 and 1978), and his other three performances were nothing to brag about. Still, give credit where credit is due: Jackson was a World Series hero.

The problem lies in the notion that Jackson is "Mr. October." Now that this widely publicized nickname adorns Jackson's plaque in Cooperstown, the myth behind it needs to be exposed.

The World Series is not the only center-stage October classic. There is also the League Championship Series (LCS). Is the LCS less important than the World Series? Hardly. Unless you win these playoffs, you watch the World Series on television. As for pressure, the LCS is watched by millions. All things considered, it is almost as good a gauge of clutch play as the World Series. And in eleven LCS, Reggie Jackson bombed.

In 163 LCS at-bats, Jackson batted a paltry .227, with just six home runs and 20 RBI. In six of the eleven playoffs, Jackson batted under .200. Projected over a full season, that comes out to roughly 20 home runs and 70 RBIs to go with the anemic batting average. This is weak for any clean up hitter, and it is certainly not "Mr. October" material.

While Jackson played superbly in his five World Series, he and his teams might have had even more chances if he had performed adequately in the play-offs. And he never would have had the opportunity for his remarkable three consecutive home runs in the 1977 World Series if his Yankee teammates hadn't compensated for his .125, one-RBI performance in the LCS.

One of those teammates, Thurman Munson, considered October the loveliest month. In the 1976 World Series, Munson had six consecutive base hits and batted .529 overall. He excelled in all three of his World Series, batting a cumulative .373. He never put on the show Jackson was capable of, but he wasn't "Mr. Schizophrenic October" either—he shone in the LCS as well as the World Series. His record over six post season series is a study in consistent excellence: a cumulative batting average of .357, with no average lower than .278 in any single series. He may be more deserving of the moniker "Mr. October" than Jackson.

Munson isn't the only one. In six League Championship Series, George Brett batted .340, with a spectacular nine home runs and 19 RBIs in 103 at bats. In his two World Series, Brett batted an overall .373 (.375 and .370 respectively).

In five post season playoffs, Steve Garvey was sensational, batting .356 with eight home runs and 21 RBIs in 90 at bats. Not surprisingly, his teams won all five. In his five World Series, Garvey batted .319. Garvey's cumulative post season batting average is .338.

Of course, not everyone gets as many opportunities

Alan Hirsch *is a freelance writer. His recent publications include pieces on Leon Spinks and Charles Barkley in* Troika *magazine.*

Transcendental Graphics

Thurman Munson: consistency made October his lovliest month.

as these folks to play in big games and establish a reputation as a clutch player. Some players have made the most out of a few opportunities. Everyone remembers Kirk Gibson limping to the plate and blasting a heroic game-winning home run against Dennis Eckersley in the first game of the 1988 series. But Gibson's October greatness was not limited to that one swing. In 1984, when his Tigers won it all, he batted .417 in the LCS and .333 with two home runs and seven RBIs in the World Series. Overall, he slugged seven home runs and drove in 21 runs in his 78 post season at bats. Those numbers surpass Mr. October's October averages.

Munson, Brett, Garvey, and Gibson, along with Dave Henderson, and Lou Brock, have been Reggie Jackson's equal or superior as post-season players. Jackson's overall post season statistics are a .278 batting average with 18 home runs and 48 RBIs in 281 at bats. That's nothing to apologize for; in fact, it is darned good. As a matter of fact, it is similar to Jackson's regular season production. Which brings us back to the central point: he's not Mr. October.

The Average Length of a World Series

Teams match up well

Bob Brown

Using the most basic probability concept, namely the "multiplication rule for independent events," I determined the chances that two evenly-matched teams would play a four, five six, or seven game World Series. The chances are as follows:

Games Required to Win Series (G)	Probability P(G)
4	2/16
5	4/16
6	5/16
7	5/16
	1

Multiplying each value of G by its corresponding probability, P(G), then summing, we obtain, in theory at least, the average length of a World Series, in the long run between two evenly matched teams:

$$\text{AVG.} = \sum G \times P(G) = 4(2/16) + \ldots + 7(5/16)$$
$$= 93/16$$
$$= 5.8125 \text{ games.}$$

Next, I looked up the results of the last 87 World Series and averaged the results. What I discovered was only slightly amazing:

Bob Brown, who grew up in the shadow of the Polo Grounds, is a statistics professor at Providence College.

Games Played to Win Series	Number of Times This has Happened
4	15
5	20
6	18
7	34
	87

Actual Average number of games played to win Series since 1903 =

$$\frac{4(15) + 5(20) + 6(18) + 7(34)}{87}$$
$$= 5.8161$$

There was virtually *no* difference between the *theoretical* and *actual* average number of games played to win the Series. This implies that over the years the World Series has been played between two essentially evenly matched teams.

Calculation of probabilities—For those of you who aren't familiar with the rule mentioned above, here's how it works. Suppose we want to figure the chances that two evenly matched teams (say, A and B) will play a six-game Series. Then one team (either team) must have a 3 games to 2 lead after five. This could happen in any one of ten equally likely ways:

1. $A_1A_2A_3B_4B_5$
2. $A_1A_2B_3A_4B_5$
3. $A_1B_2A_3A_4B_5$
4. $B_1A_2A_3A_4B_5$

5. $A_1A_2B_3B_4A_5$

6. $A_1B_2B_3A_4A_5$

7. $B_1B_2A_3A_4A_5$

8. $B_1A_2B_3A_4A_5$

9. $B_1A_2A_3B_4A_5$

10. $A_1B_2A_3B_4A_5$

Actually, there is a formula for determining how many ways these objects could be rearranged. It is:

$$\frac{5!}{3!2!} = \frac{5 \times 4 \times 3 \times 2 \times 1}{3 \times 2 \times 1 \times 2 \times 1} = 10$$

At any rate, since there are ten ways team A could win in six games, there are also ten ways in which team B could win in six, and since all ten ways are equally likely, we only have to work out the probability of one of them (say $A_1A_2A_3B_4B_5A_6$), then multiply by ten, then by two (since team B could just as easily win in six). So we get:

$P(A_1A_2A_3B_4B_5A_6) = (1/2) (1/2) (1/2) (1/2) (1/2) (1/2) = 1/64.$

Hence:

P(WS lasts six games between two evenly matched teams) =

(1/64) (10) (2) = 20/64 = 5/16

In no other major sport, not in the NHL, not even in the NBA (sports that also use a best-of-seven format to determine a champion), are the two "averages" so close. Indeed, they are not even remotely close in the NHL. (The actual average number of games played between Stanley Cup finalists since 1939 is a little over 5.3, far too low an average to support the claim that the two best teams made it to the finals.) Baseball's long season, pennant races and the brutal simplicity that requires season-long excellence have insured the integrity of the World Series—where, in most cases, the team that loses is probably just as good as the team that wins.

GAME 7 Tuesday, October 4, 1955

Brooklyn   000 101 000 - 2 5 0
New York   000 000 000 - 0 8 1

BROOKLYN (3-3)				
4/7 Gilliam	63	w	43	sc	8
6 Reese	8	8	S	k
8 Snider	43	k	e3*	k
2 Campanella	43	D	14b	7
9 Furillo	7	63+	i	8
3 Hodges	w	s'	8h'+	3^f
5 Hoak	43	53	w	s
4 Zimmer	63	k		
o Shuba 6	31			
7 Amoros 6	w			
1 Podres	43	5^f	43	8

NEW YORK (3-3)				
6 Rizzuto	2^f	wx	53	s
4 Martin	8	s	w	9
5 McDougald	43	s	sx	s+
2 Berra	8	d	763p	9
9 Bauer	43	8	63	k
3 Skowron	d	43+	63	13
8 Cerv	63	6^	63	7
7 Howard	8	7	s	63
1 Byrne	k	k		
1Grim 6				
o Mantle 7	6^			
1 Turley 8				

* 13b and e3

Pitchers: BROOKLYN, Podres W. NEW YORK, Byrne L (995xx), Grim (WP,xx42x), Turley (xxx71).

Left on Base- Bkl 8, NY 8. T- 2:44. A- 62,465.

Ump-Honochick, Dascoli, Summers, Ballanfant, Flaherty, Donatelli.

Ham Hyatt and the Development of Pinch Hitting

An early—but long-term—record-holder

John T. Hannon, Jr.

Pinch hitting was first allowed during the 1891 season. Before that, substitutions were only allowed in emergency situations. It was on such an occasion in early 1871 that Frank Norton was forced to hit for injured Doug Allison. Norton struck out, but that appearance is considered by most baseball historians to be the first use of a pinch hitter.

The use of pinch hitters evolved slowly during the next fifteen years, though the game-altering effect was evident soon after the rule change. There were over 6,000 fans in Boston on May 14, 1892, when Tom Daly of Brooklyn pinch hit for outfielder Hub Collins in the ninth inning. With Brooklyn trailing 6-5, the switch-hitting Daly, batting lefthanded against Boston righthander, John Clarkson, hit the first pich for a home run, sending the game into extra innings.

Things were beginning to change, but it would be 1907 before a player pinch hit more than twenty times in a season.

In the American League, St. Louis had a twenty-three-year-old wildness-prone righthander from Sherman, Mississippi, who could swing the bat better than he could pitch. During the 1908 season, Manager Jimmy McAleer would send the lefthand swinging Dode Criss to the plate for a record-shatter-ing 41 at bats. Twelve times, the 6' 2", 200 pounder would deliver in the pinch.

For his short four-year career, Criss would become major league baseball's first pinch-hitting specialist, collecting 35 hits in 147 at bats.

Though Criss was the first heavily used pinch hitter, it was another Southern-born young man, the same age as Criss, who would become the major league's first power pinch hitter. Beginning his career in 1909 with Pittsburgh, Robert "Ham" Hyatt, would spend seven years in the majors, including five years with Pittsburgh, as a utility first baseman and outfielder. From 1909-10 and 1912-14 he was not in the majors in 1911), 205 of his 499 at bats were as a pinch hitter. He would hit four pinch homers, including a record three during the 1913 season. In 1909, Hyatt would hit three pinch triples, which would remain a record for 61 years, until it was tied in 1970 by St. Louis' Vic Davalillo. Hyatt's five career pinch triples would last to the coming of Gates Brown, and the three pinch homers hit in the dead-ball era of 1913 would not be equaled until August 14, 1932, when Johnny Frederick hit his fourth, on his way to a still-standing record six for the Dodgers.

Ham's early days—Robert Hamilton Hyatt was born on a farm near Chandler, North Carolina on the fringes of the Smoky Mountains. He lived there until he was nineteen, when the lack of opportunity caused him to head west. With him, he carried one skill—the ability to play baseball.

John T. Hannon, Jr. is controller for a large hand tool manufacturer. He has been a SABR member since 1977. His interest in pinch hitting began when he was 10, with Elmer Valo of the Dodgers, and continued later with Gus Zernial and Jerry Lynch.

Hyatt initially settled in Hoquiam on the coast of Washington state, where he found work as a logger. It was while here that he began to refine his baseball skills with a local semipro team.

The local team was a member of the Southwest Washington State Semi-Pro League, and Hyatt would become the league's premier hitter, hitting .350 in 1905, and .375 in 1906, playing mostly in the outfield and on first base.

His 1906 season attracted the attention of the professional club in Vancouver, British Columbia, which was part of the Northwestern League. Signing with the club in 1907, Hyatt hit an even .300, and in 1908, .323. On August 30 he was sold to the Pittsburgh Pirates.

Hyatt came to the Pirates as a 6' 1", 190 pound, twenty-four year old, with above-average fielding skills and a very strong arm. One thing he lacked, though, was speed. It would be a problem that would plague him throughout his career. The problem was compounded by a tendency to let his playing weight creep up to 220 pounds.

The Pirates starting outfielders were generally fast afoot, as was the starting first baseman, Bill Abstein. Hyatt quickly found himself relegated to pinch hitting chores on the "talent loaded" team. From all indications, the quiet, good-natured Hyatt accepted his limited role, happy just to be in the majors.

Big league beginnings—Hyatt made his first major league appearance in Cincinnati in the second game of the season, when he pinch hit for pitcher Vic Willis in the ninth inning. He failed to reach base.

The next day Hyatt found himself hitting in a similar situation, two outs, ninth inning, one on, and the Pirates down 4-2. Facing Reds righthander Jean Dubuc, Hyatt tripled to right center for his first major league hit.

He was hitless in his next six pinch-hit at bats. Then, on May 29, at Pittsburgh's Exposition Park in a game against the Cubs played in front of a wild, packed house including President Taft and his ambassador brother, Hyatt connected again. The game was tied 3-3 through ten innings, when the Cubs exploded for five runs in the top half of the eleventh. Battling for pitcher Lefty Leifield in the home half, Hyatt tripled off future Hall of Famer "Three Finger" Brown with the bases empty. As with his first triple, he was left stranded.

Hyatt's next hit was on June 7, when he hit a pinch double off Philadelphia's Buster Brown in the eighth, helping Pittsburgh to a 4-3 win.

The next day Hyatt started his first major league game, playing first base and going 2 for 4, including a double. He scored two runs in another 4-3 win.

When July 4 arrived, Hyatt had appeared in 16 games with 23 at bats. He was hitting .348, with eight hits, including two triples and two doubles, very impressive statistics for a utility man.

Hyatt hit his third pinch triple of the season on August 16 in Forbes Field against the Giants. Batting for pitcher Vic Willis in the eighth, Hyatt slammed a Christy Mathewson fastball to deep right. When Hyatt walked off the field that day after Ed Abbaticchio pinch ran for him, he had unknowingly set a pinch hitting record that wouldn't be equaled for sixty-one years.

Hyatt ended the 1909 regular season hitting .299 in 48 games with a .463 slugging average. As a pinch hitter, he had appeared in 40 games with 37 at-bats, collecting nine hits, five of which were for extra bases.

He appeared in two games in the 1909 World Series against the Tigers. In game six, he appeared as a pinch hitter, grounding to second, and in the seventh game in Detroit, he played 8-1/2 innings in center field collecting an RBI sacrifice to center and a walk in five trips, as the Pirates won the series.

The quiet career continues—Hyatt appeared in 74 games in 1910, hitting .263. As a pinch hitter, he went only 6 for 31. Through he was in the field only 42 times, 38 at first base, his 175 at bats would be, by far, the largest number in his five-year career with the Pirates. On June 15 Hyatt hit his first major league home run, while playing first base in a game with the Giants in the Polo Grounds. The homer came off Christy Mathewson in the seventh inning, when Hyatt sent the ball to the top of the right field grandstand, barely inside the foul line.

Though Hyatt's pinch hitting was less than spectacular in 1910, the use of pinch hitters was gaining in popularity. Reds manager Clark Griffith used a speedy outfielder named Ward "Windy" Miller regularly as a pinch hitter. The slender lefthanded hitter was the first National Leaguer to have 40 pinch at bats in a season. He collected 11 hits. While in the American League, Dode Criss had 44 at bats, and became the first player in major league history to have more than 100 career pinch hitting at bats.

Before the start of the 1911 season, Hyatt was optioned to Kansas City of the American Association. The Pirates were favoring the speed and power of John Flynn, and the speed of 31-year-old rookie,

Newt Hunter in lieu of Hyatt. Obviously, Hyatt's future depended on his ability to pinch hit, and his .194 average in 1910 wasn't getting the job done.

Hyatt would play in 166 games in Kansas City, and bat .326 in 643 at bats, playing first base with an occasional day in the outfield. Interestingly, it was here Hyatt would say long after he had left professional baseball that his greatest thrill occurred. He started and finished the only triple play he ever saw with teammate and former St. Louis Browns shortstop Red Corriden.

Back to the majors—In 1912, Hyatt found himself back with the Pirates after neither Flynn nor Hunter worked out as expected. Manager Clarke moved second baseman Dots Miller to first, and Hyatt was back in his familiar role as a utility man. During the season, Hyatt would appear in only 46 games, mostly as a fill-in outfielder. As a pinch hitter, he was 6 for 27. The Pirates finished second, ten games back of the Giants.

In New York during 1912, the colorful McGraw did much to popularize the role of the pinch hitter with the press with his use of a 31-year-old, tall, lanky, poor-fielding outfielder by the name of Moose McCormick. McGraw's antics, such as having the trainer massage McCormick's legs before he stepped into the batter's box, made McCormick something of a pinch hitting legend and popularized the role with the fans. The college-educated McCormick responded with a league-leading 11 for 30 performance. Though in the majors for only five seasons, and used heavily as a pinch hitter only during his last two years, McCormick left the game with a .301 pinch hitting average in 93 at bats. In World Series play in 1912 and 1913, he was 2 for 6.

The 29-year-old Hyatt started the 1913 season poorly. On May 15, he found himself hitting .091 (1 for 11), all as a pinch hitter. He had appeared only once in the field as a late inning replacement. His future as a major leaguer was definitely in doubt, but that was to change quickly. May 16 would mark the beginning of an amazing streak of power for a fringe player in the "dead ball" era.

Christy Mathewson had been pitching an excellent game through seven innings at the Polo Grounds on May 16. The Giants were leading 7-1, when Hyatt was called on to pinch hit. The following is from the account of the New York *Times* the next day:

Ham Hyatt ambled up to the plate in the 8th without attracting undue notice. But Ham caused a few inquires as to his identity before again going down into the Pirate dugout. He picked one of Matty's slants to his liking and gently lifted the ball into the upper tier of right field.

Between May 16 and July 17, Hyatt went 18 for 44, and 6 for 12 as a pinch hitter. His average would climb to .345. His six pinch hits included two doubles and his second pinch homer.

The homer came on July 2 in Chicago, when he pinch hit for infielder Art Butler in the eighth. Hyatt lined one of right-hander Bert Humphries' fastballs into the right stands in the Cubs' West Side Park.

The next day, in a game back in Pittsburgh against the Cards, Hyatt would hit two triples while starting at first base.

Hyatt came close to getting another pinch triple on August 14 in Ebbets Field. Hyatt came to the plate in the fifth for pitcher Wilbur Cooper with the bases loaded. He lined a double off the right field wall, scoring two runs. Acording to the New York *Times'* account, the hit would easily have been a triple, if Hyatt hadn't been slowed down by teammate George Gibson's indecision over whether to stay at third, or head home. Nevertheless, the hit was Hyatt's third pinch double of the season. The double and Hyatt's .367 batting average got his photo in the *Times* the next day.

A week later, on August 22 in Philadelphia's Baker Bowl, Hyatt's streak continued, when he pinch hit for pitcher Babe Adams in the seventh and homered to right off right hander Erskine Mayer. It was Hyatt's fourth homer of the season and third as a pinch hitter.

At the end of the season Hyatt was hitting .333 with a .605 slugging average in 81 at bats. He was 15-52 as a pinch hitter for a .288 average, including four doubles and a record three homers.

A watershed year—1913 was a watershed year for pinch hitting. Besides Hyatt's record three homers, the Phils Doc Miller collected a record 20 hits in a league leading 56 at-bats. The 20 hits, like Hyatt's record, would last until 1932. The Giants Sam Leslie broke the record with 22 pinch hits, while across town, Brooklyn's Johnny Frederick's six pinch homers eclipsed Hyatt's record. In the American League, Washington's Germany Schaefer had 11 pinch hits in 21 at bats for a .524 average. Pinch hitting had become an important part of the game.

The Pirates finished seventh in 1914 with a team that was racked with dissent. Team president Barney

Dreyfuss became so frustrated that in late July he asked waivers on eleven players, including five starters. Hyatt finished the season with the Pirates, collecting 14 hits in 58 pinch at bats, leading the majors in both categories, but he was only 3 for 21 when not in a pinch hitting role. This lowered his combined average to .215, the worst of his career. Among the 14 pinch hits was a two-run homer on April 26 in Chicago off Jim Lavender in the eighth that began a comeback from a 4-0 defitcit to win the game, and a triple with two on against the Braves in the eighth off George Davis on July 22, his fifth in his career as pinch hitter.

Hyatt was released by the Pirates on February 28, 1915, and immediately picked up by the Cardinals. For the first time in his major league career, he played regularly, primarily at first base. The Cards finished in sixth. Hyatt hit .268 in 106 games. As a pinch hitter, he was a poor 3 for 14.

Fading out—Hyatt spent 1916 and 1917 in the minors with Chattanooga, near his boyhood home but a long way from the majors. When Hyatt's friend and former teammate Miller Huggins replaced "Wild Bill" Donovan as the Yankees manager in 1918, he signed Hyatt as a utility man and pinch hitter. For the 33-year-old Hyatt, this would mark his last year in the big-time. He hit .229 in 53 games, showing only occasional signs of power. As a pinch hitter, he was a poor 4-21. Hyatt went 6 for 12 in his last three games with the Yankees, and his last as a major leaguer. He played left field for the fourth-place Yankees in Washington. In his last appearance as a major leaguer, the quiet, unassuming Hyatt had a ground out RBI off Senator pitcher Sam Jones.

Hyatt stayed in organized ball five more years, two with Toledo and three with the Vernon Tigers of the Pacific Coast League.

During the off season in his playing days, Hyatt worked as a logger in western Washington. After retiring from baseball, he landed a job with the Washington State Patrol, where he stayed for over twenty years.

Hyatt had married May Connolly after the 1909 season and they had a daughter in 1911. Two sons and another daughter were born after he left professional ball. Shortly before his seventy-ninth birthday in 1963, Hyatt died in Spokane from heart failure following an operation.

Hyatt was not a great baseball player, but he had lived every boy's dream: he had played major league baseball, and at times, he had played it very well.

On October 4, 1914, Hyatt pinch hit for rookie Paddy Siglin, his last appearance in a Pirate uniform. He received a base on balls, and as he trotted down to first base that fall afternoon he couldn't possibly have realized that 80 years later his name would still be prominent in the Pittsburgh record book.

Fenway Doubt

Doubt has often been voiced about Fenway Park's distance to left field. The fence carries the figure '315.' Many are skeptical. Team officials have resisted efforts to obtain an exact measurement. Some years ago a Boston Globe writer asked a friend skilled in aerial photography analysis, trigonometry, and the complex computer field to solve the enigma. A shot of Fenway from the air was provided. With lenses and other sophisticated equipment the friend did his calculations. His answer: "Home plate to the 'Green Monster' is 304.779 feet." The Globe presented the story on Page One on October 18, 1975. Reaction in the Fenway front office (said with a smile): "We thought everyone knew the distance was less than 315." The sign, of course, remains.

—Jim Murphy

They Didn't Know How To Quit

Five examples of determination from the American Association

Henry C. Mayer

Professional baseball has benefitted American life in many ways. Watching a game and cheering the home team can be healthy, but this article singles out another benefit.

That is the refusal to quit under adverse, not to say depressing, conditions. Many athletes have exemplified it in many ways. This article presents five players who did their best for themselves and their teams either when their chances for promotion and fame in the majors were remote or when their teams found themselves mired in the second division, even in the cellar.

One scenario takes place between the years of the Great Depression and the end of World War II. The example of athletes not quitting in spite of personal reverses might well have said something about our nation's ability to cope with these situations.

To appreciate the quality of these players' feats, we need to recall some of the circumstances in which they played. Salaries were a modest fraction of today's.

Night games were often played with substandard illumination. During a game in Louisville during 1934 the lights went out four times before the umpires called a halt.

Travel was slow, without air conditioning, sometimes in day coaches and requiring a change of trains. Even as late as September, 1939, it took ten hours to reach Minneapolis from Louisville. Some teams resorted to buses during the deep days of the Depression.

Now, let's meet Ray French, John Niggeling, Whit Wyatt, Mel Simons, and Nick Cullop. Only Wyatt eventually made it back big in the majors. Niggeling and Cullop experienced real if modest successes there. The others simply busted their butts day after day in the American Association.

Ray French—Baseball has some highly emotional experiences. But few experiences can be as traumatic as an unconditional release. Forty-two-year-old Ray French knew the feeling in the spring of 1937, when Kansas City let him go. He was relieved when the Louisville Colonels "Cap" Neal offered him a contract. In spring training Manager Bert Niehoff asked him to double as his assistant.

French could still cover second, third, or short; he preferred the last. He shared it with two others during 1937. Then, as the 1938 regular season began, he made the opening day lineup. Soon he was alternating with 18-year-old "Pee Wee" Reese during the season's first seven weeks.

So, as our camera swings into focus the date is June 7 and the scene Louisville's Parkway Field. A stirring mound duel is under way. St. Paul's "calm, courageous, crafty" southpaw, Lloyd Brown, the winner of nearly a hundred big league games, is safeguarding his 1-0 shutout over a more youthful "Yank" Terry.

Some faithful fans were still trying to cheer the Colonels into a ninth-inning rally as an error, a single

Henry C. Mayer is one of three researchers preparing a history of professional baseball in Louisville. He invites correspondence with those who have memories of the city's years in the American Association.

and a useless peg to the wrong base had put Koster and Bell on third and second with no outs. That brought up thirty-eight-year-old Mel Simons. St. Paul skipper "Babe" Ganzel well knew Mel's ability to hit in the clutch, so he ordered Brown to walk him. Sturm then hit a fielder's choice allowing Koster to tie the game. French now moved into the batter's box.

He fouled off Brown's first pitch, then smiled as the count went to two and one. Fourteen long years had elapsed since Ray had worn a big league uniform, but he still had a reputation for not swinging at questionable pitches. Instinctively, Ray glanced quickly at Niehoff in the coaching box at third and picked up his new sign. Brown stretched as two runners edged off their bases. If Bell's lead from third was a little daunting, it was too late to react. But what's this? Shifting his grip on the bat, French was laying down a bunt. Bell had crossed the plate and French was safe at first. A beaming Niehoff chortled to himself as he led the triumphant Colonels to the clubhouse while the stunned Saints, some perhaps uttering unsaintly language, slunk off toward theirs in somber silence.

John Niggeling—One lazy sunny afternoon in early August, 1939 John Niggeling of the Indianapolis Indians was summoned to manager Wes Griffin's room.

The thirty-four-year-old, dark-haired Niggeling responded with a touch of anxiety, but Griffin came to the point. "We're selling you—to the Cincinnati Reds!" The quiet Niggeling looked up in disbelief. The Cincinnati Reds—the team apparently headed for the National League pennant! He was to leave ASAP.

Soon he was shaking hands and saying his good-byes. Though he didn't realize it, he was also saying so long forever to eleven years of minor league baseball. Niggeling hadn't started playing professional baseball until he was twenty-four. He'd had three successful years in the lower minors before a queasy stomach had sidelined him in 1932. He'd had the thrill of being named Kansas City's opening day pitcher in 1933 and sending home copies of the picture of himself that appeared in the Louisville *Courier Journal*. But he'd suffered the disappointment of not being able to finish the game and of winning only four games and losing eleven for the Blues. It had taken him three more seasons, mostly in lower leagues, to make their regular mound staff. He couldn't marry Ruth, his hometown sweetheart, because his modest salaries would only support his widowed mother and himself.

And just when he thought his 1936 record of eighteen wins and fifteen losses seemed to say he had made it, 1937 had brought new doubts with a lackluster 7-12 for Kansas City.

Then things began to move fast: a late season transfer to the Newark Bears, followed quickly by purchase by the Boston Bees of the National League. Scarcely had he begun to savor the fact that in his first brief appearance, he had gotten credit for his first big league win when the Bees dispatched him to Indianapolis, where he became the winning pitcher in the Association's All Star Game and finished at a respectable 14- 11. Then came 1939, a 15-7 slate, and this sudden elevation to Cincinnati. He must have felt that his career had something in common with a roller-coaster ride.

There was more to come. John contributed two victories to the Reds' victory drive but sat out the World Series. Then in the off-season, Cincinnati put him on the waiver list. A former opposing manager from Association days, Fred Haney, now managing the St. Louis Browns, claimed him as a steady, hard-working pitcher with good control.

John hung in there to win seven games in each of the next two seasons. Then in 1942, at the age of 37, he won fifteen and lost eleven, started twenty-seven and completed sixteen games and whiffed 107 batters. His improving salary and a bonus now let him take the faithful Ruth down the aisle.

In all he spent seven consecutive years in the majors. He broke his own season mark for strikeouts, whiffing 121 batters in one season and in only one of his big league seasons (his last at age 42), did he walk more men than he fanned. He closed out his big league record with a respectable 64-69, playing with second division teams.

Whit Wyatt—Unlike the other players in this article, Whit Wyatt first saw big league action just before his twenty-second birthday—and the stock market crash. Also unlike them, his most frustrating years were six seasons in the American League. It certainly depressed him to win a mere twenty-six games while losing forty-three, and to experience high ERAs including a career high of 7.14. And to top off this record, after his 1936 season with Kansas City had earned him another trip to the majors, his 1937 record with Cleveland included twenty-nine appearances, two wins and three losses.

So a badly shaken thirty-year-old athlete reported to Milwaukee Brewer Manager Al Sothoron for spring training in 1938. Wyatt began winning and was named to the Association All-Stars at midseason. Sensing a story, Louisville *Courier-Journal*'s Bruce Dudley interviewed Wyatt. "To get to the big leagues you got to be lucky," Wyatt began, "and you have to be lucky to stay there. I believe I will be able to stick now. I have learned a lot about pitching from Al Sothoron. I have much more confidence in myself than I ever had before." Another article emphasized that Sothoron had helped Wyatt perfect a change-up to increase the effectiveness of his fast ball.

Wyatt's 1938 stats proved the change. He led the league in wins (23, with only seven defeats); he pitched the most innings and led the pack in strikeouts (208) and ERA (2.37). No wonder he was purchased as a part in MacPhail's rebuilding of Brooklyn's Dodgers.

Wyatt was 8 and 3 in his first year in Flatbush, with an ERA of 2.31. His 1940 record was a modest 15 and 14. Yet his appearance in the 1940 All-Star game gave him heart, for in a two-inning stint, he limited the powerful American Leaguers to one hit.

But 1941 was to be his year. His achievement of twenty-two wins and ten reverses was a major factor in the Dodgers winning the league title. He also paced National League moundsmen in shutouts, tying a record for Brooklyn pitchers in so doing. This time he held the American League All-Stars hitless and later achieved the Dodgers' only triumph from the Yankees in the World Series. The Baseball Writers Association of America selected him to the prestigious *Sporting News* Major League All Star Team.

Wyatt also had two more highly successful seasons after 1941. He closed his career with three times as many wins in the National League as he had had in the American League.

Mel Simons—He was a singles hitter in a home run era but twice he made more hits than any other Association batter. His .371 average led Louisville to its pennant in 1930 and he was voted the best outfielder in the league. This drew attention from both the Yankees and the White Sox. Chicago gave the Colonels $22,000 and two players for him. But with a .275 average in 68 games in 1931 and a hitless start in 1932, he was back in a Louisville uniform.

A Greek tag, "character is destiny," sums up the rest of Simons' career. In the following seven seasons, only once did the Colonels rise out of the second division. In contrast, Mel's averages were .314, .324,

.328, .352, .353, .316 and .272. It was his ninth-inning, two-out single on the last day of the 1934 season that let the Colonels creep into the first division and each player collect a $250 bonus.

But it was his 1936 season that stood out. Though the team's oldest regular, the thirty-six-year-old Simons set a personal career season mark both with twenty-two steals and thirty-eight attemps, led the team in hitting and paced the league in total hits. He also made the league's All-Star team while the local fans named him the team's most valuable player.

Nick Cullop—His published photo and my contact with him as a clubhouse boy would not even hint at it. But Nick Cullop had to cope with more difficult troubles than his failure to make five big league teams by the age of thirty. Here is what happened.

Purchased by Minneapolis at the end of the 1929 season, Cullop was confronted during the offseason with the deaths of two of his children and his wife's nervous breakdown. The new season had hardly begun when Cullop was beaned, and in his first twenty-five games he hit only one home run. He never said publicly how he did it, but then Cullop caught fire. He set a league record for home runs (54), hit .359 and led everyone else in runs scored (150) and RBIs (152).

That got him his last best chance to make it to the majors. Cincinnati bought him and in 1931 he hit .263 in 102 games including eight homers. But two stats may indicate why he did not stick. He walked only 21 times while striking out on 86 occasions. Former big league catcher Mickey Owen once told this writer, "In the majors, you have to hit their pitches; they also find out your weakness more quickly than in the American Association and if you don't correct it promptly, you're gone!"

So back to the Association he went. There he led Columbus to two consecutive pennants (.313, 28 homers and 143 RBIs in 1933, and .303, 27 home runs and 130 RBIs in 1934). He also made the 1936 All-Stars.

But even better days were ahead. Branch Rickey had spotted a talent for managing and by 1937 Nick was managing in the Cardinals' far flung farm system. Before he was fifty years old, *The Sporting News* had twice named him Manager of the Year with two different Association teams.

Competitive Imbalance

A study of the major leagues from 1876 through 1993

Campbell Gibson

During the course of major league baseball history, there has been an increase in the competitiveness of teams. One simple indicator of this trend is the decreased frequency of teams with season winning percentages above .700 or below .300. There were 42 such occurrences during the 1876-1900 period (excluding the Union Association in 1884), 24 during the 1901-1945 period, and only three during the 1946-1993 period. It has been over 30 years since the last .700+ season (1954 Indians) or the last .300- season (1962 Mets).

The purpose of this article is to develop a good summary measure of competitive imbalance and to use it to quantify the changes that occurred from 1876 through 1993.

A high degree of imbalance does not necessarily mean that there was not a close pennant race, or vice-versa. For example, the 1942 NL season was highly imbalanced, with winning percentages of .688 for the first place team and .278 for the last. Yet there was a tight pennant race, with the second place team winning at a .675 clip. In contrast, the 1958 NL season was much more balanced, with the winners at .597 and the tail-enders at .448. There wasn't, however, a close pennant race.

Developing a measure—To develop a summary measure of imbalance, I prefer to start with the example of an eight-team league. This has been the most frequent case in major league history, including the entire 1900-1960 period. In a totally balanced regular season, each team would have a .500 winning percentage. In a totally imbalanced season (illustrated with a 154-game schedule), the first-place team would be 154-0, the second-place team would be 132-22 (losing only to the first-place team), the third-place team would be 110-44 (losing only to the first- and second-place teams), and so forth. The winning percentages of the eight teams would be 1.000, .857, .714, .571, .429, .286, 143, and .000. (Won-lost records are not needed for measuring imbalance, so the subsequent discussion is limited to distributions of winning percentages.)

Desirable qualities of a summary measure of imbalance (the imbalance index), include:

1. range from 0 (total balance) to 100 (total imbalance);

2. linearity (the average of the totally balanced and imbalanced distributions has an imbalance index of 50);

3. sensitivity to variation in distributions of winning percentages, not just to the highest and lowest values.

Experimentation with different approaches suggested that the best way to define the imbalance index is as the standard deviation of a distribution of winning percentages expressed as a percentage of the standard deviation of a totally imbalanced distribution. (The standard deviation is a basic statistical

Campbell Gibson is Senior Demographer at the U.S. Bureau of the Census. His previous BRJ article, "Simon Nicholls: Gentleman and Ballplayer," appeared in the 1989 issue.

measure of dispersion in a distribution of numerical values. It is defined as the square root of the variance, which is the average of squared deviations from the mean. For a discussion of these two measures, see an introductory textbook on statistics.)

Examples—Several examples of the imbalance index for an eight-team league are shown in the following text table and are labeled A through F.

	A	B	C	D	E	F
Win %						
1	1.000	.750	.625	.563	.625	.625
2	.857	.679	.589	.545	.615	.525
3	.714	.607	.554	.527	.605	.515
4	.571	.536	.518	.509	.595	.505
5	.429	.464	.482	.491	.405	.495
6	.286	.393	.446	.473	.395	.485
7	.143	.321	.411	.455	.385	.475
8	.000	.250	.375	.437	.375	.375
Std. dev.	.327	.164	.082	.041	.111	.064
Imb. index	100.0	50.0	25.0	12.5	33.8	19.6

Example A shows the totally imbalanced distribution of winning percentages described earlier. Example B shows an average of Example A and a totally balanced distribution (all teams at .500). Example C averages Example B with a totally balanced distribution, and Example D averages Example C with a totally balanced distribution. (In these examples, the winning percentages and standard deviations are rounded to three decimal places, but the imbalance index is based on more detailed calculations). The imbalance index is thus reduced by one-half from A to B, from B to C, and from C to D. Examples of actual seasons similar to these illustrative examples include the 1884 NL season for Example B, the 1960 NL and AL seasons for Example C, and the 1959 NL season for Example D.

Examples E and F are for comparison with Example C and show how the imbalance index can vary given the same first-place and last-place winning percentages (.625 and .375, respectively). Examples of similar actual seasons include the 1950 AL season for Example E and the 1958 AL season for Example F.

Totally imbalanced distributions for leagues with six, eight, ten, twelve, and fourteen teams are shown in the following table to cover the full range of major league experience in the 1876-1993 period.

	6-team	8-team	10-team	12-team	14-team
Win %					
1	1.000	1.000	1.000	1.000	1.000
2	.800	.857	.889	.909	.923
3	.600	.714	.778	.818	.846
4	.400	.571	.667	.727	.769
5	.200	.429	.556	.636	.692
6	.000	.286	.444	.545	.615
7		.143	.333	.455	.538
8		.000	.222	.364	.462
9			.111	.273	.385
10			.000	.182	.308
11				.091	.231
12				.000	.154
13					.077
14					.000
Std dev.	.342	.327	.319	.314	.310
Imb. index	100.0	100.0	100.0	100.0	100.0

Interdivisional play (1969-1993) presents some conceptual problems in defining an imbalance index because each team plays a significant portion of its games against teams outside its division and because the average winning percentage in a division can differ significantly from .500. I decided to compute the imbalance index for the NL and the AL to continue the historical time series, and also to compute the imbalance index separately for each division, since this is the basic level at which teams compete during the season.

Actual values—The annual imbalance indices by league and division, 1876-1993, are shown in the table at the end of this article. Distributions and averages of the imbalance index for various segments of the 1876-1993 period are summarized in the following table.

Leagues, divisions, and years	Total cases	Under 20.0	20.0-29.9	30.0-39.9	40.0 and over	Average index
LEAGUES–total	224	39	101	62	22	28.5
1876-1900, total	36	1	5	14	16	39.4
1876-1900 NL	25	1	3	9	12	40.1
1882-1891 AA	10	-	2	4	4	38.4
1890 PL	1	-	-	1	-	31.9
1901-1920, total	42	5	12	21	4	30.6
1901-1920 NL	20	3	3	11	3	31.6
1901-1920 AL	20	1	8	10	1	30.5
1914-1915 FL	2	1	1	-	-	21.8
1921-1940, total	40	3	24	12	1	28.4
1921-1940 NL	20	3	11	6	-	27.4
1921-1940 AL	20	-	13	6	1	29.5

1941-1960, total	40	5	23	11	1	26.9
1941-1960 NL	20	2	13	5	-	26.1
1941-1960 AL	20	3	10	6	1	27.6
1961-1968, total	16	4	10	2	-	23.9
1961-1968 NL	8	1	6	1	-	24.9
1961-1968 AL	8	3	4	1	-	23.0
1969-1993, total	50	21	27	2	-	21.8
1969-1993 NL	25	12	12	1	-	21.5
1969-1993 AL	25	9	15	1	-	22.0
DIVISIONS–total	100	45	51	4	-	20.8
1969-1993 NL-E	25	13	11	1	-	20.0
1969-1993 NL-W	25	11	13	1	-	21.5
1969-1993 AL-E	25	10	14	1	-	21.6
1969-1993 AL-W	25	11	13	1	-	19.9

For the entire 1876-1993 period, the average imbalance index for leagues is 28.5. The average index dropped from 39.4 in the 1876-1900 period to 21.8 in the 1969-1993 period. There was a corresponding change in the distribution of index values. In the 1876-1900 period, there were 16 cases of 40.0 and over and only one case under 20.0. In the 1969-1993 period, there were 21 cases under 20.0, zero cases of 40.0 and over, and only one case in the 30.0-39.9 range.

For the 1969-1993 period, the average imbalance index for divisions is 20.8. This is similar to the average of 21.8 for leagues during the same period.

As shown in the final table at right, the imbalance index for leagues in the 1876-1968 period ranged from a high of 66.7 in the NL's inaugural season of 1876 to a low of 13.9 in the NL in 1968. Since 1969, with divisional play, the league imbalance index has been lower in two cases: 1974 AL and 1983 NL, both 13.7.

The imbalance index for divisions in the 1969-1993 period was highest in the NL East in 1969 at 33.4. The index was below 10.0 (which never occurred at the league level) on four occasions, with the lowest index of 7.3 occurring twice: in the NL East in 1973 and the AL West in 1987.

Imbalance over time—While this article has focused on the imbalance index by season, it should be noted that the index can be calculated for longer periods of time. One example is given here to show a high degree of imbalance over a decade.

During the 1903-1912 period in the NL, Chicago, New York, and Pittsburgh dominated. They had a combined winning percentage over .600 in every year and finished in the top three places 28 out of a possible 30 times. The average winning percentages for the eight teams during this decade were Chicago,

.647; New York, .631; Pittsburgh, .614; Cincinnati, .489; Philadelphia, .481; Brooklyn, .400; St. Louis, .387; and Boston, .351. The imbalance index of 33.7 for the decade is higher than has occurred in even a single season since the 1962 NL had an index of 36.9.

In general, the major factor underlying the long-term decline in the imbalance index over the 1876-1993 period is probably the increased balance in financial resources among the teams. In the 1876-1891 period, cases of extremely noncompetitive teams (with winning percentages below .250) and franchise shifts were fairly frequent. In the past two generations, draft procedures and free agency have probably contributed to the continued slow decline in the average imbalance index. At the divisional level, it of course remains to be seen what effect, if any, the change to three divisions per league will have on the competitive balance of regular season play.

Imbalance Index by League and Division: 1876-1993

Yr.	NL	AL	AA	PL
1876	66.7			
1877	39.4			
1878	41.8			
1879	48.6			
1880	49.1			
1881	25.0			
1882	38.8		37.2	
1883	43.3		46.4	
1884	50.7		51.5	
1885	50.7		28.9	
1886	57.5		28.6	
1887	34.5		39.3	
1888	27.3		40.9	
1889	31.0		44.9	
1890	48.2		32.7	31.9
1891	24.3		33.7	
1892	34.7			
1893	30.3			
1894	38.9			
1895	40.0			
1896	37.0			
1897	41.7			
1898	38.5			
1899	45.4			
1900	19.1			
1901	31.1	26.0		
1902	33.8	26.3		
1903	34.7	29.0		
1904	37.8	36.3		
1905	40.5	25.2		
1906	43.7	31.0		

Yr.	NL	AL	FL		Yr.	NL	AL		NL-E	NL-W	AL-E	AL-W
1907	34.4	30.1			1951	24.3	29.1					
1908	38.3	26.1			1952	33.4	27.1					
1909	45.4	34.7			1953	32.0	32.5					
1910	30.9	32.4			1954	27.6	42.0					
1911	31.5	31.3			1955	21.5	31.7					
1912	35.3	36.0			1956	24.5	28.7					
1913	30.2	27.4			1957	22.1	26.5					
1914	19.1	27.8	18.5		1958	14.5	16.2					
1915	14.1	40.1	25.0		1959	14.3	19.4					
1916	27.8	32.3			1960	24.9	24.3					
1917	25.6	29.4			1961	27.9	30.0					
1918	24.4	19.9			1962	36.9	18.6					
1919	33.2	35.5			1963	25.7	25.1					
1920	19.8	33.7			1964	24.1	26.7					
1921	27.1	28.1			1965	26.9	26.8					
1922	26.4	22.3			1966	22.3	16.1					
1923	30.9	21.3			1967	21.4	18.4					
1924	30.5	20.0			1968	13.9	21.9					
1925	19.0	28.2			1969	30.5	27.1		33.4	27.2	27.1	23.7
1926	19.6	28.1			1970	18.7	28.8		11.7	23.5	24.6	30.0
1927	30.8	35.2			1971	19.4	25.4		20.1	17.1	29.5	20.3
1928	36.4	29.7			1972	24.9	20.7		24.5	25.4	15.2	24.9
1929	25.7	29.5			1973	19.4	20.5		7.3	25.6	17.4	22.6
1930	27.8	31.5			1974	23.5	13.7		15.5	28.6	13.8	13.5
1931	26.3	35.8			1975	22.5	22.5		12.0	29.3	26.0	18.0
1932	17.2	42.4			1976	26.2	18.8		29.3	22.6	20.0	17.2
1933	24.3	26.9			1977	24.5	30.6		24.4	23.9	33.2	27.7
1934	29.1	29.0			1978	19.1	26.9		17.8	18.7	27.7	23.2
1935	38.3	23.1			1979	22.0	28.2		22.8	18.7	29.9	22.3
1936	23.7	29.0			1980	19.0	24.9		20.8	15.0	22.4	22.7
1937	28.3	34.0			1981	25.9	23.5		26.1	24.8	23.2	22.2
1938	26.5	31.1			1982	18.8	21.6		18.6	19.0	13.8	24.6
1939	31.0	38.9			1983	13.7	22.7		14.9	11.2	17.4	22.2
1940	28.1	25.0			1984	16.6	18.0		14.3	16.4	21.2	9.4
1941	35.2	21.0			1985	26.5	22.6		28.9	23.4	25.6	18.6
1942	39.7	29.6			1986	22.7	17.1		27.4	16.9	13.9	16.6
1943	28.4	26.4			1987	18.0	19.9		14.0	16.8	26.7	7.3
1944	29.8	16.5			1988	23.0	23.6		21.5	24.5	22.9	24.3
1945	32.8	21.0			1989	17.9	20.2		17.0	18.8	18.9	19.7
1946	26.0	31.7			1990	17.4	17.7		17.1	17.2	13.1	19.9
1947	22.8	22.7			1991	18.7	18.8		16.5	20.7	22.2	8.7
1948	20.0	34.5			1992	20.1	19.7		17.6	22.4	17.6	21.2
1949	25.4	35.2			1993	29.0	17.0		26.9	30.8	15.6	17.7
1950	23.4	36.1										

Masaoka Shiki, 1898

hisakata no   *Under the heavens*
amerikabito no   *of distant America*
hajimenishi   *it was created:*
besuboru wa   *this game of baseball*
miredo akanu ka mo   *I never tire of watching.*

—Submitted by Dan Johnson

How Voters Decide

The Cy Young Award

Stuart Miller

The pen hovers above the blank ballot as the mind mulls the merits of the league's premier pitchers. This guy had the lowest ERA and the third-most wins despite pitching for a mediocre team. Let's see, five points for first place, three for second, or one for third. Hmm. He gets...ZERO. Now, how about that guy who didn't crack the top ten in ERA, but had the most wins, thanks to his team's pennant-winning offensive powerhouse? High five for him.

Unfortunately, this befuddled and thoroughly illogical voter is more the rule than the exception. That's why the 1993 Cy Young Award went to Jack McDowell of the Chicago White Sox (22-10, 3.37) won, while Kevin Appier of the Kansas City Royals (18-8, 2.56) finished a distant third, omitted by ten voters. How do the very people paid to report on and interpret games for the public so thoroughly misunderstand the essence of what makes a great pitcher?

The most frequent defense is that writers make the best of an impossible situation. "In team sports, you cannot [pick the best] statistically. It is a waste of time," insists Tom Hirdt of the Elias Sports Bureau. A variety of variables, from home field dimensions to pitching with a big lead, render "scientific analysis" impossible. "It might not be what you'd expect from Elias, but observation, not numbers, is what gives you the best qualitative judgment."

"Numbers by their nature ignore certain conditions," agrees veteran beat writer and author Leonard Koppett. Writers base votes on observation, conversations with players, scouts and executives, and then stats, Koppett says.

There may be no absolute truths but the numbers reveal more definitive answers than Koppett or Hirdt allow. "Intangibles always translates into statistics," says John Schuerholz, Atlanta Braves general manager. If a pitcher bears down with runners in scoring position, it "filters down to the bottom line."

In 1993, Appier had the best bottom line. McDowell's ERA was second worst of any Cy Young winner (LaMarr Hoyt of the '83 White Sox won 24 with a 3.66 ERA). Flame-thrower Randy Johnson, whose 308 strikeouts propelled him to second in the voting, finished at 3.24, also well above Appier's league-leading 2.56. McDowell yielded 11.6 hits and walks per nine innings, Johnson and Appier each permitted only 10.0 per game. McDowell's .687 winning percentage was only .107 higher than his club's, Appier's .692 was .161 higher than the Royals', and Johnson's .703 (19-8) was .197 higher than the Seattle Mariners'.

Interpretation is the problem—Yet Black Jack grabbed twenty-one first place votes and was on all twenty-eight ballots, tallying 124 points. Johnson had six votes for first and seventy-five points. Appier totalled a mere thirty. Thirteen of his eighteen voters pegged him third. The problem is not that statistics lie, it's that writers don't know how to read them,

Stuart Miller is co-author of Island Hopping: A Journey to New York City's Other Islands, *which will be published by Countryman in spring, 1996.*

overemphasizing wins, which often tell more about the team than the individual.

"The biggest thing I look for is wins," explains McDowell-voter Paul Hoynes, who covers the Indians for the Cleveland *Plain Dealer*. (Two writers from each city vote; different writers select Rookie-of-the-Year, Cy Young, and MVP). "Cy Young is also tied in to team performance—how close a club stays in contention influences me."

While pennant race pitching is more challenging, Hoynes and others have inexplicably changed the award from "best" pitcher to "most valuable."

That's wrong, says Schuerholz. Take the hurler you'd want, "if somebody is going to take [your] house away unless you win this one game. That's a pretty good litmus test." But base that decision on "individual capabilities and productivity, not tied to the fortunes of the team."

Why presume McDowell makes the White Sox winners, not vice versa. This chicken-or-the-egg question defies solution, but Appier's stats suggest he'd have won even more on the White Sox. In other words, writers were casting their Cy Young votes for Frank Thomas and the explosive 1993 Chicago offense over a lackluster Royal attack.

"Kevin Appier was the best pitcher in the league," says stats guru Bill James. "To ignore the run support McDowell got is horse hockey."

"I watched them both pitch and Appier gets my vote ten times out of ten," says Joe Horlen, former White Sox hurler, who was similarly ignored in 1967, when Jim Lonborg won.

"Jack had a great year," Appier says, "But I definitely thought I deserved stronger consideration. I was disappointed, but not surprised—after seeing how they voted in the past, I didn't think I had a good chance."

Appier, it turns out, is not only an ace pitcher, but an astute history student. In 1990, Bob Welch (27-6, 2.95, 11.7) routed Roger Clemens (21-6, 1.93, 9.7) in the voting. Welch's Oakland A's were baseball's supreme team—he received over five runs a game, compared to Clemens' 4.2. From June through August, when Welch racked up a 15-3 record, his monthly ERAs were 3.83, 4.78 and 3.47. Clemens gained three fewer wins those months with ERAs of 2.38, 1.00, and 1.09. (Clemens was injured in September.)

How about the Dutch Leonard Award?—Writers have overemphasized wins and pennants since the award began in 1956. Some of the blame rests with Commissioner Ford Frick, who named the award after the man remembered for achieving the most wins (in a career). Perhaps voting would have followed a different pattern if he'd called it the Dutch Leonard Award, for the Red Sox hurler whose 1914 ERA of 1.01 has never been matched.

Through 1966, with one award for both leagues, only Dean Chance, with the 1964 L.A. Angels won on a team finishing lower than a first-place tie. In 1967, when each league began selecting winners, AL writers, under the same old spell, committed one of the worst errors in the history of Cy Young voting. They chose Jim Lonborg over Horlen by an 18-2 margin (pre-point system). Lonborg, who pitched the pennant clincher on the final day of the season, led the league in wins, at 22-9, but Horlen, whose White Sox finished fourth in a four-team chase, was tops in winning percentage at .731 (19-7). Lonborg's 3.16 ERA and 10.3 runners per nine innings were respectable, his 246 strikeouts unsurpassed, but Horlen dominated hitters, leading the league in ERA, 2.06, and ratio at 8.6.

"I definitely should have gotten the Cy Young," reflects Horlen, saying the press often misses the game's nuances. "I had a far superior year and the numbers back me up."

The idiosyncrasies and inconsistencies of the writers became most apparent when the 5-3-1 point system was implemented in 1970 (after Mike Cuellar and Denny McLain shared 1969 AL award). Even when deserving pitchers win, the writers' faulty logic is on display, with three-time winner Tom Seaver highlighting the writers' follies.

When Bob Gibson, 23-7, 3.12, won the 1970 NL award with 118 points, Seaver's league-leading 2.81 ERA earned him only four points since he won *only* eighteen games and the Mets fell from Series champs to third-place. On Series-bound Cincinnati, Jim Merritt's twenty wins and bloated 4.08 ERA garnered eight points, although he "didn't pitch very well," according to Paul Meyer, who now covers the Pirates for the Pittsburgh *Post-Gazette*. "It shouldn't be how many they won, it should be how they pitched—getting twenty wins is different than winning twenty games."

In 1971, Seaver produced stats Cy Young would have envied— 20-10, a league-low 1.76 ERA, 289 strikeouts, 8.5 baserunners per nine innings. But Chicago Cub Ferguson Jenkins, 24-13, won his first Award in his fifth-straight twenty-win campaign. Jenkins, with a better offense, allowed a full run more per game (2.77), yet crushed Seaver 97-61 as five writers inexplicably omitted Seaver from their ballots.

1977 was a difficult year for Seaver—New York columnist Dick Young ripped him publicly and Seaver was shipped to Cincinnati in midseason. Through it all, Seaver posted a 21-6 record and 2.58 ERA. He finished a distant third behind winner Steve Carlton and Tommy John, despite a higher winning percentage and lower ERA. (They each won twenty on first-place teams.) In strike-shortened 1981, when Fernando Valenzuela won, Meyer says two San Diego writers ignored Seaver's 14-2, 2.55 season.

"Seaver had a reputation for being aloof and arrogant," says Meyer. "I never heard a guy say 'I can't vote for so-and-so,' but look at the votes. It's inconceivable that personality didn't come into it."

In the end, judging the Cy Young Award should be in the numbers—yes, a pitcher who shines in a pennant race gets a slight edge, as should a team's ace (always facing the opponent's best pitcher), but ERA and baserunners allowed per nine innings reveal the most dominant pitcher. (Many writers get sidetracked by strikeouts—although a strikeout is no more valuable than a popup. Relievers have also become part of the equation. They didn't win their first Cy Young until Sparky Lyle in 1977, but have captured seven since. However, their role is so different, they should only compete for the Fireman of the Year Award.)

Joel Horlen

Transcendental Graphics

Appier points to quality starts as an indicator, "if you took wins and losses away from pitchers, that's what their job is." James says ERA should get 30 percent of the weight, baserunners ratio 30 percent, win-loss 20 percent and the rest 20 percent (strikeouts, innings per start, park factor).

Enter the numbers guys—The good news is that the fossilized views of older hands are gradually giving way to a more sophisticated generation. "There are more younger guys now, and they're looking inside the numbers," observes Meyer. "They're more willing to go beyond 20-10 to see how a guy really pitched."

However, just as they're getting the hang of this system, a new dilemma has arisen. With more and more players receiving cash bonuses based on how they fare in the voting (for MVP as well as Cy Young), Koppett and other writers have begun wondering if their votes could cost them access to a player who may be miffed if he thinks the writer cost him hundreds of thousands of dollars. (Writers used to perform official scoring duties until contentious athletes forced newspapers to change their policies.)

"It is increasingly uncomfortable to have my writers do it," says Bill Dwyre, sports editor for the Los Angeles *Times*. "It's close to being a conflict of interest, when they have to go down into the locker room and [interview] players who they voted on."

However, Dave Smith, executive sports editor for the Dallas *Morning-News*, says that while everyone is concerned about it, there's been nothing more than minor flare-ups.

Despite their qualms about problems looming on the horizon, both editors say the current system is the best option— fans are by their very nature too partisan while players and managers become consumed by internal politics.

"I don't know anyone more legitmate to vote on it than the baseball beat writers," says Smith. "They're very objective and they take it very seriously."

"There is no viable alternative," Dwyre concludes. "So we'll go on, but with a wrench in the gut."

Tim McNamara

Fordham, the Braves, the Giants...and SABR

Jim Kreuz

In 1910 Tim McNamara, future National League pitcher and SABR member, played on a grade school team called the Millville Bluejays, just outside his home town of Woonsocket, Rhode Island. His coach was a man by the name of Fred Hartnett. Fred's son, Charles Leo, began playing in 1912, and was the team's catcher. Most of his friends, though, knew him as "Gabby." McNamara and Hartnett played on through high school, and, according to Tim, "we remained good friends until Gabby's death on December 20, 1972, which also happened to be his birthday." Tim once said that his battery mate, a Hall of Fame catcher but not an overwhelmingly successful manager, was "too nice to everyone, including his players. To be a winning manager, you have to be tough at times with your players, and Gabby was too kind-hearted."

Tim graduated from high school, and sat out for two years before going off to Fordham University in 1918, where he was a teammate of Frank Frisch for a season.

"I can still picture one game during my freshman year. Frisch was standing in the batter's box, digging in and going through his usual motion of wringing the bat handle while glaring at the pitcher on the mound. We all busted out laughing when one of our teammates said that he could see sawdust falling to the ground from Frisch wringing the bat so hard."

Tim graduated from college in 1922 and immedi-

ately signed with the Boston Braves. "I enjoyed playing in Boston. It was a one-hour drive to the ballpark, so I could live in my home town. And Braves Field was a pitcher's park, with no short fences. We had good fans at Boston, very loyal. The club management also treated us real well. They honored Gabby, 'Jigger' Statz and myself one day before a ballgame, because the three of us grew up in the area, and gave us some nice gifts. This was typical of the Braves management—I never had any problems with them."

McNamara's favorite teammate also happened to be his favorite manager, Casey Stengel. Stengel was his teammate on the Braves in 1924 and 1925, and his manager at Toledo in 1926. The two hit it off well from the beginning. "Casey was always talking baseball, twenty-four hours a day, at the park and away from it. He understood the game better than anyone else on the team. And he did not hesitate to give the younger ballplayers a few pointers, either, which was unusual back then because everyone lived in fear of losing their starting position to another teammate."

McNamara liked Stengel's wife, Edna, too. "I thought she was a saint for putting up with Casey all those years. You know, they had what I considered to be the perfect marriage. He treated her like his brand new bride every minute they were together."

This comment led me to ask Tim how he had met his wife. "Typically, after most home Braves games, when I would arrive home, there would be two young high-school-aged girls in my yard, waiting to play ball with me, "Charlie" Hartnett, Gabby's younger sister

---

Jim Kreuz spends all of his spare time searching for old ballplayers in need of attentive ears for their stories.

and her friend Helen. Both were pretty fair ballplayers. Well, in 1931, Helen and I got married."

Tim found himself with the Giants in 1926. McNamara's memory of manager John McGraw is very clear. "When he said something, you did it!" Tim learned something about the Giants' future manager, too. Besides being an outstanding batter and slick fielding first baseman, Bill Terry could sing. "During a rain delay at Pittsburgh's Forbes Field, Billy Southworth, Jack Bentley, Bill Terry, and I began singing. We liked the way we sounded, which is to say that we didn't sound terrible, so we sang a few more. After three songs, we quit and, to our amazement, the fans of Pittsburgh showed their appreciation by giving us a round of applause."

Tim really never had a chance to prove himself before being shipped down to Toledo. As he was packing his bags, Eddie Brannick, the secretary of the Giants, told him, "With our need for your strong pitching arm down the stretch, you'll be back on the club soon." McNamara is still waiting for the call.

Back with Stengel, he had a great time with the Mudhens, even when things weren't going well. "I came to bat for the first time in a particular game, and was facing future Giants pitcher Roy Parmelee. The first three pitches were all fastballs, all right down the middle, and they were all called strikes. They were so fast I never had the opportunity to take my bat off my shoulder. Well, I walked back to the dugout and took my place on the bench. Casey got up and walked down to my end of the dugout, and, in a loud, joking voice said, 'Well, young man, it looks like we're goin' to have to take you to the hospital.' I asked him what for? He replied, 'Why, to have a doctor surgically remove the bat that's attached to your shoulder, so that you can swing at a ball, that's what for!'" The Toledo bench burst into laughter.

McNamara believes that Stengel got the most out of his players, was an excellent motivator, and his joking behavior did not distract his teams from playing at their best. He was there one day when Stengel was trying to explain to a couple of rookies how to execute the hook slide. He wasn't having much luck. In his frustration, he gazed around the crowded lobby, looking for some sort of inspiration. All at once, he blurted out, "Watch closely!" to the two rookies, and took off in his street clothes toward a marble pillar. The entire lobby turned to watch as the manager of the Mudhens executed a perfect slide on the slick marble floor by hooking the instep of his foot around the pillar. Amid a roar of laughter, Casey got up, walked over to the two rookies, and asked if there were any more questions. None. They understood completely. "And you know what," said Tim, "Casey never seemed to notice all the hotel patrons laughing at him. He was only concerned with teaching his players, and he never quit doing it."

Tim McNamara passed away on November 4, 1994, two weeks shy of his ninety-sixth birthday. My friendship with him had begun several years before, while I was searching for surviving members of the 1926 Giants. The father of a friend of mine, Jim Boyle, had his one official appearance in a major league game with that club, and I was trying to find out more about him. Tim was one of three living players from that team, none of whom, unfortunately, remembered Boyle. But that contact led to one of the best friendships I've formed in my years of baseball research—and I have Tim to thank for telling me about SABR, too.

Consecutive Shutouts Against One Team (Season)

Since 1900 only four pitchers have shut out one team in one season four or mor consecutive times. Jaster's five straight shutouts against Los Angeles is the record. Technically, however, Mel Stottlemyre, if one counts a 1971 shutout, had five straight against California over two seasons. The four pitchers who have achieved this feat are listed in the table below. CSI stands for Consecutive Scoreless Innings against this particular opponent during the streak, even if it started or ended in another season.

Pitcher	Year	Opponent	Con. ShO	Lifetime ShO	CSI
Larry Jaster, St.L.	1966	LA	5	7	52
Lefty Leifield, Pitts.	1906	Boston	4	33	41
Dizzy Trout, Det.	1944	Philadelphia	4	28	44
Mel Stottlemyre, NY	1972	California	4	40	46

—William Ruiz, with the assistance of Ray Gonzalez

From a Researcher's Notebook

Al Kermisch

Paschal batted for Babe Ruth *and* Lou Gehrig

Ben Paschal never appeared in more than 96 games in a major league season, but he was a super sub for the New York Yankees from 1924 through 1929. His best year was in 1925, when he hit .360 in 89 games, with 12 home runs and 56 RBIs. Overall, he batted .309 for his six years with the Yanks.

Paschal had the unique experience of pinch hitting for the two great Yankee sluggers—Babe Ruth and Lou Gehrig. Gehrig began his consecutive game streak on June 1, 1925, when he pinch hit for Pee-Wee Wanninger against Walter Johnson and flied out to Goose Goslin. But Lou was himself hit for six times in the next two months, three times by Paschal.

On June 18, when the Tigers beat the Yanks 6-3 at Yankee Stadium, Paschal batted for Gehrig in the seventh inning and fanned. In an 8-1 loss at Washington on June 23, Ben hit for Lou in the fourth inning and sacrificed. On August 2 at New York, Paschal again batted for Gehrig in the ninth inning and grounded out as the Indians won, 3-2. In all three instances left-handers were on the mound for the opposition.

Paschal batted for Ruth in the opening game of the 1927 season, the year in which the Babe became the first player in major league history to hit 60 home runs. The game was played at Yankee Stadium on April 12, and the Yanks defeated the Philadelphia Athletics, 8-3, before 63,060. In the bottom of the seventh inning Ruth, who had had fanned twice and popped up once, complained to Manager Miller Huggins that he felt sick, and with the game nearly in the bag Huggins told his star slugger to take a rest. Paschal was sent up to bat for him and singled off Lefty Grove.

Umpire listed in lineup of "Casey" game

When Chicago broke Tim Keefe's 19-game winning streak on August 14, 1888, the baseball reporter for the New York *Press* expressed his displeasure with umpire Tom Lynch. He wrote: "Incidentally, it might be mentioned that New York was not robbed of the game by the umpire but Mr. Lynch gave Anson's pitcher the earth and a part of the sky. He proved of immense assistance to Chicago in this way." The reporter added insult to injury by placing Lynch's name in the box score following the Chicago pitcher as follows:

	AB	R	H	PO	A	E
Lynch, Umpire	0	0	0	*	*	0

*Complete record not kept

The game drew a fine Monday crowd of 10,240 to the Polo Grounds to see the league-leading Giants take on the second-place Chicagos. There was a carnival atmosphere at the Polo Grounds. The New York

Al Kermisch is an original member of SABR, whose "Notebook" has been a popular regular feature of The Baseball Research Journal for many years.

management had invited the members of Colonel McCaull's Opera Company to the contest. The company, headed by McCaull and DeWolf Hopper, entered the grounds in Tally-ho coaches.

That evening the players of both teams were guests of the Opera Company at Wallack's Theatre to see the play "Prince Methusalem." The house was packed to the doors, and when the clubs came in they were cheered to the rafters. Also in attendance was General William T. Sherman, who drove his Union troops through Georgia in 1864. As the general walked to his seat he was recognized by the players in the boxes and by many others in the audience. Some of the players began to applaud and everyone joined in and the general bowed quietly to the impromptu reception. As expected Hopper took care of the baseball skits and recited for the first time the poem "Casey at the Bat." The New York *World* covered his performance as follows:

> In honor of the occasion he [Hopper] recited with telling effect the humorous poem 'Casey at the Bat.' The audience literally went wild with enthusiasm, men got up on their seats and cheered while General Sherman laughed until the tears ran down his cheeks. It was one of the wildest scenes ever seen in a theatre, and showed the popularity of Hopper and baseball.

1906: 16 clubs in Series?

With eight clubs now eligible to vie for the right to play in the World Series, it is interesting to note that during the 1906 World Series between the White Sox and Cubs, Stanley Robison, president of the St. Louis Cardinals, was so enamored by the series that he thought it would be a great idea if all 16 teams in the majors got to participate in the series.

The following article appeared in the Toledo *News-Bee* on October 1, 1906:

> CHICAGO, Oct. 12—President Stanley Robison of the St. Louis Cardinals said today that at the December meeting of the National League he would offer a resolution cutting down the number of games from 154 to 132, and proposing a world series of games in which 16 clubs in the two major leagues should all take part. The resolution he will offer will respectfully call on the American League to co-operate in his scheme.
>
> "By my plan the regular season in both leagues will end on September 1 or soon thereafter," said Stanley. "Then the American League clubs will start out, each playing two games in the National League

city.

> "When that series had been completed the National League clubs take to the road, each playing two games in each American League city."

Needless to say, nothing ever came of the proposal.

Galan hit into no doubles, but a triple play in 1935

During the season of 1935, Augie Galan of the Chicago Cubs went through the entire season of 154 games without grounding into a double play. But while he did manage to escape the twin-killing stigma he nevertheless was one of only two players to hit into a triple play in the National League that year. On April 21, in a game at Chicago, won by Cincinnati 8-4 in twelve innings, the Reds engineered their triple play in the eleventh inning, stopping a Cub rally. Paul Derringer walked Billy Jurges to open the eleventh. Derringer pitched carefully to Clay Bryant to keep the Cub pitcher from sacrificing, but walked him on a 3-2 pitch. Galan also failed to bunt but worked the count to three and two. Cub hopes were high since Augie already had three hits in the game and when he hit a shot toward right the game seemed to be over. But Sunny Jim Bottomley jumped into the air and speared the drive for the first out. He ran to first to double up Bryant for the second out. He then threw to Alex Kampouris at second to retire Jurges to complete the triple killing.

Cy Young played first and last games for Canton

Hall of Famer Cy Young made his debut in Organized Baseball for Canton of the Tri-State League on April 30, 1890, pitching a three-hitter in defeating Wheeling, 4-2. He was 15-15 for Canton before he was sold to Cleveland (NL). He pitched in the majors for twenty-two years and won a record 511 games. In 1911, his final season in the majors, he was 3-4 with Cleveland (AL), before being released. He signed with Boston (NL) for whom he was 4-5 before ending his big league career.

On July 10, 1912, Young came out of retirement to play one game at first base for the Canton (Central League), club on Boosters Day. He went hitless and handled six chances without an error as Canton defeated Youngstown, 4-3.

Puccinelli Was Dominant Hitter in International Loop

George (Pooch) Puccinelli led the International League in batting twice in his seven years in the league. He flirted with a .400 average for Rochester in 1931 and finished with a .391 mark. In 1935, playing with Baltimore, he had one of those dream offensive years. He led the league with a .359 average. He also was tops in runs (135), hits (209), doubles (49), home runs (53), runs batted in (173), and total bases (425). Puccinelli was a terror in his home park. In 77 games at Oriole Park he hit 43 home runs, twice hitting three homers in a game.

On April 23, 1938, Puccinelli had another three-home-run game that was of the believe it or not variety. In the first game of a doubleheader against Rochester at Oriole Park, the Orioles defeated the Red Wings, 5-3. Francis Barrett and Bob Bowman held the Orioles to three hits, but all three were home runs by Puccinelli, who also drove in all five runs. He homered over the left field fence in the second inning. In the fourth, after Frank McGowan walked, Pooch hit the ball into the right-field bleachers. In the sixth Nolen Richardson drew a base on balls and Puccinelli drove one over the fence in left center.

Tom O'Brien Victim of Drinking Sea Water

In the fall of 1900, players from the New York and Brooklyn National League clubs set out for Cuba to play a series of exhibition games. Thomas J. O'Brien, who had played for Pittsburgh that year, but who had been with the Giants in 1899, was asked to go along.

On the voyage down, O'Brien was told that if he drank plenty of sea water he would immediately become seasick for a day and then would be all right. O'Brien and Kid Gleason drank the sea water and both became sick, but O'Brien got much the worst of it. He drank so much of the water that it affected his internal organs. Upon arrival in Cuba O'Brien went to a hotel and stayed there for a long time, still very sick. He did not take part in any of the games.

On his return to New York, a specialist told O'Brien that his stomach, heart and kidneys had been affected. In addition, his lungs were not in the best of condition. After spending a few days with his parents in Verona, PA, O'Brien decided to go to Arizona to regain his health. He showed improvement for a while, but then grew worse and died in Phoenix on February 4, 1901, sixteen days before his twenty-ninth birthday. His body was shipped home for burial.

Corcoran Received Shabby Treatment in 1885

Larry Corcoran was a star pitcher with the Chicago White Stockings of the National League from 1880 through 1884, winning a total of 170 games, including four seasons of 30 or more victories. He also pitched three no-hitters in that span. Larry came up with a sore arm in 1885 and received shabby treatment from the Chicago club. When the White Stockings took off on a month-long road trip in early 1885, Corcoran was left behind to work the kinks out of his arm. After several weeks Larry's funds were running low and he went to Al Spalding, who was running the club at that time, to ask for a portion of his salary. Spalding gave him the runaround and finally asked Corcoran if he couldn't get along until June 8. Larry had no choice but to agree to that date.

Corcoran went back on June 8, and this time Spalding told him that he had checked into the matter and that the Chicago club did not owe him anything since they had cut off his salary when he was not able to pitch. Corcoran then asked to be released, but had to make promises that he would return to the White Stockings at a later date. Spalding did give Corcoran some money so that he could get to his home on the East Coast, but it was in the form of a loan at six per cent interest.

Corcoran's arm never came around and after short stints with New York, Washington and Indianapolis he drifted to the minors in 1887.

Doubling Up

Not only did Johnny Vander Meer forever etch his name in the baseball record books with his two consecutive no-hitters June 11 and 15, 1938, but he also—within five days—doubled what every other pitcher in the National League accomplished in the ten years of the 1930s. Besides Johnny's double no-hit feat, only one other NL pitcher spun a no-hitter during the entire decade of the '30s: Paul Dean of the Cardinals no-hit Brooklyn, 3-0, on September 21, 1934. You could look it up.

—Don Nelson